PostgreSQL 9.6
Performance Story

PostgreSQL 9.6
Performance Story

Siyeon Kim

SIYEON Academy

PostgreSQL 9.6 Performance Story

First Published: April 2017

http://siyeonacademy.wordpress.com

This book is dedicated to my wife and joule.

About the Author

Siyeon Kim has been an Oracle performance consultant for 19 years. In particular, he performed Oracle performance monitoring, diagnosis, tuning and EXADATA tuning. He has been devoted to PostgreSQL research and knowledge sharing (siyeonacademy.wordpress.com) over the past year. This book is the result of his research.

Introduction

Contents of the book

This book is about PostgreSQL performance.

To discuss performance, various contents such as structure, shared buffer operation principle, IO processing method, optimizer operation principle, statistical information, explain analysis method, access method, join method, query rewrite, hint, histogram, index, you need to know.

In addition to this, this book describes the Vacuum, HOT required for PostgreSQL MVCC features. And BRIN is explained in detail.

Who This Book Is For

It is great if you have a couple of years of experience with PostgreSQL and those who are familiar with another DBMS and are starting PostgreSQL. And those who are interested in the principles of operation will be of great help.

Characteristics of Books

We conducted various tests and source analyzes to ensure accuracy of the study.

To make it easy for the reader to understand, I explained about the operation principle with about 60 pictures.

All examples are reproducible using a script.

How to read a book

We recommend that you read books in order from the first chapter.

Chapter 1 is very basic. If you are familiar with PostgreSQL, you can skip it.

The source analysis section of Chapter 2 is recommended only for those interested. There is no big problem in reading the rest, without knowing the details. However, you should be familiar with the terms that appear in the middle of the source description.

Scripts for configuring the test environment can be downloaded from http://siyeonacademy.wordpress.com.

Table of Contents

chapter **1**.

Architecture overview

Architecture overview

This section will explain several characteristics of the PostgreSQL structure and PostgreSQL.

PostgreSQL architecture

The physical structure of PostgreSQL is very simple. Shared memory, and very few background processes and data files. (See Figure 1-1)

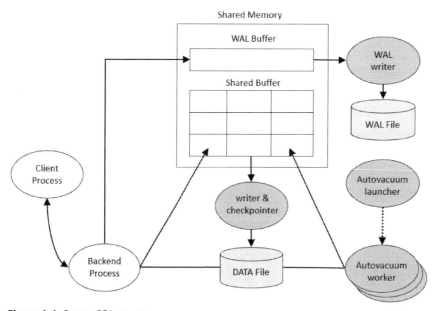

Figure 1-1. *PostgreSQL structure*

Shared Memory

The most important elements in shared memory are Shared Buffer and WAL buffers.

Shared Buffer

The purpose of Shared Buffer is to minimize DISK IO. For this purpose, the following principles must be met. This is covered in 'Chapter 2. Understanding Shared Buffer'

- You need to access very large (tens, hundreds of gigabytes) buffers quickly.

- You should minimize contention when many users access it at the same time.

- Frequently used blocks must be in the buffer for as long as possible.

WAL Buffer

The WAL buffer is a buffer that temporarily stores changes to the database. The contents stored in the WAL buffer are written to the WAL file at a predetermined point in time. From a backup and recovery point of view, WAL buffers and WAL files are very important. However, the subject of this book is somewhat different. Therefore, this book does not cover.

Process type

PostgreSQL has four process types.

- Postmaster (Daemon) Process

- Background Process

- Backend Process

- Client Process

Postmaster Process

The Postmaster process is the first process started when you start PostgreSQL. At startup, performs recovery, initialize shared memory, and run background processes. It also creates a backend process when there is a connection request from the client process. (See Figure 1-2)

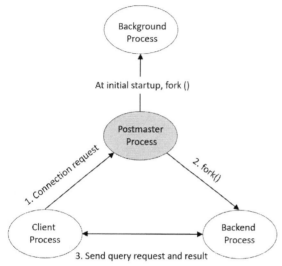

Figure 1-2. *Process relationship diagram*

If you check the relationships between processes with the `pstree` command, you can see that the Postmaster process is the parent process of all processes. (For clarity, I added the process name and argument after the process ID)

```
$ pstree -p 1125
postgres(1125) /usr/local/pgsql/bin/postgres -D /usr/local/pgsql/data
                    ┬postgres(1249)  postgres: logger process
                    ├postgres(1478)  postgres: checkpointer process
                    ├postgres(1479)  postgres: writer process
                    ├postgres(1480)  postgres: wal writer process
                    ├postgres(1481)  postgres: autovacuum launcher process
                    ├postgres(1483)  postgres: stats collector process
```

Background Process

The list of background processes required for PostgreSQL operation is as follows. (See Table 1-1) Other processes except `Autovacuum launcher` are easily found in ORACLE.

Table 1-1. *List of PostgreSQL background processes*

Process	Role
logger	Write the error message to the log file.
checkpointer	When a checkpoint occurs, the dirty buffer is written to the file.
writer	Periodically writes the dirty buffer to a file.
wal writer	Write the WAL buffer to the WAL file.
autovacuum launcher	Fork autovacuum worker when vacuum is needed. Vacuum is described in 'Chapter 4. Understanding Vacuum'.
archiver	When in Archive log mode, copy the WAL file to the specified directory.
stats collector	DBMS usage statistics such as session execution information (pg_stat_activity) and table usage statistical information (pg_stat_all_tables) are collected.

Backend Process

The maximum number of backend processes is set by the max_connections parameter, and the default value is 100. The backend process performs the query request of the user process and then transmits the result. Some memory structures are required for query execution, which is called local memory. The main parameters associated with local memory are:

work_mem

Space used for sorting, bitmap operations, hash joins, and merge joins. The default setting is 4 MiB.

maintenance_work_mem

Space used for Vacuum and CREATE INDEX. The default setting is 64 MiB.

temp_buffers

Space used for temporary tables. The default setting is 8 MiB.

Database structure

Let's look at some of the things you need to understand the database structure.

Things related to the database

1. PostgreSQL consists of several databases. This is called a database cluster.
2. When `initdb()` is executed, `template0`, `template1`, and `postgres` databases are created.
3. The `template0` and `template1` databases are template databases for user database creation and contain the system catalog tables.
4. The list of tables in the `template0` and `template1` databases is the same immediately after `initdb()`. However, the template1 database can create objects that the user needs.
5. The user database is created by cloning the template1 database.

Things related to the tablespace

1. The `pg_default` and `pg_global` tablespaces are created immediately after `initdb()`.
2. If you do not specify a tablespace at the time of table creation, it is stored in the `pg_dafault` tablespace.
3. Tables managed at the database cluster level are stored in the `pg_global` tablespace.
4. The physical location of the `pg_default` tablespace is `$PGDATA\base`.
5. The physical location of the `pg_global` tablespace is `$PGDATA\global`.
6. One tablespace can be used by multiple databases. At this time, a database-specific subdirectory is created in the table space directory.
7. Creating a user tablespace creates a symbolic link to the user tablespace in the `$PGDATA\tblspc` directory.

Things related to the table

1. There are three files per table.

2. One is a file for storing table data. The file name is the OID of the table.
3. One is a file to manage table free space. The file name is `OID_fsm`.
4. One is a file for managing the visibility of the table block. The file name is `OID_vm`.
5. The index does not have a _vm file. That is, `OID` and `OID_fsm` are composed of two files.

📄 **Note** The file name at the time of table and index creation is OID, and OID and `pg_class.relfilenode` are the same at this point. However, when a rewrite operation (`Truncate`, `CLUSTER`, `Vacuum Full`, `REINDEX`, etc.) is performed, the relfilenode value of the affected object is changed, and the file name is also changed to the `relfilenode` value. You can easily check the file location and name by using `pg_relation_filepath` ('`<object name>`').

---

template0, template1, postgres database

Let's take a look at the tests we've done.

If you query the `pg_database` view after `initdb()`, you can see that the `template0`, `template1`, and `postgres` databases have been created.

```
select oid, datname, datistemplate, datallowconn
from    pg_database order by 1;
  oid  |  datname  | datistemplate | datallowconn
-------+-----------+---------------+---------------
     1 | template1 | t             | t
 13321 | template0 | t             | f
 13322 | postgres  | f             | t
```

- Through the `datistemplate` column, you can see that the `template0` and `template1` databases are database for template for user database creation.

- The `datlowconn` column indicates whether the database can be accessed. Since the `template0` database can't be accessed, the contents of the database can't be changed either.

- The reason for providing two databases for the template is that the `template0` database is the initial state template and the `template1` database is the template added by the user.

- The `postgres` database is the default database created using the `template1` database. If you do not specify a database at connection time, you will be connected to the `postgres` database.

The database is located under the `$PGDATA/base` directory. The directory name is the database `OID` number.

```
[postgres@pgserver data]$ ls -l $PGDATA/base
drwx------. 2 postgres postgres 8192 Nov  4 19:34 1
drwx------. 2 postgres postgres 8192 Nov  4 19:34 13321
drwx------. 2 postgres postgres 8192 Nov  4 19:34 13322
```

Create user database

The user database is created by cloning the `template1` database. To verify this, create a user table `T1` in the `template1` database. After creating the `mydb01` database, check that the `T1` table exists.

```
-- Create a T1 table in the template database.
template1=# create table t1 (c1 integer);

-- Create the mydb01 database.
postgres=# create database mydb01;

-- After connecting to mydb01 database, check if T1 table exists.
mydb01=# \d t1
      Table "public.t1"
 Column |  Type   | Modifiers
--------+---------+-----------
 c1     | integer |
```

See Figure 1-3.

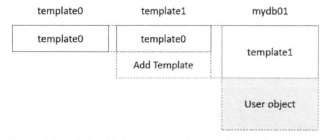

Figure 1-3. *Relationship between Template Database and User Database*

pg_default tablespace

If you query `pg_tablespace` after `initdb` (), you can see that the `pg_default` and `pg_global` tablespaces have been created.

```
postgres=# select oid, * from pg_tablespace;
 oid  |   spcname    | spcowner | spcacl | spcoptions
------+--------------+----------+--------+------------
 1663 | pg_default   |       10 |        |
 1664 | pg_global    |       10 |        |
```

- The location of the pg_default tablespace is $PGDATA\base. There is a subdirectory by database OID in this directory. (See Figure 1-4)

```
[postgres@pgserver ~]$ ls -l $PGDATA/base
drwx------. 2 postgres postgres 8192 Nov  4 20:06 1
drwx------. 2 postgres postgres 8192 Nov  4 20:02 13321
drwx------. 2 postgres postgres 8192 Nov  4 20:02 13322
drwx------. 2 postgres postgres 8192 Nov  4 20:06 16396
```

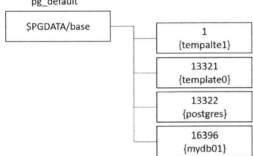

Figure 1-4. *Pg_default tablespace and database relationships from a physical configuration perspective*

pg_global tablespace

The `pg_global` tablespace is a tablespace for storing data to be managed at the 'database cluster' level.

- For example, tables of the same type as the `pg_database` table provide the same information whether they are accessed from any database. (See Figure 1-5)

- The location of the pg_global tablespace is $PGDATA\global.

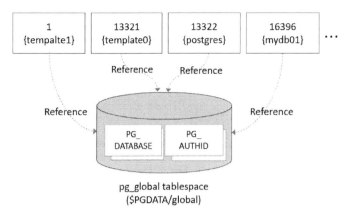

| 1
{tempalte1} | 13321
{template0} | 13322
{postgres} | 16396
{mydb01} | ... |

Reference   Reference

Reference   Reference

PG_DATABASE   PG_AUTHID

pg_global tablespace
($PGDATA/global)

Figure 1-5. *Relationship between pg_global tablespace and database*

Create user tablespace

Create a user tablespace.

```
postgres=# create tablespace myts01 location '/data01';
```

The `pg_tablespace` shows that the `myts01` tablespace has been created.

```
postgres=# select oid, * from pg_tablespace;
  oid  |   spcname   | spcowner | spcacl | spcoptions
-------+-------------+----------+--------+------------
  1663 | pg_default  |       10 |        |
  1664 | pg_global   |       10 |        |
 24576 | myts01      |       10 |        |
```

Symbolic links in the `$PGDATA/pg_tblspc` directory point to tablespace directories.

```
[postgres@pgserver ~]$ ls -l $PGDATA/pg_tblspc
lrwxrwxrwx. 1 postgres postgres 7 Nov  8 15:10 24576 -> /data01
```

Connect to the `postgres` and `mydb01` databases and create the table.

```
[postgres@pgserver ~]$ psql -p 5436 -d postgres
-- Create a table.
postgres=# create table t1 (c1 integer) tablespace myts01;

-- Check the OID.
postgres=# select oid from pg_class where relname='t1';
  oid
-------
 24577
```

```
[postgres@pgserver ~]$ psql -p 5436 -d mydb01

-- Create a table.
mydb01=# create table t1 (c1 integer) tablespace myts01;

-- Check the OID.
mydb01=# select oid from pg_class where relname='t1';
  oid
-------
 24580
```

If you look up the /data01 directory after creating the table, you will see that the OID directory for the postgres and mydb01 databases has been created and that there is a file in each directory that has the same OID as the T1 table.

```
[postgres@pgserver ~]$ ls -Rl /data01
/data01:
drwx------. 4 postgres postgres 30 Nov  8 15:19 PG_9.6_201608131

/data01/PG_9.6_201608131:
drwx------. 2 postgres postgres 18 Nov  8 15:18 13322
drwx------. 2 postgres postgres 18 Nov  8 15:19 16396

/data01/PG_9.6_201608131/13322:
-rw-------. 1 postgres postgres 40960 Nov  8 15:40 24577

/data01/PG_9.6_201608131/16396:
-rw-------. 1 postgres postgres 40960 Nov  8 15:41 24580
```

How to change tablespace location

PostgreSQL specifies a directory when creating tablespace. Therefore, if the file system where the directory is located is full, the data can no longer be stored. To solve this problem, you can use the volume manager. However, if you can't use the volume manager, you can consider changing the tablespace location. The order of operation is as follows.

```
-- Shutdown PostgreSQL.
/usr/local/pgsql/bin/pg_ctl  -D /usr/local/pgsql/data stop

-- Copy the myts01 tablespace to the new file system.
[postgres@pgserver data01]$ cp -rp /data01/PG* /data02

-- Check the contents of the pg_tblspc directory.
[postgres@pgserver pg_tblspc]$ ls -l
lrwxrwxrwx. 1 postgres postgres 7 Nov  8 15:52 24576 -> /data01
```

```
-- Delete the symbolic link.
[postgres@pgserver pg_tblspc]$ rm 24576

-- Create a new symbolic link.
[postgres@pgserver pg_tblspc]$ ln -s /data02 24576

-- Confirm the contents
[postgres@pgserver pg_tblspc]$ ls -l
lrwxrwxrwx. 1 postgres postgres 7 Nov  8 15:53 24576 -> /data02

-- Startup PostgreSQL.
/usr/local/pgsql/bin/pg_ctl -D /usr/local/pgsql/data start
```

🗋 **Note**   Tablespaces are also very useful in environments that use partition tables. Because you can use different tablespaces for each partition table, you can more flexibly cope with file system capacity problems.

What is Vacuum?

Vacuum does the following:

1. Gathering table and index statistics
2. Reorganize the table
3. Clean up tables and index dead blocks
4. Frozen by record XID to prevent XID Wraparound

#1 and #2 are generally required for DBMS management. But #3 and #4 are necessary because of the PostgreSQL MVCC feature. (This is discussed in detail in 'Chapter 4. Understanding Vacuum')

Differences between ORACLE and PostgreSQL

The biggest difference I think is the MVCC model and the existence of a shared pool. This is also a feature of PostgreSQL. (See Table 1-2)

Table 1-2. *The biggest difference between ORACLE and PostgreSQL*

Item	ORACLE	PostgreSQL
MVCC model implementation method	UNDO Segment	Store previous record within block
Shared Pool	existence	it does not exist

Differences in the MVCC model

To increase concurrency, you must follow the principle that "read operations do not block write operations and write operations should not block read operations". To implement this principle, a Multi Version Concurrency Control (MVCC) is required. ORACLE uses UNDO segments to implement MVCC. On the other hand, PostgreSQL uses a way to store previous records in a block. This section is covered in 'Chapter 4. Understanding Vacuum'.

Shared Pool

PostgreSQL does not provide a shared pool. This is somewhat embarrassing for users familiar with ORACLE. Shared Pool is a very important and essential component in ORACLE.

PostgreSQL provides the ability to share SQL information at the process level instead of the Shared Pool. In other words, if you execute the same SQL several times in one process, it will hard-parse only once. This part is described in Chapter 3. Understanding Optimizer'.

Summary

The PostgreSQL structure is very simple. From a physical point of view, it consists of shared memory, processes, and data files. The main components of shared memory are Shared Buffer and WAL buffers.

Process is divided into Postmaster process, background process, backend process and client process.

Background processes exist for error logging, buffer writes, WAL buffer writes, and there is a process for `autovacuum`. The backend process executes the query requested by the client process, and there is a local memory area for performing the task.

PostgreSQL can create multiple databases, and clone the contents of the template database when creating a user database.

From a physical point of view, the relationship between a database and a tablespace is the way in which tablespaces are located in the table space directory.

The `pg_global` tablespace stores data that must be managed at the database cluster level.

chapter **2**.

Understanding Shared Buffer

Understanding Shared Buffer

Shared buffer is an essential component for efficient IO processing.

Because of this importance, the DBMS buffer manager will be highly optimized. In other words, if you set the Shared Buffer to a reasonable size (several Gb or tens of Gb, or even hundreds of Gb), there may not be a performance problem caused by Shared Buffer.

Then why? Do I need to know how Shared Buffer works? It is doubtful.

This is also the question I had when I started the Shared Buffer study.

However, as the research on Shared Buffer was repeated, it was found that Shared Buffer has characteristics. IO strategy, ring buffer, and clock sweep algorithm. Without knowing these characteristics accurately, it can be difficult to determine the cause of sudden slowing of IO processing.

So, let's get to the point.

Three goals of Shared Buffer for performance improvement

The purpose of Shared Buffer is to improve IO performance by minimizing DISK IO. To accomplish this, we must accomplish the following three goals.

1. Very large (tens, hundreds of gigabytes) buffers should be accessed quickly.
2. Contention should be minimized when many users access at the same time.
3. Frequently used blocks should be in the buffer for as long as possible.

The first and second targets are related to the shared buffer structure, and the third target is related to the shared buffer algorithm. Let's take a closer look.

Very large (tens, hundreds of gigabytes) buffers should be accessed quickly.

To accomplish this goal, you should be able to find blocks in the shared buffer very quickly. Also, if the block is not in the Shared Buffer, you should be able to quickly see that the block does not exist. The details are described in 'Shared Buffer Architecture'.

Contention should be minimized when many users access at the same time.

Shared Buffer is a shared resource used by many users simultaneously. A lock mechanism is required to protect shared resources. In order to minimize the contention at the time of acquiring the lock, a method using several locks is required. The details are described in 'Shared Buffer Architecture'.

Frequently used blocks should be in the buffer for as long as possible.

This goal is related to the efficiency of Shared Buffer management. In terms of performance, it is very important to keep frequently accessed blocks in shared buffers for as long as possible. To do this, PostgreSQL uses the Clock Sweep algorithm. The details are described in 'Clock Sweep Algorithm'.

Shared Buffer Architecture

Shared buffers consist of four major components.

1. Hash table
2. Hash elements (and element keys)
3. Buffer descriptor to manage buffer status
4. Buffer pool to store the actual block

Shared Buffer structure is as follows.

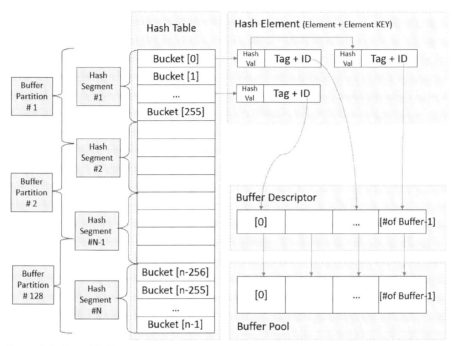

Figure 2-1. *Shared Buffer structure*

Hash Table

Hash tables are a very effective data structure when managing (retrieving, inputting) buffers in memory. However, a hash table has a problem in that performance is degraded when a hash collision occurs.

▢ **Note**   Hash collision is a computational term which means that the same hash value is output for different input values. From a Buffer perspective, this means that different blocks are connected to the same hash bucket.

One way to reduce the hash collision problem is to divide the hash table into logical N segments. This is called a 'segmented hash table', and PostgreSQL uses this method. (See Figure 2-2)

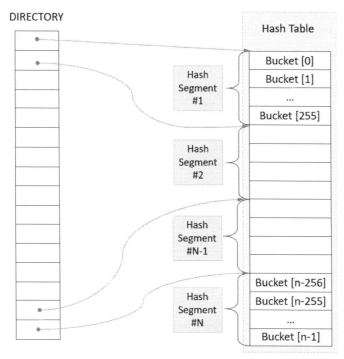

Figure 2-2. *Segmented hash table structure*

What is DIRECTORY?

A segmented hash table is a hash table divided by N logical hash segments. Therefore, another array is needed to indicate the starting position of each segment divided by N. This array is called a 'directory'. The default directory setting is 256, and if you set Shared Buffer to bigger, the directory size will increase. For more information, see 'Hash table size and number of hash segments?'.

What is the size of the hash segment?

One hash segment consists of 256 buckets.

📄 **Note** A bucket is an array element. That is, the number of buckets is the length of the array.

Hash table size and number of hash segments?

Through the source, let's see how to calculate the hash table size. (Readers who are not interested in the internal structure can skip this part)

Src 2-1. src/backend/utils/hash/dynahash.c

```
#define DEF_SEGSIZE              256
#define DEF_SEGSIZE_SHIFT          8     /* must be log2(DEF_SEGSIZE) */
#define DEF_DIRSIZE              256
#define DEF_FFACTOR                1     /* default fill factor *
```

Src 2-2. src/include/storage/lwlock.h

```
#define NUM_BUFFER_PARTITIONS   128
```

Src 2-3. src/backend/utils/hash/dynahash.c

```
nbuckets = next_pow2_int((nelem - 1) / hctl->ffactor + 1);
hctl->max_bucket = hctl->low_mask = nbuckets - 1;
nsegs = (nbuckets - 1) / hctl->ssize + 1;
nsegs = next_pow2_int(nsegs);
```

The variables needed to understand the calculation method are as follows.

- **nelem**: Number of buffers + NUM_BUFFER_PARTITIONS

- **hctl->ffactor**: Means fill factor. The default setting is 1

- **hctl->max_bucket**: Number of hash table buckets

- **nsegs**: Number of hash segments

Let's take a closer look at the formula. (Assuming that the block size is 8 KiB and the shared buffer is 1 GiB)

nelem

The nelem value is 'number of buffers + NUM_BUFFER_PARTITIONS'.

This value is used as an input value to calculate the number of hash table buckets. In the case of 1 GiB, the number of buffers is 131,072 and the value of NUM_BUFFER_PARTITIONS is 128. Therefore, the value of nelem is 131,200.

```
nelem = (1 GiB / 8KiB = 131,072) + (NUM_BUFFER_PARTITIONS=128)
= 131,200
```

nbuckets

The nbuckets value represents the number of hash table buckets.

If you apply the following formula, the number of hash table buckets is 262,144. This value is twice the actual buffer count of 131,072. The reason why the number of hash table buckets is set to be large is to minimize hash collisions.

```
nbuckets = next_pow2_int((nelem - 1) / hctl->ffactor + 1);
= next_pow2_int((131,200 - 1) / 1 + 1)
= next_pow2_int(131,200)
= 262,144
```

In the above equation, hctl-> ffactor means Fill Factor and the default value is 1. And next_pow2_int () is a function that returns an exponent of 2 greater than the input value. Therefore, it returns 2^{18} (262,144) which is larger than the input value 131,200.

▫ **Note**   The formula shows that the larger the fill factor, the smaller the number of buckets, and the smaller the fill factor, the greater the number of buckets. The number of buckets can be increased or decreased by adjusting the fill factor. To minimize the hash collision, it is preferable to use a default value of '1'.

---

hctl->max_bucket

The value of hctl-> max_bucket means the size of the hash table array. The array index is zero-based, so set nbuckets -1.

nseg

`nseg` means the number of hash segments. From the results below, it can be seen that the number of hash segments is 1,024 when the shared buffer is 1 GiB. Since the number of hash segments is 1,024, the directory size is also set to 1,024.

```
nsegs = (nbuckets - 1) / hctl->ssize + 1
      = (262,144 - 1) / 256 + 1
      = 1,024
nsegs = next_pow2_int(nsegs);
      = next_pow2_int(1,024)
      = 1,024
```

In the above formula, `hctl-> ssize` represents the number of buckets per hash segment, and the default value is 256.

What is a buffer partition?

Directories, hash segments, and hash tables are all shared resources in the shared buffer. Shared resources are protected using LW (Light Weight) locks. That is, the backend process must acquire LW locks to access shared memory. Although there is a positive aspect that LW lock protects shared resources, there is a problem that performance degradation may occur due to LW lock contention.

For example, if there is one LW lock that manages a hash table, most processes accessing the hash table will wait for the LW lock. To solve this problem, PostgreSQL uses a method of dividing the hash table into N 'buffer partitions' and allocating one LW lock per buffer partition.

What is the number of buffer partitions?

Up to version 9.4, there were only 16 buffer partitions. As a result, LW lock contention is likely to occur during buffer partition access in high concurrency environments, and this has actually caused performance problems. To solve this problem, the number of buffer partitions has been increased to 128 since 9.5. As a result, the number of LW locks to manage buffer partitions has also increased from 16 to 128. The number of buffer partitions can be set with the `NUM_BUFFER_PARTITIONS` variable.

Hash Element

Let's take a closer look at source analysis. (You may skip this part if you are not interested in the internal structure.) A hash element consists of an element and an element key. Let's take a look at the element first.

Element component

The element consists of an element pointer to the Next element and a hashvalue. (See Sources 2-4) The hashvalue is calculated using the `BufferTag`.

Src 2-4. src/include/utils/hsearch.h

```
typedef struct HASHELEMENT
{
    struct HASHELEMENT *link; /* link to next entry in same bucket */
    uint32 hashvalue;         /* hash function result for this entry */
} HASHELEMENT;
```

Element KEY component

The element KEY is constructed as follows. (See Figure 2-3)

- The element KEY consists of a `BufferTag` structure and a buffer descriptor array index. (See Sources 2-5)

- The BufferTag structure consists of the `RelFileNode` structure, `forkNum`, and `blockNum`. (See Sources 2-6)

- The `RelFileNode` structure consists of a tablespace number, a database number, and an object number. (See Sources 2-7)

Src 2-5. /src/backend/storage/buffer/buf_table.c

```
typedef struct {
    BufferTag   key;        /* Tag of a disk page */
    int         id;         /* Associated buffer ID */
} BufferLookupEnt;
```

Src 2-6. /src/include/storage/buf_internals.h

```
typedef struct buftag {
    RelFileNode rnode;          /* physical relation identifier */
    ForkNumber  forkNum;
    BlockNumber blockNum;       /* blknum relative to begin of reln */
} BufferTag;
```

Src 2-7. /src/include/storage/relfilenode.h

```
typedef struct RelFileNode {
    Oid         spcNode;    /* tablespace */
    Oid         dbNode;     /* database */
    Oid         relNode;    /* relation */
} RelFileNode;
```

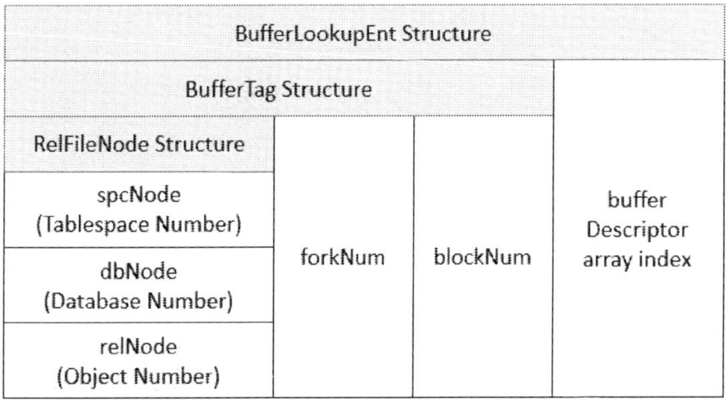

BufferLookupEnt Structure			
BufferTag Structure			buffer Descriptor array index
RelFileNode Structure	forkNum	blockNum	
spcNode (Tablespace Number)			
dbNode (Database Number)			
relNode (Object Number)			

Figure 2-3. *Element KEY component*

BufferTag

BufferTag is the same concept as the social secret number of a block. In other words, it consists of data that can uniquely identify each block in the cluster database. To do this, we use the following structure.

- The BufferTag is stored in the `BufferTag` structure.

- The `BufferTag` structure consists of the `RelFileNode` structure, `forkNum`, and `blockNum`.

- The `RelFileNode` structure consists of a tablespace number, a database number, and an object number. That way, you can get a unique object number in the cluster database.

- `forkNum` refers to the object type. 0 is the table (or index), 1 is the FSM, 2 is the VM. (See Sources 2-8)

- `blockNum` means block number.

Src 2-8. /src/include/common/relpath.h

```
typedef enum ForkNumber
{
    InvalidForkNumber    = -1,
    MAIN_FORKNUM         =  0,
    FSM_FORKNUM,
    VISIBILITYMAP_FORKNUM,
    INIT_FORKNUM
} ForkNumber;
```

Hash element memory allocation

Let's take a quiz before proceeding. At what point is the hash element memory structure allocated?

1. Pre-allocate a certain number of times at DB start
2. Allocation at the time of request after DB startup

The correct answer is number one.

PostgreSQL pre-allocates 'buffer number + `NUM_BUFFER_PARTITIONS`' hash element arrays at DB startup. And every time a buffer is allocated, it is pulled out from the last one.

Multiple freeList

Up to version 9.5, one freeList managed the entire hash element array. Therefore, if many processes request buffers at the same time, freeList bottlenecks have occurred. To solve this problem, increased the number of freelists to 32 from 9.6.

Therefore, if the shared buffer is 1 GiB, 4,100 hash elements are managed per freeList. The formula is as follows.

```
Shared Buffer = 1 GiB
=> The number of hash element arrays that are initially allocated.
(132,000) = Number of buffers (131,072) + NUM_BUFFER_PARTITIONS (128)

=> Number of hash element arrays managed by one FreeList
(4,100) = 132,000 / NUM_FREELISTS (32)
```

And I explained that 'take it out of the back'. This is related to how the hash element is connected. As shown in Figure 2-4, each of the 32 hash element arrays has a link structure from the back to the front. And the `freeList` in the `HASHHDR` structure points to the hash element at the end of each hash element array. That is, the method of managing 32 hash element arrays using 32 `freeLists` is applied. This reduces contention when allocating buffers.

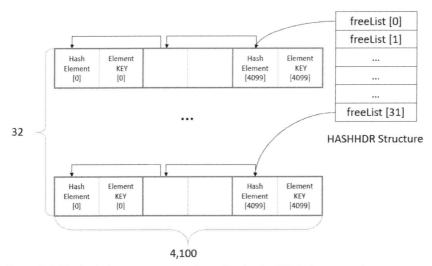

Figure 2-4. *The hash element array status immediately after DB startup*

Buffer Descriptor

The buffer descriptor is a structure for managing buffer metadata. Let's take a closer look at the components through the source. (Readers who are not interested in the internal structure can skip this part)

Buffer descriptor component

Src 2-9. src/include/storage/buf_internals.h

```
typedef struct BufferDesc {
    BufferTag   tag;                /* ID of page contained in buffer */
    int         buf_id;             /* buffer's index number (from 0) */

    /* state of the tag, containing flags, refcount and usagecount */
    pg_atomic_uint32 state;

    int         wait_backend_pid;   /* backend PID of pin-count waiter */
    int         freeNext;           /* link in freelist chain */
    LWLock      content_lock;       /* to lock access to buffer contents */
} BufferDesc;
```

The main components of the buffer descriptor structure are as follows.

- **tag**: Store BufferTag.

- **buf_id**: This is the index number in the 'buffer pool' array where the actual buffer is stored.

- **wait_backend_pid**: To access the buffer, the buffer PIN must be obtained. If the buffer PIN can't be obtained, it should wait. The column provides the process ID that waits for the buffer PIN.

- **context_lock**: It is the LW lock needed to access the buffer. The LW lock acquisition will be described in the section 'Spin lock and LW lock'.

A detailed description of the state and freeNext variable follows.

state variable

Until version 9.5, the number of processes to set the PIN to access the buffer (`refcount`), the number of buffer accesses (`usage_count`), and the buffer status (`flags`) were provided, respectively.

However, since 9.6, these three variables are provided as one state variable. (See Figure 2-5)

Figure 2-5. *State variable component*

Bit operation for information acquisition

Since the data is stored in units of bits, it is necessary to perform bit mask and bit shift operations to extract the data. The bit operation method is as follows.

Src 2-10. src/include/storage/buf_internals.h

```
#define BUF_REFCOUNT_ONE 1
#define BUF_REFCOUNT_MASK ((1U << 18) - 1)
#define BUF_USAGECOUNT_MASK 0x003C0000U
#define BUF_USAGECOUNT_ONE (1U << 18)
#define BUF_USAGECOUNT_SHIFT 18
#define BUF_FLAG_MASK 0xFFC00000U

/* Get refcount and usage_count from buffer state */
#define BUF_STATE_GET_REFCOUNT(state) ((state) & BUF_REFCOUNT_MASK)
#define BUF_STATE_GET_USAGECOUNT(state) (((state) & BUF_USAGECOUNT_MASK) >> BUF_USAGECOUNT_SHIFT)
```

For example, it can be seen that a bit mask operation and a right shift operation are used to extract the BUF_STATE_GET_USAGECOUNT value. (See Figure 2-6)

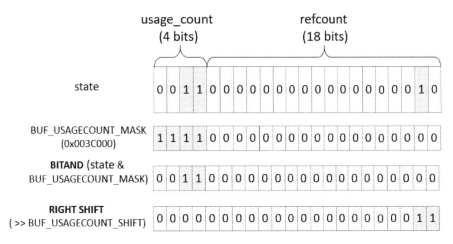

Figure 2-6. *Procedure for obtaining usage_count using bit operation*

flags

The flags field shows 10 buffer states using 10 bits.

For example, the BM_IO_IN_PROGRESS bit, which is the fifth bit (the 27th bit among 32 bits), manages the 'disk IO in progress' state. Therefore, if the buffer is in disk I/O, the corresponding bit must be set to '1'. To do this, shift 1 to the left 26 times. (1U means Unsigned Integer 1)

Src 2-11. src/include/storage/buf_internals.h

```
#define BM_LOCKED                 (1U << 22)
#define BM_DIRTY                  (1U << 23)
#define BM_VALID                  (1U << 24)
#define BM_TAG_VALID              (1U << 25)
#define BM_IO_IN_PROGRESS         (1U << 26)
#define BM_IO_ERROR               (1U << 27)
#define BM_JUST_DIRTIED           (1U << 28)
#define BM_PIN_COUNT_WAITER       (1U << 29)
#define BM_CHECKPOINT_NEEDED      (1U << 30)
#define BM_PERMANENT              (1U << 31)
```

freeNext variable

FreeNext is a pointer to the next empty buffer.

Immediately after DB startup, all buffers are empty, so freeNext points to the next array element. After receiving the buffer allocation request, it operates as shown in Figure 2-7.

That is, the `firstFreeBuffer` entry in the `BufferStrategyControl` structure points to the `freeNext` link header, and the `lastFreeBuffer` entry points to the `freeNext` link tail.

After all buffers have been allocated, there is no empty buffer. Therefore, if a buffer allocation request is received after this point, a victim buffer should be selected. (Here, `firstFreeBuffer` has a value of -1.) The details will be explained in the 'Clock Sweep Algorithm' section.

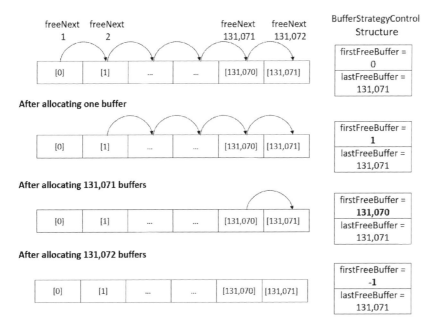

Figure 2-7. *FreeNext link changes due to buffer allocation*

Spin lock and LW lock

Spin lock and LW lock must be acquired when accessing Shared Buffer. If you're familiar with ORACLE, think of a spin lock as a `mutex` and an LW lock as a `latch`.

The reason for distinguishing spin lock from LW lock is to improve performance. LW lock is a very light lock, and Spin lock is a lighter lock. Therefore, it is advantageous to use Spin Lock if possible. The two differences are summarized as follows. (See Table 2-1)

Table 2-1. *Difference between spin lock and LW lock*

Item	Spin lock	LW lock
Work Load	Very very low	Very low

Context Switching	Does not occur	May happen
How it works	Spin	Queuing & Posting
purpose of use	Used when accessing variables in the structure	Used when accessing a structure
Lock Mode	EXCLUSIVE	SHARE & EXCLUSIVE

Spin lock

Spin lock works very lightly.

Spin locks are used for operations that can be performed in a very short time. Even if another process has already acquired a Spin lock, it is very likely to acquire a Spin lock after doing a few Spin loops. Spin does not fall into Sleep state, so there is no context switching.

Spin lock implementation method

There are two ways to implement spin locks.

- Use mutex

- Use TAS (Test & Set) with an inline assembly language

PostgreSQL uses the second method.

LW lock

PostgreSQL uses the 'queueing & posting' approach to acquire LW locks.

- Suppose you want to retrieve a hash element with a hash bucket. In this case, LW lock should be acquired in SHARED mode because it is in read mode.

- Assume that you enter `BufferTag` information in a hash element. In this case, LW lock must be acquired in EXCLUSIVE mode because it is write mode.

LW lock acquisition procedure

The pseudo code for LW lock acquisition is as follows.

```
LWLockAcquire(LWLock *lock, LWLockMode mode)
LOOP
  Attempt to acquire LW lock by calling LWLockAttemptLock () function.
  Acquire the lock, escape the LOOP.
  If the lock can't be acquired, it is registered in the waiting queue.
  Call the LWLockAttemptLock () function one more time.
  If the lock is acquired, the entry registered in the waiting queue is
  deleted and the LOOP is escaped.
  If it can't acquire the lock, it will start waiting.
  (Waits until another process wakes up.)
END LOOP
```

Reading buffers from Shared Buffer

So far, we have looked at the major components of Shared Buffer. The main points are summarized as follows.

- Shared Buffer consists of hash table, hash element, buffer descriptor and buffer pool.

- The hash table is an array structure, and uses a segmented hash table structure to minimize hash collisions.

- Also, manage the logical partitions to increase concurrency.

- At this time, there is one LW lock per partition.

- The hash element consists of an element and an element key.

- The element consists of a hashvalue for the BufferTag and a pointer to the next element.

- The element key stores the BufferTag and the buffer id.

- BufferTag is equal to the Social Secrete Number for the block.

- BufferTag consists of database number, table space number, object number, fork number and block number.

- MAIN object fork number is 0, FSM is 1, VM is 2.

- Beginning with version 9.6, hash elements are managed as 32 `freeLists`. This is for the purpose of eliminating contention.

- The buffer descriptor is a structure array that manages the buffer meta information. At this time, the number of arrays is equal to the number of buffers.

- The main meta information managed by the buffer descriptor is `refcount`, `usage_count`, `flags`, `freeNext`, and so on.

In this section, let's look at the following two flow charts.

1. Reading a block in the Shared Buffer
2. When Disk Read occurs

When reading blocks in Shared Buffer

It is assumed that the shared buffer size is 256 MiB and that the number of blocks currently loaded in the shared buffer is three. The BufferTag of the buffer to read is assumed to be 'Tag_B'. (See Figure 2-8)

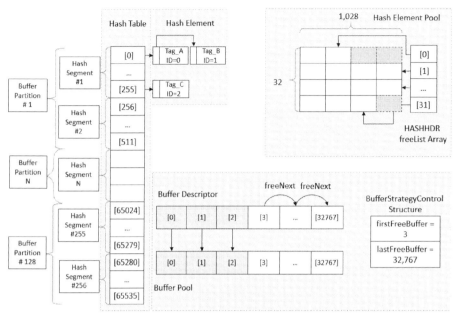

Figure 2-8. *Current Shared Buffer Status*

🗋 **Note** The values stored in the actual BufferTag are not the same values as 'Tag_A' and 'Tag_B'. As described earlier, the BufferTag stores a value that can uniquely identify a block. However, for convenience of explanation, a value equal to 'Tag_A' is used.

The size of each element shown in Figure 2-8 is shown in Table 2-2.

Table 2-2. *Size of each element*

Item	Calculation method	Value
Number of buffers	256 MiB / 8 KiB	32,768
Number of buffer partitions	`#define NUM_BUFFER_PARTITIONS`	128
`nelem`	Number of buffers + Number of buffer partitions	32,896
`hctl->ffactor`	`#define DEF_FFACTOR`	1
Hash table array (Number of buckets)	`nbuckets = next_pow2_int((nelem - 1) / hctl->ffactor + 1);`	65,536
Hash Segment Size	`#define DEF_SEGSIZE`	256

Number of hash segments	Hash table array size / Hash Segment Size	256
Number of FreeList	#define NUM_FREELISTS	32
Hash element Pool Size	nelem	32,896 = 1,028 * 32
Buffer descriptor array	Number of buffers	32,767
Array of buffer pools	Number of buffers	32,767

Processing order

The order of reading the buffers in the Shared Buffer is as follows. (See Figure 2-9)

1. Create a BufferTag. ('Tag_B' is generated)
   A. Calculate the hashvalue using the generated BufferTag.
   B. Calculate the buffer partition number using the generated hashvalue.
2. Obtain the LW lock for the buffer partition # in SHARE mode.
3. Compute the hash table bucket number using hashvalue.
   A. Replace the bucket number with the hash segment number and index number.
   B. Search for 'Tag_B' along the hash chain.
4. Since the buffer ID of Tag_B is 1, set the PIN in the buffer descriptor array index [1]. (In this case, increase refcount and usage_count by 1 respectively)
5. Release LW lock on buffer partition #.
6. Read buffer pool array index [1].
7. Release the PIN. (At this time, reduce refcount by 1)

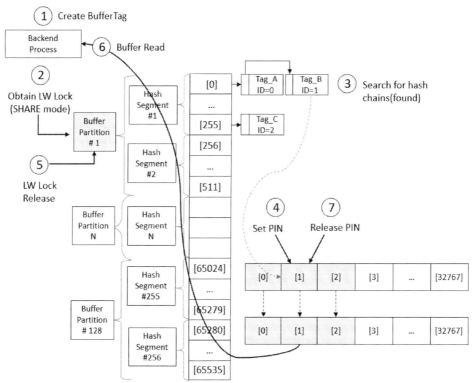

Figure 2-9. *Block read processing order in Shared Buffer*

CALC_BUCKET function

Let's look closely at the source to find the bucket number in the hash table during the execution. The function to find the hash bucket is `calc_bucket` (). (See Sources 2-12)

Src 2-12. src/backend/utils/hash/dynahash.c

```
/* Convert a hash value to a bucket number */
calc_bucket(HASHHDR *hctl, uint32 hash_val){
        uint32           bucket;
        bucket = hash_val & hctl->high_mask;
        if (bucket > hctl->max_bucket)
            bucket = bucket & hctl->low_mask;
        return bucket;
}
```

The processing logic of `cacl_bucket` () is very simple. Obtain the bucket number by performing the BITAND operation with the input `hash_val` and `hctl-> high_mask`. If the bucket value is greater than `hctl-> max_bucket`, perform a BITAND operation with `hctl-> row_mask`. The values used at this time are shown in Table 2-3.

Table 2-3. *HASHHDR value*

Item	Value	Calculation formula
`hctl->high_mask`	131,071	`(nbuckets << 1) - 1`
`hctl->row_mask`	65,535	`nbuckets -1`

The calc_bucket () caller calculates the hash segment number and the index number through the following operation. (See Table 2-4)

```
HASHHDR    *hctl = hashp->hctl;
bucket      = calc_bucket(hctl, hashvalue);
segment_num = bucket >> hashp->sshift;
segment_ndx = MOD(bucket, hashp->ssize);
```

Table 2-4. *HASHHDR value*

Item	Value	Calculation formula
`hashp->sshift`	8	`#define DEF_SEGSIZE_SHIFT 8`
`hashp->ssize`	256	`#define DEF_SEGSIZE 256`

To obtain the hash segment number, shifting the 8-bit right shift is equivalent to dividing by 256. The index in the hash segment is the remainder of dividing the bucket value by 256. This can be expressed as follows. (See Figure 2-10)

```
(hash_val: 2230457782)     10000100111100100001010110110110
(hctl->high_mask: 131071)  00000000000000011111111111111111

                        BITAND Operation
                             ⇩
(bucket: 5558)             00000000000000000001010110110110

                         Right Shift >> 8
                             ⇩
(segment_num: 21)          00000000000000000000000000010101

(segment_ndx: 182)         MOD(5558, 256)
```

Figure 2-10. *Procedure for finding bucket numbers in a table*

When DISK Read occurs

To read blocks that do not exist in Shared Buffer, Disk Read must be performed. That is, after loading the corresponding block into the shared buffer through Disk Read, the corresponding buffer is read. Assume that the current shared buffer state is shown in Figure 2-8. At this time, the order of reading the block whose `BufferTag` is 'Tag_D' is as follows.

Processing Order (Part -1)

1. Create a `BufferTag`. ('Tag_D' is generated)
   A. Calculate the hashvalue using the generated `BufferTag`.
   B. Calculate the buffer partition number using the generated hashvalue.
2. Obtain the LW lock for the buffer partition # in SHARE mode.
3. Compute the hash table bucket number using hashvalue.
   A. Replace the bucket number with the hash segment number and index number.
   B. It searches for 'Tag_D' while following the hash chain, but fails the search.
4. Release LW lock on buffer partition #.

This is the same as reading a block in the Shared Buffer. The only difference is that there is no block in the hash chain. The processing procedure so far is shown in Figure 2-11.

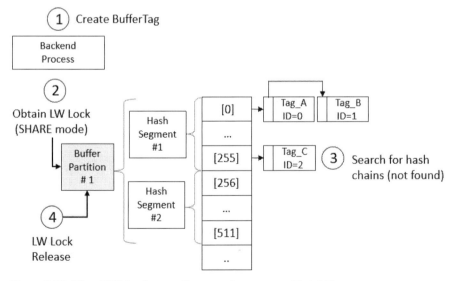

Figure 2-11. *When DISK Read occurs, the processing sequence (Part # 1)*

Processing Order (Part-2)

The following processing sequence is as follows. (See Figure 2-12)

5. Obtain the `firstFreeBuffer` value of the `BufferStrategyControl` structure.

   A. Obtain a spin lock to change the value of `firstFreeBuffer`.

   B. Change the value of `firstFreeBuffer` from 3 to 4.

   C. C. Release the spin lock.

6. Set the PIN in the buffer descriptor array index [3]. (Set `refcount` to 1 at this time)

After that, we do the work of connecting the hash element to the hash table.

7. Obtain the LW lock for the buffer partition # in EXCLUSIVE mode.

8. In the hash element pool, one element is assigned.

   A. Change the `freeList` pointer to the previous element of the element assigned in step 8

9. Attach the hash element to the hash chain and copy the record.

10. Set the buffer header lock on the buffer descriptor array index [3].

    A. Increase `usage_count` by 1

    B. Release buffer header lock.

11. Release the LW lock set in the buffer partition #.

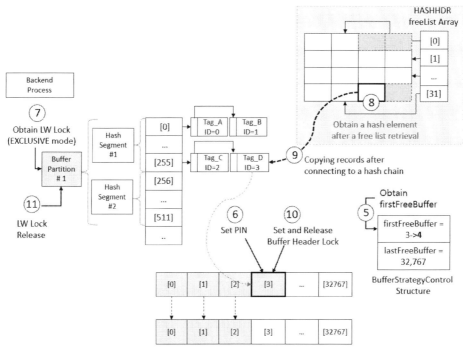

Figure 2-12. *When DISK Read occurs, the processing sequence (Part # 2)*

Processing Order (Part-3)

The following processing sequence is as follows. (See Figure 2-13.)

12. Acquires the LW lock in EXCLUSIVE mode to access `BufferIOLockArrary` array index [3].

13. Set the buffer header lock on the buffer descriptor array index [3].

    A. Set the `BM_IO_IN_PROGRESS` flag bit to 1.

    B. Release buffer header lock.

14. Load the block into the buffer pool array index [3].

15. Set buffer header lock on buffer descriptor array index [3].

    A. Set the `BM_IO_IN_PROGRESS` flag bit to zero.

    B. Release buffer header lock.

16. Release the LW lock acquired to access the `BufferIOLockArrary` array index [3].

17. Read buffer pool array index [3].

18. Release the PIN. (At this time, reduce refcount by 1)

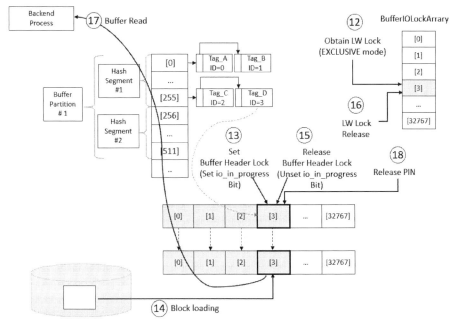

Figure 2-13. *When DISK Read occurs, the processing sequence (Part # 3)*

Clock Sweep Algorithm for Buffer Replacement

In the previous example, there was an empty buffer in the shared buffer. If there is no empty buffer, the buffer in the shared buffer must be written to disk. In this case, the buffer written to the disk is called the victim buffer, and the algorithm for selecting the victim buffer is called the buffer replacement algorithm. Since the purpose of Shared Buffer is to improve performance by minimizing DISK Read, it is very important to use a Buffer Replacement algorithm that can manage buffers efficiently.

Description of the Clock Sweep algorithm

PostgreSQL uses a clock sweep algorithm for buffer replacement. This algorithm is a kind of NFU (Not Frequently Used) algorithm that selects less used buffers as victim buffers. To select a less used buffer, it is necessary to manage the number of accesses per buffer. The number of buffer accesses has been described as a bit operation in the `state` variable in the buffer descriptor. And that the `usage_count` in the `state` variable is incremented by 1 each time the buffer is accessed.

More precisely, it only increases up to the value defined in `BM_MAX_USAGE_COUNT`, and does not increase more. `BM_MAX_USAGE_COUNT` The default setting is 5. There are readers who wonder that the value of 5 is very small. I thought so.

However, once you understand the Clock Sweep algorithm, you will think it is a very reasonable value. The reason for setting the maximum value with such a small value is for the purpose of 'fair competition'. A more detailed explanation will be given while explaining the Clock Sweep algorithm.

The 'Clock' of the clock sweep algorithm is an intuitive representation of the algorithm's operating principle. This algorithm searches the buffer clockwise to find the victim buffer. Since the buffer descriptor is an array, the index 0 and the maximum index are concatenated into a logical circle. That is, it searches the victim buffer from array 0 first. If it finds a victim buffer, it returns a victim buffer and stops the search. In the next search, the search starts from the next index.

The 'Sweep' of the Clock Sweep algorithm means that you perform a sweep while performing a search. If you look at the source code, reduce `usage_count` by 1. This is analogous to cleaning.

That is, the clock sweep algorithm selects a buffer with zero `refcount` and `usage_count` as the victim buffer. If the victim buffer is a dirty buffer (`BM_DIRTY` bit is 1), the content of the buffer is written to disk.

Clock Sweep Algorithm

The clock sweep algorithm consists of very simple code. Some of the real sources are: (For the convenience of explanation, only a part was extracted)

Src 2-13. src/backend/storage/buffer/freelist.c

```
for (;;) {
(1)     buf = GetBufferDescriptor(ClockSweepTick());
(2)     local_buf_state = LockBufHdr(buf);

(3)     if (BUF_STATE_GET_REFCOUNT(local_buf_state) == 0)
```

```
(4)        if (BUF_STATE_GET_USAGECOUNT(local_buf_state) != 0)
           local_buf_state -= BUF_USAGECOUNT_ONE;
(5)        else  return buf;
(6)    UnlockBufHdr(buf, local_buf_state);
}
```

A description of the source follows.

1. Call the `ClockSweepTick` () function to determine where to start searching for victim buffers. The function returns the `nextVictimBuffer` value in the `BufferStrategyControl` structure.
2. Perform buffer header lock.
3. If `refcount` is 0, perform Step (4). Otherwise, perform Step (6).
4. If `usage_count` is not 0, decrease `usage_count` by 1
5. If `usage_count` is zero, it returns a buffer.
6. Release the buffer header lock and repeat Step (1).

Now readers have understood the basic principles of the Clock Sweep algorithm. The clock sweep algorithm is illustrated in Figure 2-14.

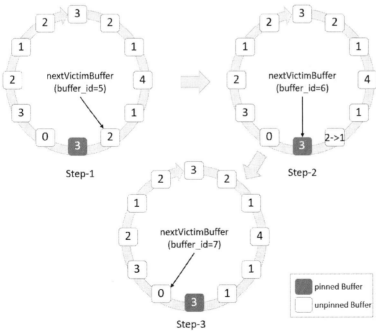

Figure 2-14. *Clock Sweep Procedure*

Step by step explanation is as follows.

Step-1

NextVictimBuffer, buffer_id = 5 is not a pinned buffer. However, since usage_count is 2, change usage_count to 1 and move to next buffer

Step-2

The nextVictimBuffer, buffer_id = 6, is the pinned buffer. Therefore, it moves to the next buffer.

Step-3

NextVictimBuffer buffer_id = 7 is an unpinned buffer and usage_count is zero. Therefore, it is selected as a victim buffer.

What is fair competition?

I mentioned earlier that the reason for setting the BM_MAX_USAGE_COUNT default setting slightly smaller is because of 'fair competition'. If you understand the Clock Sweep algorithm and are familiar with ORACLE's touch count algorithm, you might have some sense of 'fair competition'.

To understand 'fair competition', think about when 'unfair competition' occurs. For example, suppose you have accessed a particular buffer a few hundred thousand times in a very short time, and there is no access after that. In this case, is it fair to put the buffer in Shared Buffer for a long time? Of course, not. Therefore, the Buffer Replacement algorithm using the access count should include logic to eliminate unfair competition.

For example, ORACLE does not increment touch_count for accesses occurring in the same buffer within N seconds. Also, when the buffers move to the HOT area, touch_count is initialized to zero.

PostgreSQL has the same effect as ORACLE by setting the BM_MAX_USAGE_COUNT to a somewhat smaller value of 5. In other words, usage_count is 5 even though accesses to the same buffer occur thousands of times in N seconds. Thus, no matter how many accesses at any point in time, the buffer is chosen as the victim buffer if it is not accessed again before the clock has rotated six times. (See Figure 2-15)

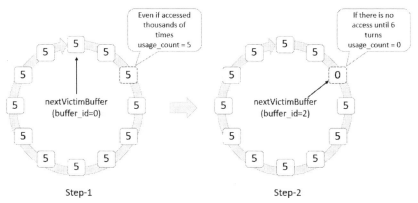

Figure 2-15. *Fair competition*

From another perspective, it is also fair to reduce usage_count by 1 each time a clock sweep is performed. This is because the usage_count of the buffer always maintains a value greater than 1 if it is regularly accessed frequently.

IO Strategy and Ring Buffer for Bulk IO Processing

PostgreSQL has used the Clock Sweep algorithm to improve the efficiency of shared buffers. If so, how do I solve the problem that Seq Scan can flood the shared buffer?

PostgreSQL uses the IO strategy and Ring Buffer to solve this problem.

What is IO strategy?

The IO strategy implies a different strategy depending on the IO type. PostgreSQL has four IO types. (See Sources 2-14)

Src 2-14. src/include/storage/bufmgr.h

```
typedef enum BufferAccessStrategyType {
    BAS_NORMAL,      /* Normal random access */
    BAS_BULKREAD,    /* Large read-only scan */
    BAS_BULKWRITE,   /* Large multi-block write (e.g. COPY IN) */
```

```
    BAS_VACUUM          /* VACUUM */
} BufferAccessStrategyType;
```

That is, IO requests are classified into NORMAL (for random access), BULK READ (for large segment scan), BULK WRITE (for bulk write), and VACUUM. All requests except NORMAL request use Ring Buffer.

Ring Buffer

Ring Buffer means a logically circular array.

That is, it uses a circular array of a predetermined size, thereby preventing a shared buffer flooding due to Seq Scan. Of course, Ring Buffer also exists in Shared Buffer.

Ring Buffer Size

The size of the ring buffer is slightly different depending on the IO type. (See Sources 2-15)

Src 2-15. src/backend/storage/buffer/freelist.c

```
switch (btype)
{
    case BAS_NORMAL:
            return NULL;
    case BAS_BULKREAD:
            ring_size = 256 * 1024 / BLCKSZ;
            break;
    case BAS_BULKWRITE:
            ring_size = 16 * 1024 * 1024 / BLCKSZ;
            break;
    case BAS_VACUUM:
            ring_size = 256 * 1024 / BLCKSZ;
            break;
```

The Ring Buffer size for BULK READ is 256 KiB (32 blocks).

BULK READ Definition

So, what is the definition of BULK READ? Is all Seq Scan BULK READ?

Not like that. PostgreSQL uses the BULK READ method only for Seq scans on tables that are at least one-fourth the size of the shared buffer. At this time, the table size uses statistical information.

How Ring Buffer works in BULK READ

The ring buffer size for BULK READ is 256 KiB (32 blocks). But if you think a bit more, there are some questions. Let's answer the following questions.

Question 1

There is a table that performs BULK READ very frequently.

If the table is read 100 times repeatedly, is the ring buffer size for that table 32 blocks? 3,200 blocks?

Question 2

If the same table is read twice with UNION ALL, is the ring buffer size 32 blocks? Or is it 64 blocks?

The correct answer is as follows.

1) 3,200 blocks

The reason why 32 more ring buffers are allocated for each SQL execution is due to the fairness of buffer usage. We have introduced Ring Buffer to prevent the risk of Seq Scan on a large table, but allocating only 32 blocks of Ring Buffer is out of equality if you frequently access the table in many SQLs.

---

2) 64 blocks

Whenever BULK READ target table appears in one SQL, allocate 32 ring buffers each time.

Let's test it.

Check Ring Buffer operation principle

1. Install the `pg_buffercache` extension for testing.

```
create extension pg_buffercache;
```

2. Since Shared Buffer is 256 MiB, it creates a table that is larger than 1/4 of 256 MiB.

```
drop table b1;
create table b1 (c1 char(1000), c2 char(1000));
insert into b1 select i, i from generate_series(1,35000) a(i);
analyze b1;

select relname, relpages, relpages*8192/1024/1024 as size
from    pg_class where relname='b1';
 relname | relpages | size
---------+----------+------
 b1      |     8750 |   68
```

3. Restart the DB for testing.

4. Seq Scan B1 table.

```
select count(*) from b1;
```

5. As a result of executing the check script, you can see that 32 blocks have been loaded into the shared buffer.

```
Shared Buffer check script execution result (see below for script contents)
buffers
---------
     32
```

6. Perform one more time.

```
select count(*) from b1;
```

7. As a result of executing the check script, you can see that 64 blocks have been loaded into Shared Buffer.

```
buffers
---------
     64
```

If you repeat the test several times, you can see that it is loaded into the shared buffer by the number of 'execution * 32 blocks'.

8. Restart the DB for testing.

9. Perform a `UNION ALL` statement.

```
select count(*) from b1
union all
select count(*) from b1;
```

10. As a result of executing the check script, you can see that 64 blocks have been loaded into Shared Buffer.

```
buffers
---------
      64
```

11. Perform one more time.

```
select count(*) from b1
union all
select count(*) from b1;
```

12. As a result of executing the check script, 128 blocks are loaded into the shared buffer.

```
buffers
---------
     128
```

Script. *Query for Shared Buffer check*

```
select count(*) as buffers
from    pg_buffercache a, pg_class b
where   a.relfilenode = pg_relation_filenode(b.oid)
and     a.reldatabase in (0, (select oid
                              from   pg_database
                              where  datname=current_database()))
and     b.relname='b1';
```

Risk of Ring Buffer

So far, PostgreSQL has been using Ring Buffer to prevent damage to shared buffers caused by large BULK READs. In addition, if BULK READ is repeatedly performed, it increases the ring buffer size to improve table access efficiency.

But there is still a risk.

For example, suppose that the data suddenly increases and the table size is larger than one quarter of the shared buffer. In this case, after the DB restart (or after the buffer for the corresponding table is aged out of the shared buffer), the Seq Scan for the corresponding table is performed in the BULK READ manner. That is, the ring buffer is used. Therefore, the query performance may be slow. Let's test it.

1. Creates a table that is less than one-fourth the size of the shared buffer.

```
drop table s1;
create table s1 (c1 char(1000), c2 char(1000));
insert into s1 select i, i from generate_series(1,32000) a(i);
analyze s1;

select relname, relpages, relpages*8192/1024/1024 "SIZE"
from   pg_class where relname='s1';
 relname | relpages | SIZE
---------+----------+------
 s1      |     8000 |   62
```

2. Restart the DB for testing.

3. For testing, we create a function that iteratively performs Seq Scan.

```
CREATE or replace FUNCTION loop_fullscan(v_begin integer, v_end integer)
RETURNS VOID AS $$
DECLARE
rval integer;
BEGIN
    FOR i in v_begin..v_end LOOP
        SELECT COUNT(*) FROM s1 INTO rval;
    END LOOP;
END;
$$ LANGUAGE plpgsql;
```

4. Measure the performance of 100 times Seq scan of the table.

```
select loop_fullscan(1,100);
 loop_fullscan
---------------

(1 row)
Time: 605.653 ms
```

5. Enter an additional 1,000 to make the table size 1/4 of the shared buffer size.

```
insert into s1 select * from c1 limit 1000;
```

```
analyze s1;

select relname, relpages, relpages*8192/1024/1024 "SIZE"
from   pg_class where relname='s1';
 relname | relpages | SIZE
---------+----------+------
 s1      |     8250 |   64
```

5. Restart the DB for testing.

6. Measure the performance of 100 times Seq scan of the table.

```
select loop_fullscan(1,100);
 loop_fullscan
---------------
(1 row)
Time: 1689.020 ms
```

Test results show that using Ring Buffer degrades performance.

Of course, there will be some differences depending on the table size and test environment. However, it is obvious that Ring Buffer slows down the execution speed.

So how can we solve this problem?

Fortunately, PostgreSQL provides a way to solve this problem by providing the pg_prewarm extension.

pg_prewarm Extension

The pg_prewarm extension provides the ability to load tables and indexes into shared buffers. (You can also load a table that is larger than one-fourth the size of the shared buffer.) However, it is not a permanent buffer to reside in the shared buffer.

Let's try the previous test again using pg_prewarm ().

1. Create the pg_prewarm extension.

```
create extension pg_prewarm;
```

2. Restart the DB for testing.

3. Perform pg_prewam.

```
select pg_prewarm('s1');
 pg_prewarm
------------
       8250
Time: 51.789 ms
```

4. Measure the performance of 100 times Seq scan of the table.

```
select loop_fullscan(1,100);
 loop_fullscan
---------------
Time: 545.811 ms
```

Test results show that performance of `pg_prewarm` () greatly improves query performance. Therefore, you should use pg_prewarm () appropriately when working on batch program performance improvements.

Summary

Let's briefly summarize what we learned in this chapter.

First, you learned the Shared Buffer structure. A Shared Buffer consists of a hash table, a hash element, a buffer descriptor, and a buffer pool.

And we learned the order of memory read and DISK read. I hope that I can draw the IO processing flow after closing the eyes and drawing the Shared Buffer structure.

Also, we learned the clock sweep algorithm for efficient shared buffer management. Through the understanding of the algorithm, we can think about why the `BM_MAX_USAGE_COUNT` value is not set too large and fair competition.

Finally, you learned about IO strategies and ring buffers to protect shared buffers from BULK READ. We also learned about the principle of ring buffer operation and its disadvantages, and the `pg_prewarm` () extension to overcome this.

chapter **3**.
Understanding Optimizer

Understanding Optimizer

The Query Optimizer is not perfect. In other words, if the Query Optimizer can completely establish the execution plan of all the queries, we will not have to learn the Query Optimizer. But there are still slow queries.

Of course, not all problems with slow queries are due to the Query Optimizer. There may be a variety of causes, including inaccurate statistical information, inefficient index configuration, system overload, and lack of CPU resources. However, in order to accurately understand the causes of such performance degradation, it is necessary to understand the operation principle of the Query Optimizer.

In other words, you need to understand the query execution order, query rewrite, access method, join method, histogram, and various indexes.

In this chapter, we will learn about these contents.

Overview of the Cost Based Optimizer (CBO)

There are two types of Query Optimizer. One is the RBO (Rule Based Optimizer) and the other is the CBO (Cost Based Optimizer). PostgreSQL provides a CBO.

The RBO creates an execution plan by a set of rules (Rule). For example, if an index exists, it creates an execution plan that uses an index rather than a Seq Scan. The advantage of RBO is that it is very simple and intuitive. For this reason, RBO was preferred to the work environment when it was simple. However, as the complexity of work environment increases, RBO gradually disappears.

The CBO is a way of calculating the cost (COST). Use the statistical information to select an execution plan that can be executed with the least cost (COST). It is therefore very important to provide appropriate statistical information. In today's complex work environment, it is preferable to use CBO.

What is COST?

COST means cost. So, what is the unit of COST? How many IO blocks? Is it CPU time?

Neither. The unit of COST is just a number. In other words, the COST number is only a number calculated using some predefined parameter values and statistical information. Therefore, COST can't be used to invert the number of IO blocks and CPU usage time. However, the lower the COST, the lower the resource (IO, CPU) will be used to perform the query.

COST calculation method

Let's look at how COST is calculated. COST is divided into IO cost and CPU cost. Different costs are applied according to operation type (Seq Scan, Index Scan). (See Table 3-1)

Table 3-1. *Parameters and default settings for COST calculation*

Item	Parameter	Default Value
IO Cost	seq_page_cost	1
	random_page_cost	4
CPU Cost	cpu_tuple_cost	0.01
	cpu_index_tuple_cost	0.05
	cpu_operator_cost	0.0025

The description of each parameter is as follows.

seq_page_cost

It is the cost of reading one block by Seq Scan method.

random_page_cost

This is the cost of reading one block by the index scan method. More precisely, it is the cost of reading index leaf blocks and table blocks at the time of index scan. Index Root and Branch blocks are excluded from IO cost calculation. Most of these blocks are considered to be loaded into shared buffer. It can be seen that the index scan cost is calculated as 4 times of Seq Scan by the default setting value. The setting of 4 times seems to be a long experience. However, this setting may not be the optimal setting in all environments. As an extreme example, if all blocks are in shared buffer, both parameter settings can be set to 1. The parameters can also be set at the tablespace level. Therefore, if a particular tablespace is located on a very fast disk, you may set the parameter value lower.

cpu_tuple_cost

It is the cost of accessing one record at the time of Seq Scan.

cpu_index_tuple_cost

It is the cost of accessing one record at the time of index scan.

cpu_operator_cost

It is the cost of filtering one record at the time of Seq Scan and Index Scan.

Seq Scan cost calculation

Let's look at a very simple example of how Seq Scan costs are calculated.

```
drop table t1;
create table t1 (c1 integer, c2 integer);
insert into t1 select i, mod(i,10) from generate_series(1,100000) a(i);
analyze t1;

select relpages, reltuples from pg_class where relname='t1';
 relpages | reltuples
----------+-----------
      443 |    100000

explain select * from t1;
                    QUERY PLAN
--------------------------------------------------------
 Seq Scan on t1  (cost=0.00..1443.00 rows=100000 width=8)
```

The first number in cost is the cost of fetching the first record, and the second number is the cost of fetching the last record. (More information on how to read explain results will be explained in the 'Explain Tools' section)

The cost of reading the entire T1 table by Seq Scan method is 1,443. So how was the 1,443 calculated? This is the sum of IO cost for reading 443 blocks with Seq Scan and CPU cost for extracting 100,000 rows. That is, use the following formula.

```
COST=
select relpages  * current_setting('seq_page_cost')::float +
       reltuples * current_setting('cpu_tuple_cost')::float
from   pg_class where relname='t1';
= 443 * 1.0 + 100,000 * 0.01
= 1,443
```

Let's look at a case where a filter condition is added. This example fetches 300 rows by adding a C1 column condition.

```
explain select * from t1 where c1 <= 300;
                    QUERY PLAN
-----------------------------------------------------------
 Seq Scan on t1  (cost=0.00..1693.00 rows=277 width=8)
   Filter: (c1 <= 300)
```

The cost was increased to 1,693 by adding the C1 column condition. Compared to the previous results, 250 increased. You might be a little puzzled by this result. Since the number of records satisfying the filter condition is 300, is it reasonable to increase only 0.75 (300 rows * 0.0025)?

However, Seq Scan is a way to read all records in a table. Therefore, filter processing is performed on all records. That is, the processing cost increases by 250 (100,000 rows * 0.0025). The calculation formula is as follows.

```
COST=
select relpages  * current_setting('seq_page_cost')::float +
       reltuples * current_setting('cpu_tuple_cost')::float +
       reltuples * current_setting('cpu_operator_cost')::float
from   pg_class where relname='t1';
= 443 * 1.0 + 100,000 * 0.01 + 100,000 * 0.0025
= 1,693
```

Let's check COST after adding C2 column condition.

```
explain select * from t1 where c1 <= 300 and c2=1;
                    QUERY PLAN
--------------------------------------------------------
 Seq Scan on t1  (cost=0.00..1943.00 rows=28 width=8)
   Filter: ((c1 <= 300) AND (c2 = 1))
```

With the addition of the C2 column condition, the cost increased to 1,943. This is also an increase of 250 compared to the previous processing cost. This shows that the same cost increases with each additional filter condition. The calculation formula is as follows.

```
COST=
select relpages  * current_setting('seq_page_cost')::float +
       reltuples * current_setting('cpu_tuple_cost')::float +
       reltuples * current_setting('cpu_operator_cost')::float +
       reltuples * current_setting('cpu_operator_cost')::float
from   pg_class where relname='t1';
= 443 * 1.0 + 100,000 * 0.01 + 100,000 * 0.0025 + 100,000 * 0.0025
= 1,943
```

Index Scan cost calculation

Let's do a test after creating an index on the C1 column. Cost calculation of Index Scan is somewhat complicated. So we will not look at all these formulas in detail. Through a basic explanation, we will check what step the cost of the index scan is calculated.

```
create unique index t1_uk on t1(c1);
explain select * from t1 where c1 <= 300;
                       QUERY PLAN
--------------------------------------------------------------
 Index Scan using t1_uk on t1   (cost=0.29..14.28 rows=285 width=8)
   Index Cond: (c1 <= 300)
```

The cost after index creation is 14.28. This is a very low cost compared to the Seq Scan cost of 1,693. Since the number of rows satisfying the condition is only 3% of the total, it is reasonable that the Index Scan cost is calculated to be much lower than the Seq Scan cost. So how is the figure of 14.28 calculated?

The method of calculating the index scan cost is more complicated than we thought. Index scan cost can't be calculated using the number of blocks, the number of records and several parameters. Therefore, source analysis is needed to confirm accurate index scan cost calculation method. This is somewhat complicated, but it's a lot to do with what's going to be explained in the future.

Cost I have calculated

Before analyzing the source, I tried to calculate the cost. Of course, the cost I have calculated is different from the cost calculated by the optimizer. However, the reason I have calculated my own is because I want to know which part is different.

1) Install the `pageinspect` extension for block dump.

```
create extension pageinspect;
```

2) The index Blevel is 1.

```
select level from bt_metap('t1_uk');
 level
-------
     1
```

3) The first Leaf block stores 367 keys. Therefore, 300 keys corresponding to 'C1 <= 300' are stored in the first leaf block.

```
select blkno, live_items, avg_item_size from bt_page_stats('t1_uk', 1);
 blkno | live_items | avg_item_size
-------+------------+---------------
     1 |        367 |            16
```

4) CTID means {table block number, offset}. As a result, it can be seen that the records corresponding to the keys 1 to 226 are stored in the block 0 of the table and the records corresponding to the keys 227 to 300 are stored in the block 1 of the table. Figure 3-1 shows the contents.

```
select * from bt_page_items('t1_uk', 1);
 itemoffset |  ctid   | itemlen | nulls | vars |          data
------------+---------+---------+-------+------+-------------------------
          2 | (0,1)   |      16 | f     | f    | 01 00 00 00 00 00 00
... skip
        227 | (0,226) |      16 | f     | f    | e2 00 00 00 00 00 00
--------------- So far, table 0 block (C1 value: 1~226)
        228 | (1,1)   |      16 | f     | f    | e3 00 00 00 00 00 00
... skip
        301 | (1,74)  |      16 | f     | f    | 2c 01 00 00 00 00 00
```

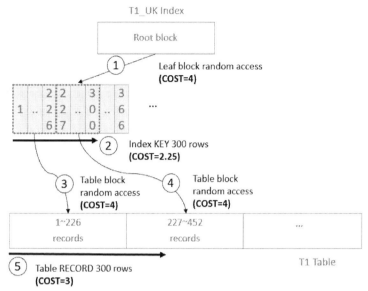

```
--------------- So far, table 1 block (C1 value: 227~300)
```

Figure 3-1. *Index Scan Cost I Calculated*

The index scan cost I calculated is 17.25. The calculation method is as follows.

- The random access cost generated in step (1) (3) (4) is 12.
  3*4=12 (random_page_cost=4)

- The cost of 300 key extraction and filter processing stored in the Leaf block is 2.25.
  300*(0.005 +0.0025) =2.25
  (cpu_index_tuple_cost=0.005, cpu_operator_cost=0.0025)

- The cost for extracting 300 records stored in a table block is 3.
  300*0.01=3 (cpu_tuple_cost=0.01)

The cost I have calculated is somewhat different from the cost calculated by the optimizer.
Where did the difference occur? Let's see how the optimizer calculated it.

How the optimizer calculates the cost

The optimizer uses three functions to calculate the cost of the index scan.

- **genericcostestimate()** : Calculate cost of index block access and key extraction

- **btcostestimate()** : Applying a weighted cost for index block access

- **cost_index()** : Table block access cost and record extraction cost calculation

genericcostestimate() analysis

Source analysis is as follows.

(1) Calculate the random access cost for the index Leaf block. The result is 4.

```
indexTotalCost = numIndexPages * spc_random_page_cost;

numIndexPages        = 1 block
spc_random_page_cost = 4 (random_page_cost parameter value)
```

∴ **indexTotalCost = 4**

(2) Index key extraction costs are summed. The calculation result is 6.1375. There is a slight difference from my calculations of 6.25 (Step 1 + Step 2). In fact, this part of my calculations is more accurate. Because I know that there are exactly 300 'C1 <= 300' conditions, but the optimizer counts 285 instead of 300. That is, the optimizer can use the statistical information to calculate the number, which can cause some gaps.

```
indexTotalCost += numIndexTuples * num_sa_scans *
                  (cpu_index_tuple_cost + qual_op_cost);
numIndexTuples       = 285
num_sa_sacns         = 1       (Repeat once)
cpu_index_tuple_cost = 0.005   (cpu_index_tuple_cost parameter value)
qual_op_cost         = 0.0025  (cpu_operator_cost parameter value)
```

∴ **indexTotalCost = 6.1375**

btcostestimate() analysis

Let's look at the calculation method following the explanation above.

(3) Two values are applied. (Please look at the formula below if you are interested.)

- Add CPU cost to find key value in index Root block

- CPU cost required to access Root and Branch blocks (IO cost is not calculated because Root and Branch blocks are loaded in Shared Buffer as mentioned above)

The primary correction value is 0.0425. Therefore, the total cost is 6.18.

```
descentCost = ceil(log(index->tuples) / log(2.0)) * cpu_operator_cost;
costs.indexTotalCost += costs.num_sa_scans * descentCost;


index->tuples        = 100,000 rows
log(index->tuples) = 11.512925
log(2.0)             = 0.693147
ceil(log(index->tuples) / log(2.0)) = 17
cpu_operator_cost  = 0.0025 (cpu_operator_cost parameter value)
costs.num_sa_scans = 1 (Repeat once)


∴ descentCost          = 0.0425
∴ costs.indexTotalCost = 6.18
```

The secondary correction value is 0.25. Therefore, the total cost is 6.43.

```
descentCost = (index->tree_height + 1) * 50.0 * cpu_operator_cost;
costs.indexTotalCost += costs.num_sa_scans * descentCost;


costs.num_sa_scans = 1 (Repeat once)
index->tree_height = 1
cpu_operator_cost  = 0.0025 (cpu_operator_cost parameter value)


∴ descentCost          = 0.25
∴ costs.indexTotalCost = 6.43
```

cost_index() analysis

The previous steps are not much different from my calculations. In fact, this step is the biggest difference. So, you need to look very carefully at this part.

(4-1) Calculate maximum cost for table access. The maximum cost is the cost assuming that the records are scattered and stored. For computation, use the `index_pages_fetched()` function to calculate the number of blocks and then multiply by 4.

```
pages_fetched = index_pages_fetched(tuples_fetched,...);
max_IO_cost   = pages_fetched * spc_random_page_cost;


pages_fetched          = 216 (index_pages_fetced() Function return result)
spc_random_page_cost = 4
∴ max_IO_cost           = 864
```

(4-2) Calculate the minimum cost for accessing the function return result table. The minimum cost is the cost assuming that records are stored in contiguous table blocks. That is, only the first table block is accessed by random access, and thereafter by Seq Scan.

```
pages_fetched = ceil(indexSelectivity * (double) baserel->pages);
min_IO_cost = spc_random_page_cost;
min_IO_cost += (pages_fetched - 1) * spc_seq_page_cost;

indexSelectivity      = 0.00285 (285 rows/100,000 rows)
baserel->pages        = 443 (Number of T1 table blocks)
∴ pages_fetched          = 2

spc_random_page_cost  = 4 (random_page_cost parameter value)
spc_seq_page_cost     = 1 (seq_page_cost parameter value)

∴ min_IO_cost         = 5
```

(4-3) The maximum cost and minimum cost are values that do not take into account the sort order of the records. Therefore, it is necessary to correct the formula by considering the sorting order of the C1 column. The sort order of the columns is based on the correlation column value of the pg_stats table. A value of '1' is perfectly sorted. We have entered 100,000 successively using the generate_series() function, so the pg_stats.correlation value of the C1 column is 1.

```
csquared = indexCorrelation * indexCorrelation;
indexTotalCost += max_IO_cost + csquared * (min_IO_cost - max_IO_cost);

indexCorrelation = 1    (pg_stat.correlation value of column c1)
∴ csquared       = 1

max_IO_cost      = 864
min_IO_cost      = 5
∴ max_IO_cost + csquared * (min_IO_cost - max_IO_cost) => 5

∴ indexTotalCost = 11.43 (6.43 + 5)
```

> ▢ **Note** If the column sort order is bad, the correlation has a small value. For example, assuming a correlation value of 0.01, the value of csquared is 0.0001. At this time, the cost of the index scan increases greatly. Therefore, the optimizer may choose Bitmap Index Scan instead of Index Scan or even Seq Scan. In other words, the column sorting order is the largest proportion of the cost of the index scan.

(5) Finally, calculate the cost of extracting the table records. The final calculated cost is 14.28. This value is the same as the Explain result.

```
indexTotalCost += cpu_per_tuple * tuples_fetched;

cpu_per_tuple   = 0.001
tuples_fetched  = 285

∴ cpu_per_tuple * tuples_fetched = 2.85
∴ indexTotalCost = 14.28   (11.43 + 2.85)
```

Statistics

The optimizer calculates the cost using statistics about tables, indexes, and columns. Therefore, it is necessary to provide optimal statistics in order for the optimizer to establish an optimal execution plan. In this section, we will look at statistical information collection methods, statistics checking methods, and control methods.

Unit for generating statistics

The units for generating statistics are database, table, and column.

Statistics can't be generated by schema or index unit. The inability to generate statistics on a per-schema basis is expected to cause some inconveniences in operation.

Indexes are automatically generated at the time of creation. Thereafter, it is automatically updated every time the table statistics is updated.

⊡ **Note**   Users familiar with ORACLE can be surprised that indexes can't generate statistics separately. At first I thought so. However, from the optimizer's point of view, updating index-only statistics is a strange operation. The need to update statistics means that the data has changed. However, keeping the table statistics in the old state and updating the index statistics only means that only the latest information is applied. For reference, ORACLE also automatically generates statistical information at the time of index creation starting from 11*g*.

Manually generate statistics

Let's look at how to generate statistics manually using the ANALYZE command.

You can generate statistics at the database level, the table level, and the column level, and you can use the VERBOSE option to check the details.

Database level

```
analyze;
```

Table level

```
analyze t1;
```

Column level

```
analyze t1 (c1, c2);
```

Verbose option

```
analyze verbose t1
INFO:  analyzing "public.t1"
INFO:  "t1": scanned 443 of 443 pages, containing 100000 live rows and 0
dead rows; 60000 rows in sample, 100000 estimated total rows
```

Automatically generate statistics

Autovacuum is a process for automatically collecting statistics. The time of collecting the statistics is calculated by using the following parameters. (See Table 3-2)

Table 3-2. *Parameters for automatic generation of statistics*

Parameter	Description	Value
autovacuum	Whether to use the autovacuum process	on
autovacuum_analyze_scale_factor	Ratio of record change in table	0.1
autovacuum_analyze_threshold	minimum number of change records	50

Automatically generates statistics only if you set the `autovacuum` parameter to on. If set to off, not only automatic statistics collection but also automatic vacuuming is performed. Therefore, when changing parameter setting value to off, it is necessary to confirm the necessity of automatic vacuum operation.

🗋 **Note**　Even if the `autovacuum` parameter is set to off, an autovacuum operation is performed to prevent transaction XID wraparound. This section is covered in 'Chapter 4. Understanding Vacuum'

The `autovacuum_analyze_scale_factor` parameter is the primary criterion for automatically statistics. That is, records in the table must be changed by 0.1 (10%) or more.

The `autovacuum_analyze_threshold` parameter is a secondary criterion for automatically generating statistics. That is, at least 50 records must be changed. The reason for setting this parameter is to avoid unnecessary automatic statistics generation that can occur during frequent changes to a small table.

When a record is changed (`INSERT`, `DELETE`, `UPDATE`) by more than two criteria, statistics is automatically collected.

Let's take an example. Enter 10,000 rows in the table.

```
drop table t2;
create table t2 (c1 integer, c2 integer);
insert into t2 select generate_series(1,10000);
```

Since the initial input is more than 50 rows, statistical information is automatically generated.

```
select a.relname, a.relpages, a.reltuples, b.last_autoanalyze
from   pg_class a, pg_stat_user_tables b
where  a.relname = b.relname and a.relname='t2';
 relname | relpages | reltuples |       last_autoanalyze
---------+----------+-----------+------------------------------
 t2      |       45 |     10000 | 2016-12-16 03:35:14.677969+09
```

An additional 1,000 rows (10%) were inserted, but the statistics was not updated.

```
insert into t2 select generate_series(1,1000);
```

After inserting 51 rows, statistics is automatically generated. That is, if the number of records is 10,000, statistics is automatically generated after 1,051 rows (10% + 51 rows) are inserted.

```
insert into t2 select generate_series(1,51);

select a.relname, a.relpages, a.reltuples, b.last_autoanalyze
from   pg_class a, pg_stat_user_tables b
where  a.relname = b.relname
and    a.relname='t2';
 relname | relpages | reltuples |        last_autoanalyze
---------+----------+-----------+--------------------------------
 t2      |       49 |     11051 | 2016-12-16 03:37:14.833936+09
```

Viewing statistics

The dictionary tables for statistics are pg_class and pg_stats.

pg_class provides table-level statistics, and pg_stats provides column-level statistics. The statistics that is considered important in each table is as follows.

Table 3-3. *pg_class key statistical information*

Column	Description
relpages	Number of blocks
reltuples	Number of Records

표 3-4. *pg_stats key statistical information*

Column	Description
null_frac	Means the ratio of NULL values
	1 if all are NULL, 0 if none are NULL. If 75% is NULL, it is 0.75.
avg_width	The average length of the column.
n_distinct	NDV (Number of Distinct Value). It has a positive or negative value depending on the NDV value.
	If NDV is less than 10% of the number of tables, NDV is displayed as it is. However, if the NDV is 10% or more, the NDV = - (NDV / number of records) formula applies. For example, the n_distinct value of the Unique column is -1.
correlation	Indicates the sort status of the record. It is displayed as a value between −1 and 1. 1 if perfectly sorted, −1 if perfectly sorted in reverse order

Let's take a closer look at the `n_distinct` and `correlation` columns through testing.

n_distinct example

Enter four types of values and check the `n_distinct` column value.

```
drop table t3;
create table t3 (c1 integer, c2 integer, c3 integer, c4 integer);

insert into t3
select i,                 -- Unique column
       mod(i,2000),       -- NDV is 2,000 (20% of the total)
       mod(i,1001),       -- NDV is 1,001 (10.01% of total)
       mod(1,1000)        -- NDV is 1,000 (10% of total)
from   generate_series(1,10000) a(i);
analyze t3;

select attname, n_distinct from pg_stats where tablename='t3';
attname | n_distinct
---------+------------
 c1      |         -1
 c2      |       -0.2
 c3      |    -0.1001
 c4      |       1000
```

As described in Table 3-4, when the NDV is 10% or more, the formula '- (NDV / number of records)' is used, and 10% or less is indicated as the actual NDV.

correlation example

Let's check the `correlation` value if the case is well sorted, the case is sorted in reverse order, and the sorting is not working well.

When perfectly sorted

```
drop table t1;
create table t1 (c1 integer, dummy char(100));
insert into t1 select generate_series(1,10000), 'dummy';
analyze t1;
```

When perfectly reverse sorted

```
drop table t2;
```

```
create table t2 (c1 integer, dummy char(100));
insert into t2 select generate_series(1,10000), 'dummy' order by 1 desc;
analyze t2;
```

If the sorting is not working well

```
drop table t3;
create table t3 (c1 integer, dummy char(100));
-- Enter in the order of 1,201,401 ... 2,202,402 in the table.
do $$
begin
  for i in 1..200 loop
    for j in 0..49 loop
        insert into t3 values (i+(j*200),'dummy');
    end loop;
  end loop;
end$$;
analyze t3;
```

Let's check the `correlation` value.

```
select tablename, attname, correlation
from   pg_stats
where  tablename in ('t1','t2','t3') and attname='c1';
 tablename | attname | correlation
-----------+---------+-------------
 t1        | c1      |           1
 t2        | c1      |          -1
 t3        | c1      |   0.0249975
```

A case with good sorting is 1, a case with good sorting with reverse is -1, and a case with poor sorting has a very small value. (We have previously learned that `correlation` values are very important in Index Scan cost calculation) Let's check the Explain result after creating the index.

```
create unique index t1_uk on t1(c1);
create unique index t2_uk on t2(c1);
create unique index t3_uk on t3(c1);

explain select * from t1 where c1 between 1 and 500;
                     QUERY PLAN
-----------------------------------------------------------------
 Index Scan using t1_uk on t1  (cost=0.29..30.29 rows=500 width=105)
   Index Cond: ((c1 >= 1) AND (c1 <= 500))

explain select * from t2 where c1 between 1 and 500;
                     QUERY PLAN
-----------------------------------------------------------------
```

```
Index Scan using t2_uk on t2   (cost=0.29..30.29 rows=500 width=105)
  Index Cond: ((c1 >= 1) AND (c1 <= 500))

explain select * from t3 where c1 between 1 and 500;
                      QUERY PLAN
---------------------------------------------------------------------
Bitmap Heap Scan on t3   (cost=13.41..193.91 rows=500 width=105)
  Recheck Cond: ((c1 >= 1) AND (c1 <= 500))
   -> Bitmap Index Scan on t3_uk   (cost=0.00..13.29 rows=500 width=0)
        Index Cond: ((c1 >= 1) AND (c1 <= 500))
```

A case with good sorting and a case with good sorting in reverse order is done by index scan method and the cost is the same. However, cases with bad sorting are performed by Bitmap Index Scan method and the cost is higher than Index Scan method. It can be seen that the index access method can be changed according to the `correlation` value.

Statistics control

Let's look at some ways to control statistics.

How to Control Automatic Generation of Table Statistics

Parameters related to statistics generation can also be set in table level.

Below is an example of setting up statistics to be updated every 100,000 rows.

```
alter table t1 set (autovacuum_analyze_scale_factor = 0.0);
alter table t1 set (autovacuum_analyze_threshold = 100000);
```

Below is an example of setting up to update statistics when 10% of table records are changed.

```
alter table t1 set (autovacuum_analyze_scale_factor = 0.1);
alter table t1 set (autovacuum_analyze_threshold = 0);
```


How to control the number of histogram buckets

The number of buckets for storing the histogram is set with the `default_statistics_target` parameter. The default value is 100. This value can be changed at the parameter level or column level. Below is an example of setting the number of buckets for storing the histogram to 200 and 0. If set to 0, the histogram is not collected. (The histogram will be explained in detail in the section 'Histogram')

```
alter table t1 alter column c1 set statistics 200;
alter table t1 alter column c2 set statistics 0;
```

How to change n_distinct

The Number of Distinct Value (NDV) is very important information in the execution plan. However, NDV on very large tables are likely to be inaccurate. This is because the sampling method is used for statistics collection. If the NDV is incorrect, you can manually change the NDV. Let's look at the example below.

```
drop table t1;
create table t1 (c1 integer, dummy char(200));

do $$
begin
  for i in 1..2000000 loop
    for j in 1..5 loop
        insert into t1 values (i, 'dummy');
    end loop;
  end loop;
end$$;

analyze t1;

select relpages, reltuples::integer from pg_class where relname='t1';
 relpages | reltuples
----------+-----------
   294118 |  10000012

select attname, n_distinct from pg_stats where tablename='t1';
 attname | n_distinct
---------+------------
 c1      |     264394
 dummy   |          1
```

The actual NDV is 2 million, but NDV of statistics is only 264,394. This value is only 1/7 of the actual NDV. Therefore, the following query will calculate rows as 38. (The actual rows are 5)

```
explain select * from t1 where c1=10;
                      QUERY PLAN
-----------------------------------------------------------
 Seq Scan on t1  (cost=0.00..419118.15 rows=38 width=208)
   Filter: (c1 = 10)
```

Now, let's modify the statistical information manually.

The number of records is 10 million, and NDV is 2 million. Since NDV is more than 10% of the number of records, set NDV to '-0.2' (- (NDV / number of records)) and analyze. The manual says that only the ALTER command should be executed. However, in my test environment, statistics has been changed only by running analyze command.

```
alter table t1 alter column c1 set (n_distinct=-0.2);
analyze t1;

select attname, n_distinct from pg_stats where tablename='t1';
 attname | n_distinct
---------+------------
 c1      |      -0.2
 dummy   |         1
```

If you run the same query again, you can see that the rows have been changed to 5.

```
explain select * from t1 where c1=10;
                    QUERY PLAN
-----------------------------------------------------------
 Seq Scan on t1  (cost=0.00..419118.15 rows=5 width=208)
   Filter: (c1 = 10)
```

Caution

After changing the value of n_distinct manually, the value is not changed. For example, if you run analyze after updating all records with the same value, the value of n_distinct will not change.

That is, the optimizer believes in the correctness of the n_distinct value that the user has manually changed. However, if the NDV is drastically reduced or increased due to insert, update, or delete after manually changing the NDV, this also causes an inaccurate NDV. Thus, manually changing n_distinct would be appropriate for read-only tables.

To reset the manually set n_distinct value:

```
alter table t1 alter column c1 reset (n_distinct);
analyze t1;
```

Number of sampling blocks

The larger the table, the less accurate the statistics is because the sampling method is used to collect statistics.

The maximum number of sampling blocks in my system was 30,000 blocks. In other words, statistics can be collected by scanning all the blocks only for tables smaller than 30,000 blocks (approximately 234 MiB). For this reason, the larger the table, the more inaccurate the statistics.

The easiest way to determine the maximum number of sampling blocks is to use the `verbose` option when `analyze`. The result shows that the scanned page is 30,000.

```
analyze verbose t1;
INFO:  analyzing "public.t1"
INFO:  "t1": scanned 30000 of 294118 pages, containing 1020000 live rows and 0 dead rows;
30000 rows in sample, 10000012 estimated total rows
```

The reason for limiting the sampling maximum block to 30000 blocks is to collect statistics quickly. But what if you want to collect more accurate statistics even if you spend more time?

The only way I've found is to modify the source. But modifying the source can be an unexpected danger, even if it is a trivial part. Therefore, modifying the source is not recommended. Please note that this is for training or testing purposes only.

How to increase the number of sampling blocks by changing the source

The simplest way is to hard coding the `stats->minrows` value into the desired number of blocks

Src 3-1. *src/backend/commands/analyze.c*

```
bool
std_typanalyze(VacAttrStats *stats)
{
        if (OidIsValid(eqopr) && OidIsValid(ltopr))
        {
                /* Seems to be a scalar datatype */
                stats->compute_stats = compute_scalar_stats;
                /*--------------------
                 * The following choice of minrows is based on the paper
                 * "Random sampling for histogram construction: ...
                 * know it at this point.
                 *--------------------
```

```
                */
            /* Comment stats->minrows = 300 * attr->attstattarget; */
            /* Hard-coding with 200,000 blocks */
            stats->minrows = 200000;
    }
```

If you run `analyze` after source change, compile, and DB restart, you can see that the number of sampling blocks has been increased to 200,000 blocks, resulting in more accurate statistical information.

```
analyze verbose t1;
INFO:  analyzing "public.t1"
INFO:  "t1": scanned 200000 of 294118 pages, containing 6800000 live rows and 0 dead
rows; 200000 rows in sample, 10000000 estimated total rows
```

As the number of sampling blocks increases, `n_distinct` becomes a bit more accurate. (The existing figure is 264,394 and -0.147045 means 1,470,450, which is five times more accurate)

```
select attname, n_distinct from pg_stats where tablename='t1';
 attname | n_distinct
---------+------------
 c1      |  -0.147045
 dummy   |          1
```

> **Note** Modifying the source to change the number of sampling blocks is a hard practice. In future versions, users will be offered the ability to specify the number of sampling blocks.

Explain Tool

Explain is an essential tool for query tuning. Explain can be used to identify problems with the execution plan. Therefore, it is the beginning of query tuning to understand Explain usage and explain output results well.

Test environment

Configure the following test environment.

```
drop table t1;
drop table t2;
```

```
create table t1 (c1 integer, c2 integer);
create table t2 (c1 integer, c2 char(100));

-- Insert 10,000 rows.
insert into t1
select i, mod(i,100)+1 from generate_series(1,10000) a(i);

-- Insert 1,000,000 rows. (The relationship with the T1 table is 1: 100)
insert into t2
select mod(generate_series(1,1000000),10000)+1, 'dummy';

analyze t1;
analyze t2;
```

Explain Usage mode

Explain can be used in two modes.

- Prediction mode: Provides the expected execution plan without actual execution.

- Execution mode: Provides execution plan, execution time, and IO block count after actual execution.

Prediction mode

Prediction mode usage is very simple. Just add the explain keyword before the query.

```
explain select * from t2;
                    QUERY PLAN
-----------------------------------------------------------
 Seq Scan on t2  (cost=0.00..18334.00 rows=1000000 width=37)
```

Execution mode

Execution mode is also very simple to use. Just add the keyword 'explain analyze' before the query.

Note that execution mode performs the query. That is, if you perform an explain analyze on the DML statement, the data is changed. Therefore, rather than using the DML statement itself, it is desirable to test the DML statement by converting it to a SELECT. If you want to see the results of the `explain analyze` for DML. After applying '`\ set AUTOCOMMIT off`', you should run the test and execute the `rollback` command.

`Explain analyze` provides execution plan step-by-step execution time, query parsing time, and total execution time. However, `explain analyze` does not display the query results on the screen, so the display time is not included.

```
explain analyze select * from t2;
                      QUERY PLAN
---------------------------------------------------------------
 Seq Scan on t2  (cost=0.00..18334.00 rows=1000000 width=37)
         (actual time=0.010..152.993 rows=1000000 loops=1)
 Planning time: 0.121 ms
 Execution time: 246.248 ms
```

How to check the number of IO blocks

For query tuning, it is very important to reduce the number of IO blocks as well as the query execution time. To check the number of IO blocks, use the BUFFERS option. The BUFFERS option should be used with the ANALYZE option.

```
explain (analyze, buffers) select * from t2;
                      QUERY PLAN
---------------------------------------------------------------
 Seq Scan on t2  (cost=0.00..18334.00 rows=1000000 width=37)
         (actual time=0.008..173.641 rows=1000000 loops=1)
   Buffers: shared hit=8334
 Planning time: 0.023 ms
 Execution time: 286.944 ms
```

How to Analyze Explain Results

Let's analyze the `explain` results below.

```
explain (analyze, buffers) select * from t2 where c1=1;
                      QUERY PLAN
---------------------------------------------------------------
 Seq Scan on t2  (cost=0.00..20834.00 rows=98  width=37)
         (actual time=1.087..101.167 rows=100 loops=1)
   Filter: (c1 = 1)
   Rows Removed by Filter: 999900
   Buffers: shared hit=8334
```

Startup Cost and Total Cost

`Explain` provides two costs.

One is Startup Cost and the other is Total Cost. Startup Cost is the cost of fetching the first record, and Total Cost is the cost of fetching the entire record. In the example, Startup Cost is 0 and Total Cost is 20,834.

Actual Time

It provides the time it takes to fetch the first record and the time it takes to fetch the entire record. The unit is Milli-second (1 / 1,000th of a second)

Estimated Cardinality and Actual Cardinality

Estimated cardinality is the value calculated by the optimizer using statistics. This value is calculated using N

DV and histogram. (This section will be covered in detail in the section 'Histogram'). This may differ from the Actual Cardinality because it is predicted using statistics. If the difference between Estimated Cardinality and Actual Cardinality is large, the optimizer is likely to establish an inefficient execution plan.

- The Estimated Cardinality of the example is 98.

- The Actual Cardinality of the example is 100.

Width and Loops

`Width` is the average length of the record. In the example, the `Width` is 37, which is the sum of the `avg_width` columns of `pg_stats`.

```
select attname, avg_width from pg_stats where tablename='t2';
 attname | avg_width
---------+-----------
 c1      |         4
 c2      |        33
```

`Loops` is the number of loops. In this example, `Loops` value is 1 because Seq Scan is performed once.

Filter

'`Rows Removed by Filter`' means the number of records that do not match the filter condition.

In the example, you can see that 99,900 rows have been filtered. When many records are filtered compared to the number of processes, it is necessary to consider index creation. Let's take a look at the changes in Explain after creating the index. As a result of accessing records using the index, you can see that '`Rows Removed by Filter`' has disappeared.

```
create index t2_idx01 on t2(c1);
explain (analyze, buffers) select * from t2 where c1=1;
                            QUERY PLAN
-----------------------------------------------------------------
 Index Scan using t2_idx01 on t2 (cost=0.42..398.08 rows=98  width=37)
                         (actual time=0.019..0.142 rows=100 loops=1)
   Index Cond: (c1 = 1)
   Buffers: shared hit=103
 Planning time: 0.080 ms
 Execution time: 0.179 ms
```

Index Cond

`Index Cond` means an index access condition. As a result of performing the same query after creating the index, it is performed by the index scan method, and it is found that the `filter` is changed to `Index Cond`.

Buffers

The number of IO.

- **shared read**: Number of blocks read by disk Read

- **shared hit**: Number of times to read the buffer

- **dirtied**: Number of dirty blocks read

- **written**: Number of dirty blocks written to disk

Planning Time and Execution Time

Planning Time is the query parsing time and Execution Time is the query execution time. The query execution time does not include query parsing time. Therefore, the total query execution time is the sum of Planning Time and Execution Time.

How to read the execution plan

Understanding the processing order of the execution plan is the basis of query tuning. Depending on the complexity of the query, the execution plan may seem complex, but the basic principle is very simple.

- Principle 1: Read from the inside.

- Principle 2: When joining, the OUTER table is placed on top.

Principle 1: Read from the inside.

This principle is very easy and clear. Consider the example below.

```
drop table t1;
create table t1 (c1 integer, dummy char(1000));

insert into t1 select mod(i,1000)+1, 'dummy'
from    generate_series(1,10000) a(i);

create index t1_idx01 on t1(c1);
analyze t1;

explain select * from t1 where c1 between 1 and 10;
                      QUERY PLAN
-----------------------------------------------------------------
(2) Bitmap Heap Scan on t1   (cost=5.31..318.99 rows=100 width=1008)
     Recheck Cond: ((c1 >= 1) AND (c1 <= 10))
(1) ->  Bitmap Index Scan on t1_idx01
```

```
Index Cond: ((c1 >= 1) AND (c1 <= 10))
```

The execution order of the above example is (1)->(2). That is, after performing the Bitmap Index Scan operation on the inner side, the Bitmap Heap Scan operation is performed.

Principle 2: When joining, the OUTER table is placed on top.

This principle is very important when determining the order of join. If you do not understand this principle correctly, there is a high probability that you will misunderstand the order of join.

The meaning of 'Outer Table' in Principle 2 is as follows.

Table 3-5. *Meaning of outer table according to join method*

Join method	Outer Table	Inner Table	First accessed table
NL Join	Driving Table	Inner Table	Outer Table
Hash Join	Probe Table	Build Table	Inner Table

This principle is confusing for users familiar with ORACLE. The principle of reading explain in ORACLE is "read from the top when joining". In other words, ORACLE places the table being accessed first. However, PostgreSQL places the Outer table on top. As a result, a Nested Loop join first places the accessed table on top (this part is the same as ORACLE), but the Sort Merge or Hash join is located below the table being accessed first. (This is the opposite of ORACLE)

The reason for this difference is that ORACLE places the 'Outer table' (on the left) in the join tree above the Explain result, while PostgreSQL places the 'Outer table' in the join relationship on top. The picture below will help you understand.

(a) Examples of NL join

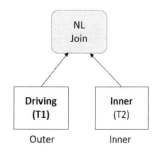
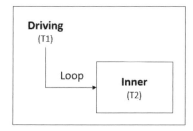

(b) Examples of hash join

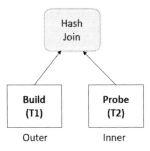

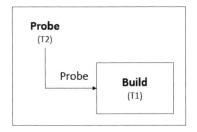

(c) Example of a Sort Merge join

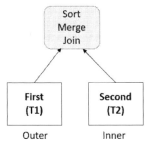

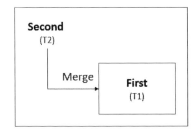

Figure 3-2. *Join Tree and Join Relationship*

Let's take an example.

Nested Loop Join Example

After looking at the Nested Loop join (NL join) between the two tables, let's look at the NL join between the three tables.

NL join example between two tables

```
drop table t1;
drop table t2;
create table t1 (c1 integer, dummy char(1000));
create table t2 (c1 integer, dummy char(1000));
insert into t1 select generate_series(1,10), 'dummy';
insert into t2 select generate_series(1,1000), 'dummy';
create index t2_idx01 on t2(c1);

analyze t1;
analyze t2;

set enable_hashjoin=off;
```

```
set enable_mergejoin=off;

explain
select *
from   t1 a, t2 b
where  a.c1 = b.c1;
                         QUERY PLAN
------------------------------------------------------------------------
Nested Loop  (cost=0.28..65.12 rows=10 width=2016)
(1) ->   Seq Scan on t1 a   (cost=0.00..2.10 rows=10 width=1008)
(2) ->   Index Scan using t2_idx01 on t2 b   (cost=0.28..6.29 rows=1..)
            Index Cond: (c1 = a.c1)
```

The order of execution in the example above is `(1)->(2)`. The processing steps are as follows.

1. Seq Scan the `T1` table which is the outer table.
2. For each record returned in step 1, access the `T2` table using the `T2_IDX01` index.

NL join example between 3 tables

```
drop table t3;

create table t3 (c1 integer, dummy char(1000));

insert into t3 select generate_series(1,10000), 'dummy';
create index t3_idx01 on t3(c1);

analyze t3;

explain
select *
from   t1 a, t2 b, t3 c
where  a.c1 = b.c1
and    b.c1 = c.c1;
                         QUERY PLAN
------------------------------------------------------------------------
Nested Loop  (cost=0.56..84.87 rows=10 width=3024)
   Join Filter: (a.c1 = b.c1)
(3) ->  Nested Loop  (cost=0.29..81.22 rows=10 width=2016)
(1)        ->  Seq Scan on t1 a   (cost=0.00..2.10 rows=10 width=1008)
(2)        ->  Index Scan using t3_idx01 on t3 c   (cost=0.28..0.35 rows=1..)
                 Index Cond: (c1 = a.c1)
(4) ->  Index Scan using t2_idx01 on t2 b   (cost=0.28..0.35 rows=1..)
            Index Cond: (c1 = c.c1)
```

The order of execution of the above example is $(1)->(2)->(3)->(4)$. The processing steps are as follows.

1. Seq Scan the T1 table which is the outer table.
2. For each record returned in step 1, access the T3 table using the T3_IDX01 index.
3. The NL join result is the Outer data source.
4. For each record returned in step 3, access the T2 table using the T2_IDX01 index.

Hash Join Example

After looking at the hash joins between the two tables, let's look at the hash joins between the three tables.

Example of a hash join between two tables

```
set enable_hashjoin=on;

explain
select *
from    t1 a, t2 b
where   a.c1 = b.c1;
                            QUERY PLAN
--------------------------------------------------------------------
Hash Join   (cost=2.23..159.07 rows=10 width=2016)
    Hash Cond: (b.c1 = a.c1)
(3) ->   Seq Scan on t2 b  (cost=0.00..153.00 rows=1000 width=1008)
(2) ->   Hash  (cost=2.10..2.10 rows=10 width=1008)
(1)          ->  Seq Scan on t1 a  (cost=0.00..2.10 rows=10 width=1008)
```

The order of execution of the above example is $(1)->(2)->(3)$. The processing steps are as follows.

1. The optimizer selects the T1 table, which is the smaller of the two tables, as the hash table. Then scan the T1 table.
2. Perform a hash build operation on the T1 table.
3. Perform a hash join while scanning the T2 table as the probe table.

Example of a hash join between three tables

```
explain
select *
from    t1 a, t2 b, t3 c
where   a.c1 = b.c1
and     b.c1 = c.c1;
                            QUERY PLAN
-------------------------------------------------------------------
Hash Join   (cost=159.20..1725.80 rows=10 width=3024)
     Hash Cond:  (c.c1 = a.c1)
(6) ->  Seq Scan on t3 c   (cost=0.00..1529.00 rows=10000 width=1008)
(5) ->  Hash   (cost=159.07..159.07 rows=10 width=2016)
(4)        ->  Hash Join   (cost=2.23..159.07 rows=10 width=2016)
                  Hash Cond:  (b.c1 = a.c1)
(3)              ->  Seq Scan on t2 b   (cost=0.00..153.00 rows=1000..)
(2)              ->  Hash   (cost=2.10..2.10 rows=10 width=1008)
(1)                   ->  Seq Scan on t1 a   (cost=0.00..2.10 rows=10..)
```

The sequence of the above example is $(1)->(2)->(3)->(4)->(5)->(6)$. The processing steps are as follows.

1. The optimizer selects the T1 table, which is the smallest of the three tables, as the hash table. Then scan the T1 table.
2. Performs a hash build operation on the T1 table.
3. Scan the T2 table, which is a probe table.
4. Perform a hash join.
5. Perform a hash build operation on the hash join result.
6. Perform a hash join while scanning the T3 table, which is a probe table.

Results of ORACLE Explain on Hash Join

Finally, let's compare it to the explain results from ORACLE. In the ORACLE example, the T1 is smaller than the T2. Therefore, the optimizer selects T1 as the hash table and T2 as the probe table. At this time, the Explain result shows that the hash table T1 is on the top. The order of execution is $(2)->(3)$.

```
SQL> select /*+ gather_plan_statistics */ *
from t1 a, t2 b where a.c1=b.c1;

SQL> select *
```

```
from table(dbms_xplan.display_cursor(null, null, 'allstats last '));
---------------------------------------------------------------------
| Id  | Operation            | Name | Starts | E-Rows | A-Rows |
---------------------------------------------------------------------
|   0 | SELECT STATEMENT     |      |      1 |        |      1 |
|*  1 |   HASH JOIN          |      |      1 |   801K |  1000K |
|   2 |     TABLE ACCESS FULL| T1   |      1 |    100 |    100 |
|   3 |     TABLE ACCESS FULL| T2   |      1 |   801K |  1000K |
---------------------------------------------------------------------
```

Query parsing

The order of execution of a query can be largely divided into parsing, query rewriting, optimizing, and execution.

The parsing step performs syntax check and semantic check steps. Then, after performing the steps to rewrite the query, perform the query optimization and then execute the query. This can be expressed as follows.

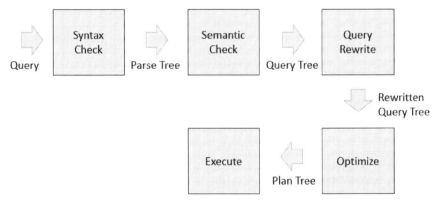

Figure 3-3. *Query execution order*

The syntax check or semantic check performed during parsing is not important from a performance standpoint. Therefore, this part is not explained.

In Chapter 1. Architecture Overview, PostgreSQL explained that there is no shared pool, and that the backend process stores SQL information. This means that if you run the same SQL multiple times within a single Backend process, you will only do Hard Parsing the first time.

Is it so? If you store SQL information in the backend process, how do you handle the invalidation? How can we prove this? It is doubtful.

Let's answer these questions through testing and source analysis.

Plan Caching Overview

Storing the 'Rewritten Query Tree' in the backend process is called Plan Caching. At the time of plan caching, 'Plan Tree' generated at the query optimization stage is not saved. Therefore, after Plan Caching, the syntax check, semantic check, and query rewrite steps are skipped, but the query optimization step is always performed.

The following is a summary of Plan Caching operation.

- Plan Caching applies only to Prepare Statements and Functions.

- Literal SQL does not apply to Plan Caching.

- Store the 'rewritten Query Tree' in the backend process when Prepare Stmt command is executed.

- Then, when you execute the Execute Stmt command, the syntax check, semantic check, and query rewrite steps are skipped and the query optimization step is performed.

- Perform a Re-Validation process to check object changes, statistics changes, etc. before executing the query optimization step.

- Performing the query optimization step every time is different from ORACLE.

- The disadvantage is that it takes time to optimize the query every time the query is executed.

- The advantage of this is that you can always perform Bind Peeking. In other words, there is an advantage that the histogram can always be used even in case of Bind SQL.

- Function saves 'rewritten Query Tree' in the backend process at the first execution, and then uses 'rewritten Query Tree' at the second execution.

Prepare Statement Processing Procedure

Prepare Statement is executed in Prepare phase and Execute phase.

The procedure is as follows. (See Figure 3-4, The source code is much more complicated than this)

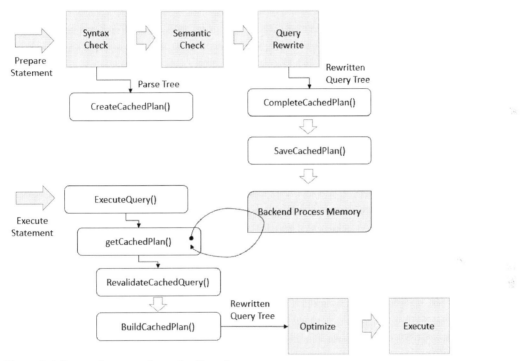

Figure 3-4. *Prepare Statement Processing Procedure*

Prepare Phase

The Prepared Statement command is executed as follows

1. Perform a syntax check.
2. Call the CreateCachedPlan() function.
3. Perform a semantic check.

4. Perform query rewriting.

5. Call the `SaveCachedPlan()` function after calling the `CompleteCachedPlan()` function. At this time, 'rewritten Query Tree' is stored in the local process.

Execute Phase

The Execute Statement command is executed as follows.

1. Call the `ExecuteQuery()` function

2. Call the `getCachedPlan()` function. At this time, the 'rewritten Query Tree' stored in the local process memory is fetched.

3. Call the `RevalidateCachedQuery()` function to check if the stored information is valid. If an object change, an index addition, statistical information update, etc. are performed, the stored information is invalidated.

4. Invoke the `BuildCachedPlan()` function to perform the query optimization step. At this time, the Bind variable is passed together. Therefore, the optimizer can build an execution plan using histogram information even in case of Bind SQL.

A Study on PostgreSQL Bind Peeking

Checking the Bind variable value at runtime is called 'Bind Peeking'.

PostgreSQL has been able to 'Bind Peek' all BIND SQL by providing Plan Caching since version 9.2. In other words, 'Bind Peeking' is possible for all Bind SQL because it stores 'rewritten Query Tree' in Plan Caching.

This has the disadvantage of having to perform the query optimization step every time, but it has the advantage of being able to perform Bind Peeking every time the query is executed. I got one and lost one.

Let's see if Bind Peeking works well with Skew data and Between Condition.

Test case 1: Skew data

The C1 column inputs the skewed data and the C2 column inputs the data evenly.

```
drop table t1;
create table t1 (c1 char(1), c2 date);

-- Enter 1 million rows of 'T' in column C1.
insert into t1 select 'T', to_date('20161201','YYYYMMDD')+mod(i,30) from
generate_series(1,1000000) a(i);

-- Enter 100 rows of 'F' in column C2.
insert into t1 select 'F', to_date('20161201','YYYYMMDD')+mod(i,30) from
generate_series(1,100) a(i);

create index t1_idx01 on t1(c1);
create index t1_idx02 on t1(c2);

analyze t1;
analyze t2;
```

In the following results, it can be seen that the Seq Scan method is performed when the 'T' value is input, and the Index Only Scan method is performed when the 'F' value is input. (The Index Only Scan method will be described in the section 'Access Method')

```
prepare stmt1(char) as select count(*) from t1 where c1=$1;

explain execute stmt1('T');
                         QUERY PLAN
--------------------------------------------------------------------
 Aggregate  (cost=19427.42..19427.43 rows=1 width=8)
   ->  Seq Scan on t1  (cost=0.00..16927.25 rows=1000067 width=0)
         Filter: (c1 = 'T'::bpchar)

explain execute stmt1('F');
                         QUERY PLAN
--------------------------------------------------------------------
 Aggregate  (cost=9.14..9.15 rows=1 width=8)
   ->  Index Only Scan using t1_idx01 on t1  (cost=0.42..9.05 rows=33..)
         Index Cond: (c1 = 'F'::bpchar)
```

> **Note** Partial indexes can be a good alternative when data skew occurs. For the partial index, see 'Chapter 5. Partial Index & BRIN'.

Test case 2: Between Condition

As a result of the below, it can be seen that Bitmap Index Scan method is performed when the Between range is narrow, and Seq Scan method is performed when the range is wide. As you can see, PostgreSQL builds an execution plan using histogram information by performing Bind Peaking in all cases.

```
prepare stmt2(char, char) as
select count(*)
from    t1
where   c2 between to_date($1,'YYYYMMDD') and to_date($2,'YYYYMMDD');

-- 2 day range
explain execute stmt2('20161201','20161202');
                        QUERY PLAN
-----------------------------------------------------------------
Aggregate  (cost=7421.48..7421.49 rows=1 width=8)
-> Bitmap Heap Scan on t1   (cost=1454.45..7250.25 rows=68490 width=0)
    -> Bitmap Index Scan on t1_idx02 (cost=0.00..1437.33 rows=68490..)

-- 15 day range
explain execute stmt2('20161201','20161215');
                        QUERY PLAN
-----------------------------------------------------------------
 Aggregate  (cost=25682.46..25682.47 rows=1 width=8)
   -> Seq Scan on t1  (cost=0.00..24428.00 rows=501784 width=0)
```

Literal SQL vs. Bind SQL Performance

Bind SQL is better than Literal SQL in every way.

Not only can the histogram always be used, but Plan Caching can reduce the hard parsing load. The benefits of reducing the hard parsing load will vary depending on the situation, but let's look at the benefits of Plan Caching through the most extreme examples.

Test case

The following example is somewhat impractical to compare the parsing time of Literal SQL and Bind SQL. This example compares only the parsing time of Literal SQL and Bind SQL while performing a million times loop. The result of the example shows that Bind SQL is four times faster than Literal SQL.

Perform Literal SQL

```
drop table t1;
drop table t2;
```

```
create table t1 (c1 integer, c2 integer);
create table t2 (c1 integer);

\timing on
do $$
declare i integer;
begin
  for i in 1..1000000 loop
     execute 'update t1 set c2=c2+1 where c1='||i||' and exists (select 1 from t2 where
t2.c1=t1.c1)';
  end loop;
end$$;
Time: 109734.846 ms
```

Perform Bind SQL

```
\timing on
do $$
declare i integer;
begin
  for i in 1..1000000 loop
     update t1 set c2=c2+1
     where c1=i and exists (select 1 from t2 where t2.c1=t1.c1);
  end loop;
end$$;
Time: 25200.883 ms
```

🗎 **One Shot Cached Plan**

If you have read Plan Caching carefully, you can see that the Literal SQL example is a bit strange. This is because Plan Caching also applies when performing a function.

So, you might have the question, " Since the Literal SQL example also uses the Anonymous Function, is this also the target of Plan Caching?" This is a very accurate indication.

In fact, the Literal SQL example is an anonymous function, so it carries out the Plan Caching routine.

However, the processing flow is slightly different. Use `CreateOneShotCachedPlan()` instead of `CreateCachedPlan()` and do not call `SaveCachedPlan()`.

In other words, we call `CreateOneShotCachedPlan()` function every time without saving the rewritten Query Tree. This is very similar to the overhead of Hard parsing. Therefore, the example of Literal SQL does not match the way Literal SQL is executed, but the test results will not be much different.

Access method

The three most important elements in query tuning are well-controlled access methods, join methods, and join order. In this section, we will look at access methods.

Seq Scan method

Seq Scan is a method of reading records while scanning all blocks. If there is no index, or if there is a large range to be read even if an index exists, this method is selected. As mentioned earlier, Seq Scan uses the BULK READ strategy according to the size of the table, and uses Ring Buffer at this time.

Index Scan method

The index scan method accesses the table record using the key stored in the index leaf block. The features of the Index Scan method are as follows.

- It is output in order of index key.

- The number of table block accesses varies greatly depending on the sort order of the records. (See Figure 3-5)

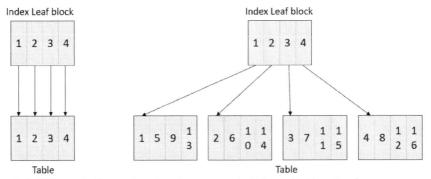

Figure 3-5. *Difference in the number of random accesses by index and table sort order*

As shown in the figure above, if the sorting order between the index and the table is the best, the table block is accessed only once. In the worst case, the table block must be accessed four times.

Analyzing Explain Results

```
drop table t1;
create table t1 (c1 integer, dummy char(100));
insert into t1 select generate_series(1,58000), 'dummy';
create index t1_idx01 on t1(c1);
analyze t1;

explain (costs false, analyze, buffers)
select * from t1 where c1 between 1 and 4000;
                         QUERY PLAN
-------------------------------------------------------------------
 Index Scan using t1_idx01 on t1 (actual time=0.016..1.166 rows=4000...)
   Index Cond: ((c1 >= 1) AND (c1 <= 4000))
   Buffers: shared hit=71 read=10
```

Explain results of Index Scan do not distinguish between table and index access. This part is a bit disappointing in performance analysis. Let's analyze the result of Explain.

- The time required to fetch the first record is 0.016ms, and the time required to fetch the entire record is 1.166ms.

- The number of memory reads is 71.

- The number of blocks read by disk read is 10.

Bitmap Index Scan method

Bitmap Index Scan is a method designed to reduce the number of table random accesses. The criterion for selecting the index scan method and the bitmap index scan method by the optimizer is the `correlation` value of the index column.

The features of the Bitmap Index Scan scheme are as follows.

- It is used when the sort order between the index and the table is bad.

- Access records after sorting by block number.

- This greatly reduces the number of table random accesses. That is, the table block is accessed only once. This is the core of the Bitmap Index Scan.

- Access by table block number order. Therefore, they are not output in key order.

Test environment

```
drop table t2;
create table t2 (c1 integer, dummy char(100));
-- Insert in the order of 1,1001,2001 ... 2,1002,2002 ... in the table.
do $$
begin
  for i in 1..1000 loop
    for j in 0..57 loop
      insert into t2 values (i+(j*1000),'dummy');
    end loop;
  end loop;
end$$;

create index t2_idx01 on t2(c1);
analyze t2;
```

When the data insert is completed, 58,000 rows are stored in 1,000 blocks. That is, 58 rows are stored for each block. (See Figure 3-6)

```
select relpages, reltuples from pg_class where relname='t2';
 relpages | reltuples
----------+-----------
     1000 |     58000
```

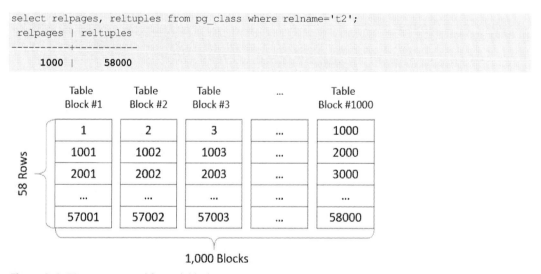

Figure 3-6. *58 rows are stored for each block*

Analyzing Explain Results

```
explain (costs false, analyze, buffers)
select * from t2 where c1 between 1 and 1000;
                        QUERY PLAN
---------------------------------------------------------------------
 Bitmap Heap Scan on t2 (actual time=0.264..0.979 rows=1000 loops=1)
   Recheck Cond: ((c1 >= 1) AND (c1 <= 1000))
   Heap Blocks: exact=1000
   Buffers: shared hit=1002 read=2
   ->  Bitmap Index Scan on t2_idx01
         Index Cond: ((c1 >= 1) AND (c1 <= 1000))
         Buffers: shared hit=2 read=2
```

From the above results, we can see that the index block accessed 4 times and the table block accessed 1,000 times. This is an easily predictable result. If so, how many times need to access the table block for the condition 'BETWEEN 1 AND 4000'? 1,000 times? 4,000 times?

```
explain (costs false, analyze, buffers)
select * from t2 where c1 between 1 and 4000;


                        QUERY PLAN
---------------------------------------------------------------------
Bitmap Heap Scan on t2 (actual time=0.642..2.011 rows=4000 loops=1)
   Recheck Cond: ((c1 >= 1) AND (c1 <= 4000))
   Heap Blocks: exact=1000
   Buffers: shared hit=1004 read=8
   ->  Bitmap Index Scan on t2_idx01
         Index Cond: ((c1 >= 1) AND (c1 <= 4000))
         Buffers: shared hit=4 read=8
```

The number of table block accesses is still 1,000 times. (However, since the BETWEEN range is widened, the number of index block accesses has increased to 12) This is the core of the Bitmap Index Scan operation principle. That is, the Bitmap Index Scan has advantages of minimizing table block access by accessing the records after sorting them in order of block numbers.

Let's compare it with the index scan method.

```
set enable_bitmapscan=off;
set enable_seqscan=off;

explain (costs false, analyze, buffers)
select * from t2 where c1 between 1 and 4000;
                        QUERY PLAN
---------------------------------------------------------------------
 Index Scan using t2_idx01 on t2 (actual time=0.011..2.939 rows=4000...)
```

```
Index Cond: ((c1 >= 1) AND (c1 <= 4000))
Buffers: shared hit=4012
```

At the time of index scan, table block is accessed 4,000 times (12 times out of 4,012 is the number of index block access).

Some questions about Bitmap Index Scan

The basic principle of the Bitmap Index Scan method is very simple. But if you think a bit more, there are some questions. The question I had was as follows.

- Use Bitmap?

- If Bitmap is used, is the unit a record? Is it a block?

- How to sort by block number using Bitmap?

- What is 'lossy' in the Explain result?

- What is 'Rows Removed by Index Recheck' in the Explain result?

Data structure for Bitmap Index Scan

If you understand the data structure used in Bitmap Index Scan, most of the above questions are solved. For reference, the description below summarizes the results of the analysis of src/backend/nodes/tidbitmap.c.

The core of the data structure is PageTableEntry

Understanding PageTableEntry solves most of the bitmap related questions.

```
typedef struct PagetableEntry
{
    BlockNumber     blockno;    /* page number (hashtable key) */
    bool            ischunk;    /* T = lossy storage, F = exact */
    bool            recheck;    /* should the tuples be rechecked? */
    bitmapword      words[Max(WORDS_PER_PAGE, WORDS_PER_CHUNK)];
} PagetableEntry;
```

The `PageTableEntry` data structure can be expressed as follows.

Figure 3-7. *PageTableEntry data structure*

Let's solve the first question.

If you look at the `PageTableEntry` structure used for Bitmap Index Scan, you can answer the first question. The `bitmapword` variable in the structure is a bitmap that stores 320 bits. It can be guessed that Bitmap is used at the time of Bitmap Index Scan.

⬚ **Note** PostgreSQL limits the maximum number of records that can be stored in a block. If there are 8 KiB blocks, about 256 ~ 300 records are stored. Therefore, it is possible to manage all the records in the block with 320 bits.

Differences between Exact mode and Lossy mode

Let's solve the second question.

The data structure for bitmap management is stored in the backend process. What if there is not enough space in the process? In this case, switch from 'exact' to 'lossy'. The description of each mode is as follows.

- **exact mode**: One bit in the bitmap points to one record. The ischunk value is set to zero. (See Figure 3-8.)

- **lossy mode**: One bit in the bitmap indicates one block. The ischunk value is set to 1 at this time. (See Figure 3-9.)

That is, each bit in the bitmap may point to a record, or to a block.

◻ Problems with Lossy Mode

In lossy mode, one bit indicates one block. That is, after accessing the table block, the query condition must be checked against all the records in the block. Because of this overhead, `lossy` mode is slower than `exact` mode. Therefore, if processed in `lossy` mode, it is necessary to increase `work_mem` size.

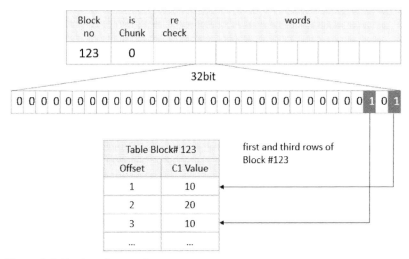

Figure 3-8. *Exact mode example*

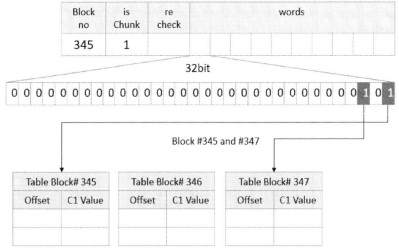

Figure 3-9. *Lossy mode example*

How to sort by block number using Bitmap?

Let's solve the third question.

Sorting by block number is very simple. Use the block number in the `PageTableEntry`. Sort results are stored in `**spages` (ordered `exact` lists) and `**schunks` (ordered `lossy` lists), respectively, in the `TIDBitmap` structure.

Performance comparison between Exact mode and Lossy mode

We learned the difference between exact and lossy modes. Now let's compare the performance of `exact` and `lossy` modes. The test is performed after loading the `T3` table and the `T3_IDX01` index into the buffer to make the other conditions the same.

Test environment

```
drop table t3;
create table t3 (c1 integer, dummy char(100));

-- Enter 58 rows for each 100,000 blocks.
do $$
begin
  for i in 1..100000 loop
    for j in 0..57 loop
        insert into t3 values (i+(j*100000),'dummy');
    end loop;
  end loop;
end$$;

create index t3_idx01 on t3(c1);
analyze t3;

select pg_prewarm('t3');
select pg_prewarm('t3_idx01');
```

Result of lossy mode

In the following results, 52,738 of the 100,000 table blocks are processed in `lossy` mode. This caused 2,531,424 'Rows Removed by Index Recheck'. (2,531,424 = 52,738 blocks * 48 rows)

```
show work_mem;
 work_mem
----------
```

```
4MB

explain (costs false, analyze, buffers)
select * from t3 where c1 between 1 and 1000000;
                        QUERY PLAN
------------------------------------------------------------------
 Bitmap Heap Scan on t3 (actual time=177.139..1026.910 rows=1000000...)
   Recheck Cond: ((c1 >= 1) AND (c1 <= 1000000))
   Rows Removed by Index Recheck: 2531424
   Heap Blocks: exact=47262 lossy=52738
   Buffers: shared hit=2736 read=99999 written=1
   ->  Bitmap Index Scan on t3_idx01
         Index Cond: ((c1 >= 1) AND (c1 <= 1000000))
         Buffers: shared hit=2735
 Planning time: 0.142 ms
 Execution time: 1131.026 ms
```

Exact mode result

After the `work_mem` size is increased, it is executed again in the exact mode, so that the execution speed is slightly faster. Therefore, it is necessary to adjust work_mem size appropriately when it is performed in lossy mode.

```
set work_mem='15MB';

explain (costs false, analyze, buffers)
select * from t3 where c1 between 1 and 1000000;
                        QUERY PLAN
------------------------------------------------------------------
 Bitmap Heap Scan on t3 (actual time=246.017..739.346 rows=1000000...)
   Recheck Cond: ((c1 >= 1) AND (c1 <= 1000000))
   Heap Blocks: exact=100000
   Buffers: shared hit=4 read=102731
   ->  Bitmap Index Scan on t3_idx01
         Index Cond: ((c1 >= 1) AND (c1 <= 1000000))
         Buffers: shared hit=3 read=2732
 Planning time: 0.154 ms
 Execution time: 840.211 ms
```

Procedure for performing Bitmap Index Scan

Now, let's summarize the procedure of Bitmap Index Scan method. The procedure of Bitmap Index Scan is as follows.

1.   Retrieve the index key satisfying the `where` condition.

2. If there is space in `work_mem`, execute it in `exact` mode.
   A. `exact` mode manages one block per `PageTableEntry` structure.
   B. One bit in the bitmap points to one record.
3. If there is no space in `work_mem`, switch to `lossy` mode.
   A. `lossy` mode manages `chunk`(Contiguous table block) per `PageTableEntry` structure.
   B. One bit in the bitmap indicates one block.
4. After the bitmap operation is completed, arrange the PageTableEntry in block number order.
5. Blocks processed in `exact` mode directly access records using bitmap information.
6. Blocks processed in `lossy` mode access block using bitmap information.
7. In `lossy` mode, scan the records in the block and extract the records that match the condition.

The above procedure is illustrated as follows. (Assume that one Leaf block is processed in `exact` mode and the other in `lossy` mode)

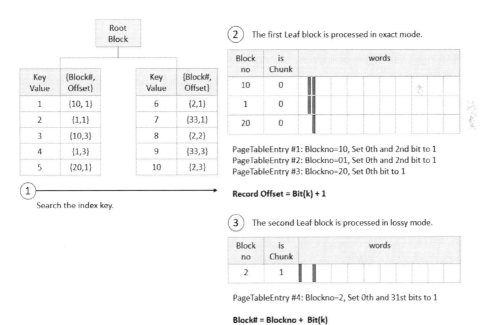

Figure 3-10. *Procedure for performing Bitmap Index Scan (#1)*

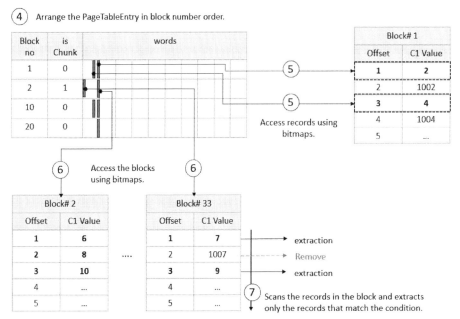

Figure 3-11. *Procedure for performing Bitmap Index Scan (#2)*

Sort table records using the CLUSTER command

Bitmap Index Scan minimizes table access through internal logic. However, this method also has overhead for bitmap processing. So, if you can reorganize the table, it is best to reorganize the table. In general, the procedure for reorganizing a table is as follows.

1. Restrict access to the original table.
2. Create a temporary table with CTAS (Create Table As Select). In this case, use the ORDER BY <index column> clause to store the records in sorted order.
3. Create an index on the temporary table.
4. Drop or rename the original table and index.
5. Change the temporary table and index names to the original table and index names.
6. Allow access to the table.

PostgreSQL can do all of the above with one CLUSTER command. (After USING, specify an index name that is an ORDER BY criterion)

```
CLUSTER T3 USING T3_IDX01;
analyze t3;
```

After executing the CLUSTER command and checking the Explain result, it can be seen that the Bitmap Index Scan method is changed to the Index Scan method. Because of the effect of sorting, the number of accesses to the block is reduced, and the query performance is faster than before.

```
explain (costs false, analyze, buffers)
select * from t3 where c1 between 1 and 1000000;
                        QUERY PLAN
-----------------------------------------------------------------
 Index Scan using t3_idx01 on t3 (actual time=0.011..274.364 ...)
   Index Cond: ((c1 >= 1) AND (c1 <= 1000000))
   Buffers: shared hit=4 read=19973
 Planning time: 0.137 ms
 Execution time: 374.013 ms
```

⧉ **Note**   The CLUSTER command is a one-time operation. Immediately after the CLUSTER command is executed, the sort order of the indexes and the tables are perfectly matched. However, after a transaction occurs, the sort order may become poor.

Cautions when using CLUSTER command

Caution for Lock waiting

The CLUSTER command is not compatible with DML (INSERT, UPDATE, DELETE) as well as with SELECT. Therefore, in order to execute the CLUSTER command, user access should be restricted. Consider the example below.

Session #1: Perform a SELECT

When SELECT is executed, 'ACCESS SHARE' lock is acquired. Therefore, you can simulate a SELECT using the LOCK TABLE command.

```
postgres=# begin;
postgres=# lock table t3 in access share mode;
```

Session #2: CLUSTER command execution

When the T3 table is in the SELECT state, CLUSTER command waits for lock.

```
CLUSTER T3 USING T3_IDX01;
```

Lock monitoring

The lock holder session of session #2 is session #1. This shows that if the CLUSTER command is executed at the time of SELECT, the lock is waited.

```
select pid, wait_event_type||'-'||wait_event wait,
       pg_blocking_pids(pid) holder, query
from   pg_stat_activity;
 pid  |      wait      | holder  |               query
------+----------------+---------+------------------------------------
15068 | Lock-relation  | {31083} | CLUSTER T3 USING T3_IDX01;
31083 |                | {}      | lock table t3 in access share mode;
```

Session #3: Perform a SELECT

A more serious problem is that SELECT at this point is waiting for lock.

```
select * from t3 limit 1;
```

Lock monitoring

The lock holder session in session# 3 is session #2. As a result, when CLUSTER command is executed, SELECT also waits for lock.

```
select pid, wait_event_type||'-'||wait_event wait,
       pg_blocking_pids(pid) holder, query
from   pg_stat_activity;
 pid  |      wait      | holder  |               query
------+----------------+---------+------------------------------------
15068 | Lock-relation  | {31083} | CLUSTER T3 USING T3_IDX01;
31083 |                | {}      | begin;
31664 | Lock-relation  | {15068} | select * from t3 limit 1;
```

▢ PG_REPACK Extension

With the pg_repack extension, CLUSTER and VACUUM FULL operations can be performed online.

pg_repack sets an exclusive lock on the table just before and after the execution of the command.

Therefore, you can perform DML as well as SELECT during command execution. If you are interested,

please visit https://github.com/reorg/pg_repack. Installation requires some trial and error. In my case, there

were errors related to the openssl library and errors related to the edit library during installation. The openssl libraries can be installed using the yum install `openssl*` command, and the `edit` libraries can be downloaded from http://thrysoee.dk/editline.

If another index exists

The `CLUSTER` operation is to sort table records based on a specific index. Therefore, when `CLUSTER` operations are performed on a specific index basis, it is necessary to consider that the sort order between other indexes and table may be deteriorated.

Index Only Scan method

The Index Only Scan method accesses only an index without accessing a table. Index Only Scan is available from version 9.2. Suppose you need to perform a wide range of index scans, and the query speed is slow because of table random access. One of the possible tuning methods is to create an index with all the columns used in the query. These indexes are called `covering index`. PostgreSQL is called index only scan using the `covering index`. Consider the example below.

Test environment

```
drop table t3;
create table t3 (c1 integer, c2 integer, c3 integer, dummy char(100));
insert into t3 select i, i, i, 'dummy'
from generate_series(1,10000) a(i);

create index t3_idx01 on t3(c1, c2);
analyze t3;
```

Index Only Scan Test

```
explain (costs false, analyze, buffers)
select count(*) from t3 where c1 between 1 and 1000 and c2 <> 0;
                              QUERY PLAN
---------------------------------------------------------------------
 Aggregate (actual time=0.455..0.456 rows=1 loops=1)
   Buffers: shared hit=21 read=2
   ->  Bitmap Heap Scan on t3
          Recheck Cond: ((c1 >= 1) AND (c1 <= 1000))
          Filter: (c2 <> 0)
          Heap Blocks: exact=19
```

```
            Buffers: shared hit=21 read=2
      ->  Bitmap Index Scan on t3_idx01
              Index Cond: ((c1 >= 1) AND (c1 <= 1000))
              Buffers: shared hit=2 read=2
```

The above results show that Covering index was created, but Bitmap Index Scan method was used instead of Index Only Scan method. As a result, 4 index blocks and 19 table blocks were accessed. Why is this?

Vacuum is required for Index Only Scan

PostgreSQL does not always perform an index only scan if a covering index exists. Vacuum must be performed in order to perform Index Only Scan method. Let's perform the test after vacuum.

```
vacuum t3;
explain (costs false, analyze, buffers)
select count(*) from t3 where c1 between 1 and 1000 and c2 <> 0;
                      QUERY PLAN
----------------------------------------------------------------
 Aggregate (actual time=0.394..0.395 rows=1 loops=1)
   Buffers: shared hit=5
   ->  Index Only Scan using t3_idx01 on t3
          Index Cond: ((c1 >= 1) AND (c1 <= 1000))
          Filter: (c2 <> 0)
          Heap Fetches: 0
          Buffers: shared hit=5
```

The above results show that the Index Only Scan method was used, and only 5 index blocks were accessed.

Index Only Scan works only when the ALL_VISIBLE bit is 1.

PostgreSQL manages one VM per table, and the VM consists of two bits per table block. The first bit is the ALL_VISIBLE bit that indicates whether the block has been changed. The ALL_VISIBLE bit is changed to 0 (False) if the record in the block is changed, and to 1 (True) after the vacuum is executed. The Index Only Scan method works only when the ALL_VISIBLE bit is all 1. From the results below, it can be seen that the ALL_VISIBLE bit of all blocks is 1.

```
create extension pg_visibility;

select * from pg_visibility_map_summary('t3');
 all_visible | all_frozen
```

```
-------------+------------
         182 |           0
```

When heap fetches occur, the table block is accessed.

If you perform an existing query after changing the record, it looks like it was done by the Index Only Scan method, but `Buffers` increased to 19 and `Heap Fetches` increased to 550. `Heap Fetches` means the number of records fetched after table block access. This means accessing the table block.

```
update t3 set c3=0 where c1 between 1 and 500;
explain (costs false, analyze, buffers)
select count(*) from t3 where c1 between 1 and 1000 and c2 <> 0;
                              QUERY PLAN
-----------------------------------------------------------------------
 Aggregate (actual time=1.008..1.008 rows=1 loops=1)
   Buffers: shared hit=1008
   -> Index Only Scan using t3_idx01 on t3
        Index Cond: ((c1 >= 1) AND (c1 <= 1000))
        Filter: (c2 <> 0)
        Heap Fetches: 550
        Buffers: shared hit=19
```

If you check the Visibility Map status now, you can see that the `ALL_VISIBLE` bit in blocks 0 through 9 has been changed to 0. Blocks with the `ALL_VISIBLE` bit set to 0 need table access.

```
select blkno, all_visible from pg_visibility('t3');
 blkno | all_visible
-------+-------------
     0 | f
...
     9 | f
```

The `ALL_VISIBLE` bit is changed to 1 after `Vacuum`. Therefore, after `Vacuum` is executed, Index Only Scan method is performed.

```
vacuum t3;
explain (costs false, analyze, buffers)
select count(*) from t3 where c1 between 1 and 1000 and c2 <> 0;
                              QUERY PLAN
-----------------------------------------------------------------------
 Aggregate (actual time=0.394..0.394 rows=1 loops=1)
   Buffers: shared hit=8
   -> Index Only Scan using t3_idx01 on t3
        Index Cond: ((c1 >= 1) AND (c1 <= 1000))
```

```
    Filter: (c2 <> 0)
    Heap Fetches: 0
    Buffers: shared hit=8
```

The above results show that after performing UPDATE, Index Only Scan, but the number of
Buffers increased to 8. Is not it strange? What we changed was the C3 column, which was not
included in the index. This will be explained in detail in the section on 'HOT'.

Tid Scan method

PostgreSQL has a CTID value consisting of "{block number, record number}" for each record. The
Tid Scan method directly accesses the record using the CTID value of the record. Since the CTID
value is unique at the table level, accessing the table using the CTID value is faster than any
other method. Consider the example below.

```
drop table t4;
create table t4 (c1 integer, c2 integer);
insert into t4 select mod(i,50), i from generate_series(1,100) a(i);

select ctid, * from t4 limit 2;
 ctid  | c1 | c2
-------+----+----
 (0,1) |  1 |  1
 (0,2) |  2 |  2

explain (costs false, analyze, buffers)
select * from t4 where ctid='(0,1)';
                        QUERY PLAN
-----------------------------------------------------------------
Tid Scan on t4 (actual time=0.003..0.003 rows=1 loops=1)
   TID Cond: (ctid = '(0,1)'::tid)
   Buffers: shared hit=1
```

As shown in the above results, it can be seen that the Tid Scan method accesses only 1 block.
The Tid Scan method can be used in data cleaning such as deleting redundant data or deleting
initial N number of data.

Controlling access methods

PostgreSQL provides the ability to turn access methods on or off. The functions provided are as
follows. (All default values are on)

Table 3-6. *Access control provided by PostgreSQL*

Item	Description
enable_seqscan	Controls whether Seq Scan is used or not.
enable_indexscan	Controls whether or not Index Scan is used
enable_bitmapscan	Controls whether Bitmap Index Scan is used or not.
enable_indexonlyscan	Controls whether Index Only Scan is used or not.
enable_tidscan	Controls whether or not to use Tid Scan.

Let's take a look at some examples.

Test environment

```
drop table t5;
create table t5 (c1 integer, c2 integer, dummy char(100));
insert into t5
select i, mod(i,2), 'dummy' from generate_series(1,100000) a(i) order by 2;
analyze t5;
```

Cost of Seq Scan

Currently, Seq Scan is the only way to access the T5 table. The cost is 3,099.

```
explain select count(*) from t5 where c2=1;
                          QUERY PLAN
-----------------------------------------------------------------
 Aggregate  (cost=3099.67..3099.68 rows=1 width=8)
   ->  Seq Scan on t5
         Filter: (c2 = 1)
```

Effect when setting Off

Even if Seq Scan method is off, it is performed by Seq Scan method. There is no other way. However, after setting off, the cost of Seq Scan becomes very high.

```
set enable_seqscan=off;
explain select count(*) from t5 where c2=1;
                          QUERY PLAN
-----------------------------------------------------------------
 Aggregate  (cost=10000003098.65..10000003098.66 rows=1 width=8)
   ->  Seq Scan on t5
         Filter: (c2 = 1)
```

Controls related to Index Scan

If you check the Explain result after creating Covering index, you can see that it is performed by Index Only Scan method

```
create index t5_idx01 on t5(c2);
vacuum t5;
explain select count(*) from t5 where c2=1;
                        QUERY PLAN
---------------------------------------------------------------
 Aggregate  (cost=1559.29..1559.30 rows=1 width=8)
   ->  Index Only Scan using t5_idx01 on t5
         (cost=0.29..1433.92 rows=50150 width=0)
         Index Cond: (c2 = 1)
```

When the Index Only Scan method is turned off, it is performed by the Index Scan method. Since records were sorted by the C2 column, the optimizer chose the Index Scan method instead of the Bitmap Index Scan method.

```
set enable_indexonlyscan=off;
explain select count(*) from t5 where c2=1;
                        QUERY PLAN
---------------------------------------------------------------
 Aggregate  (cost=2428.29..2428.30 rows=1 width=8)
   ->  Index Scan using t5_idx01 on t5
         (cost=0.29..2302.92 rows=50150 width=0)
         Index Cond: (c2 = 1)
```

At this time, if the Index Scan method is turned off, Bitmap Index Scan method is performed.

```
set enable_indexscan=off;
explain select count(*) from t5 where c2=1;
                        QUERY PLAN
---------------------------------------------------------------
 Aggregate  (cost=3422.20..3422.22 rows=1 width=8)
   ->  Bitmap Heap Scan on t5  (cost=944.96..3296.83 rows=50150 width=0)
         Recheck Cond: (c2 = 1)
         ->  Bitmap Index Scan on t5_idx01
               (cost=0.00..932.42 rows=50150 width=0)
               Index Cond: (c2 = 1)
```

Join method

There are 3 join methods provided by PostgreSQL.

- Nested Loop join

- Sort Merge join

- Hash join

Choosing the right join method is a very important factor in improving query performance.

The optimizer chooses the appropriate join method using statistics, index information, and histogram information. However, the optimizer can't always establish an optimal execution plan because it has a limitation that it must be set up in a very short time. In this case, the user needs to derive the appropriate join method. Unfortunately, PostgreSQL does not provide very precise control over the join method. It only provides a way to enable or disable specific join methods at the query level. This is a limited tuning method.

However, understanding the correct concepts and operating principles of join methods is a very important factor in tuning. Therefore, this section will detail Nested Loop joins and hash joins in detail.

Nested Loop join

A Nested Loop join (NL join) is a method of repeatedly accessing a second table using the records extracted from the first table.

The first table is called the Outer table (or Driving table), and the second table is called the Inner table. NL join is performed in a nested loop structure. Therefore, the number of loops and access efficiency to the inner table are very important. Most readers of this article know the advantages and disadvantages of NL joins. Therefore, we will not explain the general advantages and disadvantages of NL joins. Instead, we will explain how to analyze explain results, why Materialize occurs during NL joins, and why Bitmap Index Scan is used when accessing inner tables.

The most common NL join examples

Test environment

```
drop table t1;
drop table t2;
drop table t3;
create table t1 (c1 integer, c2 integer, dummy char(1000));
create table t2 (c1 integer, c2 integer, dummy char(1000));
create table t3 (c1 integer, c2 integer, dummy char(1000));

insert into t1 select i, i, 'dummy' from generate_series(1,10000) a(i);
insert into t2 select i, i, 'dummy' from generate_series(1,10000) a(i);
insert into t3 select i, i, 'dummy' from generate_series(1,1000) a(i);

create index t1_idx01 on t1(c1);
create index t2_idx01 on t2(c1);
create index t3_idx01 on t3(c1);

analyze t1;
analyze t2;
analyze t3;

select relname, relpages
from   pg_class where relname in ('t1','t2','t3');
 relname | relpages
---------+----------
 t1      |     1429
 t2      |     1429
 t3      |      143
```

Analyzing Explain Results

The following example is the most common NL join example. After extracting a small number of
rows from the driving table, the NL join is performed with the inner tables using the index.

```
explain (costs false, analyze, buffers)
select *
from   t1 a, t2 b, t3 c
where  a.c1 between 1 and 10
and    a.c1 = b.c1
and    b.c1 = c.c1;
                        QUERY PLAN
---------------------------------------------------------------
 Nested Loop (actual time=0.010..0.045 rows=10 loops=1)
   Join Filter: (a.c1 = b.c1)
   Buffers: shared hit=64
```

```
(3) ->  Nested Loop (actual time=0.006..0.023 rows=10 loops=1)
            Buffers: shared hit=34
(1)         -> Index Scan using t1_idx01 on t1 a
               (actual time=0.003..0.009 rows=10 loops=1)
                  Index Cond: ((c1 >= 1) AND (c1 <= 10))
                  Buffers: shared hit=4
(2)         -> Index Scan using t3_idx01 on t3 c
               (actual time=0.001..0.001 rows=1 loops=10)
                  Index Cond: (c1 = a.c1)
                  Buffers: shared hit=30
(4) -> Index Scan using t2_idx01 on t2 b
        (actual time=0.001..0.001 rows=1 loops=10)
         Index Cond: (c1 = c.c1)
         Buffers: shared hit=30
Planning time: 0.563 ms
Execution time: 0.089 ms
```

Order of execution

When analyzing the explain results, you should first check the order of execution. The order of execution is `(1)->(2)->(3)->(4)` and the table access order is `T1->T3->T2`.

Let's analyze it step by step.

Step (1)

Use the `T1_IDX01` index to access the outer table, the `T1` table. At this time, 10 records were returned.

Since it is located at the outermost position, the number of loops is one.

Step (2)

Use the `T3_IDX01` index to access the inner table, the `T3` table. Since the number of records returned from the Outer table is 10, it is repeated 10 times.

Step (3)

10 records were returned as a result of NL join between `T1` and `T3` tables.

Step (4)

The `T2_IDX01` index is used to access the inner table `T2`. Since 10 records were returned in Step (2), it is repeated 10 times.

Why Materialize Occurs During NL Joining

Sometimes the `Materialize` operation appears in the explain result. This operation usually occurs when there are no indexes in the Inner table. Let's perform the join with the `C2` column where the index is not created as shown below. (Other join methods have been disabled to derive the `Materialize` operation.)

```
set enable_hashjoin=off;
set enable_mergejoin=off;
explain (costs false, timing false, analyze, buffers)
select *
from    t1 a, t2 b
where   a.c1 between 1 and 10
and     a.c2 = b.c2
and     b.c2 in (10,20);
                        QUERY PLAN
---------------------------------------------------------------
 Nested Loop (actual rows=1 loops=1)
   Join Filter: (a.c2 = b.c2)
   Rows Removed by Join Filter: 19
   Buffers: shared hit=1433
   ->  Index Scan using t1_idx01 on t1 a (actual rows=10 loops=1)
         Index Cond: ((c1 >= 1) AND (c1 <= 10))
         Buffers: shared hit=4
   ->  Materialize (actual rows=2 loops=10)
         Buffers: shared hit=1429
         ->  Seq Scan on t2 b (actual rows=2 loops=1)
               Filter: (c2 = ANY ('{10,20}'::integer[]))
               Rows Removed by Filter: 9998
               Buffers: shared hit=1429
```

From the above results, we can see that 'Materialize' for `T2` table occurs because the join order is `T1->T2` and there is no proper index in `T2`. Materialize is a way to reduce the load of accessing the Inner table repeatedly. To do this, store the records in the Temp table. As a result, the Seq Scan for the `T2` table is performed only once.

As such, Materialize is a way for the optimizer to choose when there is no proper index at the time of the NL join. But Materialize is not the ultimate solution. If 'Materialize' appears in the explain result, you need to consider index creation of the join condition column.

Why use the Bitmap Index Scan method when accessing Inner tables?

The performance of the NL join is closely related to the efficiency of accessing the inner table. For this, an appropriate index should be used when accessing the inner table. Another important part is the sort order between the inner table and the index. As mentioned earlier in the Bitmap Index Scan method, if the sort order between the table and the index is bad, the Bitmap Index Scan method is used. This method also applies to NL joins. Consider the example below.

Test environment

Correlation value of C1 column becomes bad when data is input as below

```
drop table t1;
drop table t2;

create table t1 (c1 integer, dummy char(100));
create table t2 (c1 integer, dummy char(100));

insert into t1 select i, 'dummy' from generate_series(1,1000) a(i);
insert into t2 select mod(i,1000)+1, 'dummy' from generate_series(1,10000000) a(i);

create index t1_idx01 on t1(c1);
create index t2_idx01 on t2(c1);
analyze t1;
analyze t2;

select relname, relpages
from   pg_class where relname in ('t1','t2');
 relname | relpages
---------+----------
 t1      |       18
 t2      |   172414

select tablename, attname, correlation
from   pg_stats
where  tablename='t2';
 tablename | attname | correlation
-----------+---------+--------------
 t2        | c1      |  -0.0046397
 t2        | dummy   |           1
```

Analyzing Explain Results

The following query causes a Bitmap Index Scan operation to occur when accessing the Inner table. That is, when the `correlation` value of the inner table index column is bad, the bitmap index scan method may be selected.

```
set enable_hashjoin=off;
set enable_mergejoin=off;

explain (costs false, analyze, buffers)
select *
from   t1 a, t2 b
where  a.c1 between 1 and 100
and    a.c1 = b.c1;
                        QUERY PLAN
----------------------------------------------------------------
 Nested Loop (actual time=3.763..1441.674 rows=1000000 loops=1)
   Buffers: shared hit=1003036
   -> Index Scan using t1_idx01 on t1 a
         Index Cond: ((c1 >= 1) AND (c1 <= 100))
         Buffers: shared hit=4
   -> Bitmap Heap Scan on t2 b
         Recheck Cond: (c1 = a.c1)
         Heap Blocks: exact=1000000
         Buffers: shared hit=1003032
         -> Bitmap Index Scan on t2_idx01
               Index Cond: (c1 = a.c1)
               Buffers: shared hit=3032
 Planning time: 0.172 ms
 Execution time: 1529.824 ms
```

But the results of the Explain show something strange. The number of accesses of the T2 table block is one million. This is much larger than the number of blocks in the T2 table, 172,414. It seems that the same block has been accessed several times. What happened?

Check the number of buffer IO of Index Scan method

Let's do a test after disabling the Bitmap Index Scan method.

```
set enable_bitmapscan=off;
explain (costs false, analyze, buffers)
select *
from   t1 a, t2 b
where  a.c1 between 1 and 100
and    a.c1 = b.c1;
                        QUERY PLAN
----------------------------------------------------------------
 Nested Loop (actual time=0.017..986.626 rows=1000000 loops=1)
```

```
Buffers: shared hit=1003036
  ->  Index Scan using t1_idx01 on t1 a
         Index Cond: ((c1 >= 1) AND (c1 <= 100))
         Buffers: shared hit=4
  ->  Index Scan using t2_idx01 on t2 b
         Index Cond: (c1 = a.c1)
         Buffers: shared hit=1003032
Planning time: 0.120 ms
Execution time: 1075.990 ms
```

From the above results, it can be seen that both methods have the same number of buffer IO. Even Index Scan is faster. This is different from what we expected. Why? Is this the result?

Reason for the same number of buffer IO of Bitmap Index Scan and Index Scan

The Bitmap Index Scan method described in the 'Access Method' section above was to access table blocks after sorting '**all target records**' in order of table block. I also expected that the Bitmap Index Scan method that occurs at the time of NL join would work this way.

However, at the time of NL join, Bitmap Index Scan method is used for '**each record**' extracted from the Outer table. In the example above, the bitmap index scan method is performed 100 times from 1 to 100. As a result, the buffer IO is not reduced at all. Rather, it is slower than the index scan method because of the load of bitmap operation every time.

Then why? Did the optimizer choose the Bitmap Index Scan method?

Bitmap Index Scan is a way to minimize disk random IO

The Bitmap Index Scan method performed during NL join is a method of reducing disk random IO. In other words, this method works only when disk IO occurs. As shown in Figure 3-12, the Bitmap Index Scan accesses the blocks after sorting the table blocks for each record extracted from the Outer table. As a result, when disk IO occurs, random access is reduced.

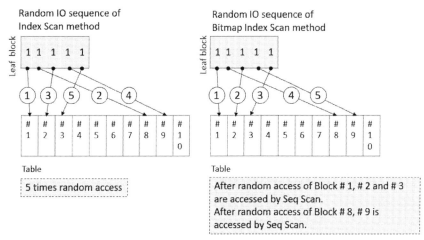

Figure 3-12. *Random access sequence according to access method*

Check the effect of Bitmap Index Scan method

To verify the effect of the Bitmap Index Scan method, perform the test after clearing the DB buffer restart and DB buffer cache each time the test is performed.

Result of Bitmap Index Scan Method

```
-- DB STOP
-- Clear the OS buffer cache by executing the following command
root # sync;  echo 1 > /proc/sys/vm/drop_caches;

-- DB START

explain (costs false, analyze, buffers)
select *
from   t1 a, t2 b
where  a.c1 between 1 and 100
and    a.c1 = b.c1;
                        QUERY PLAN
-----------------------------------------------------------------
Nested Loop (actual time=5.418..9496.744 rows=1000000 loops=1)
  Buffers: shared hit=973049 read=29987
  ->  Index Scan using t1_idx01 on t1 a
          Index Cond: ((c1 >= 1) AND (c1 <= 100))
          Buffers: shared hit=3 read=1
  ->  Bitmap Heap Scan on t2 b
          Recheck Cond: (c1 = a.c1)
          Heap Blocks: exact=1000000
          Buffers: shared hit=973046 read=29986
```

```
        ->  Bitmap Index Scan on t2_idx01
               Index Cond: (c1 = a.c1)
               Buffers: shared hit=288 read=2744
Planning time: 11.853 ms
Execution time: 9591.875 ms
```

Result of Index Scan Method

```
-- DB STOP
-- Clear the OS buffer cache by executing the following command
root # sync;   echo 1 > /proc/sys/vm/drop_caches;
-- DB START

set enable_hashjoin=off;
set enable_mergejoin=off;
set enable_bitmapscan=off;

explain (costs false, analyze, buffers)
select *
from    t1 a, t2 b
where   a.c1 between 1 and 100
and     a.c1 = b.c1;
                      QUERY PLAN
---------------------------------------------------------------
 Nested Loop (actual time=2.016..10382.576 rows=1000000 loops=1)
   Buffers: shared hit=973049 read=29987
   ->  Index Scan using t1_idx01 on t1 a
          Index Cond: ((c1 >= 1) AND (c1 <= 100))
          Buffers: shared hit=3 read=1
   ->  Index Scan using t2_idx01 on t2 b
          Index Cond: (c1 = a.c1)
          Buffers: shared hit=973046 read=29986
Planning time: 19.771 ms
Execution time: 10480.010 ms
```

From the above results, both DISK IO and buffer IO counts are the same. In this case, however, the Bitmap Index Scan method is slightly faster.

Hash join

The hash join is performed as a Build phase and a Probe phase

In the build phase, a hash table is created by applying a hash function to the join column of the first table. In the probe phase, the second table is scanned, and the hash table is searched while applying the same hash function to the join column.

At this time, the first table is referred to as a Build table, and the second table is referred to as a Probe table. Since a hash table data structure is created in the `work_mem` memory of the backend process, a small table is usually selected as the build table.

The hash join method is divided into an in-memory hash join, a Grace hash join, and a hybrid hash join. If a hash operation on the Build table can be performed within work_mem, it is performed with an in-memory hash join. If not, it is done with Grace hash join or Hybrid hash join.

PostgreSQL uses the in-memory hash join and Hybrid hash join method. If the data in the probe table skew, the histogram is referred to. (This is called 'Skew data optimization' and is sometimes called Histojoin)

In this section, we will learn about hash join methods, how to improve hash join performance, and histojoin using histograms.

The Basics of Hash Join

A hash join uses a hash function. The hash function (h) has the following characteristics.

- If $X = Y$, then $h(X) = h(Y)$.

- If $h(X) \neq h(Y)$, then $X \neq Y$.

- If $X \neq Y$, $h(X) \neq h(Y)$ is most ideal.

- If $X \neq Y$, $h(X) = h(Y)$ is also possible. This is called a hash collision.

Since hash joins apply a hash function, only Equi joins are possible.

In-Memory Hash Join

An in-memory hash join is a method used when a hash build work can be handled in `work_mem` space.

Processing procedure

In the Build step, create a hash table data structure by applying a hash function to the join column of the Build table. (See Figure 3-13.) Then, the hash table data structure is retrieved by applying the same hash function to the probe table. (See Figure 3-14.) The hash function used in the example is MOD (X, 4).

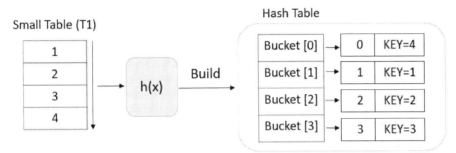

Figure 3-13. *Build phase*

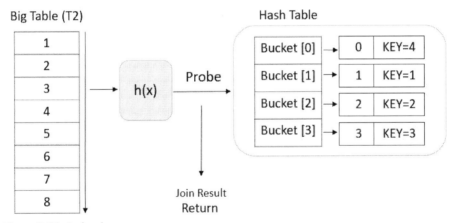

Figure 3-14. *Probe phase*

What are Buckets and Batches?

Let's check the Explain result of the in-memory hash join.

Test environment

```
drop table t1;
drop table t2;
create table t1 (c1 integer, dummy char(10));
```

```
create table t2 (c1 integer, dummy char(10));

insert into t1 select i, 'dummy' from generate_series(1,10) a(i);
insert into t2 select i, 'dummy' from generate_series(1,1000) a(i);

analyze t1;
analyze t2;
```

Analyzing Explain Results

```
explain (costs false, analyze, buffers)
select *
from    t1 a, t2 b
where   a.c1 = b.c1;
                          QUERY PLAN
------------------------------------------------------------------
 Hash Join (actual time=0.131..13.996 rows=10 loops=1)
   Hash Cond: (b.c1 = a.c1)
   Buffers: shared hit=10
   ->  Seq Scan on t2 b (actual time=0.006..0.211 rows=1000 loops=1)
         Buffers: shared hit=6
   ->  Hash (actual time=0.090..0.090 rows=10 loops=1)
         Buckets: 1024   Batches: 1   Memory Usage: 9kB
         Buffers: shared hit=1
         ->  Seq Scan on t1 a (actual time=0.001..0.004 rows=10 loops=1)
               Buffers: shared hit=1
```

In the above results, we should pay attention to `Buckets`, `Batches`, and `Memory Usage`.

- **Buckets**: The number of hash table buckets. The minimum value is 1,024..

- **Batches**: It is 1 when processed by an in-memory hash join. If an in-memory hash join can't handle it, a value greater than or equal to 2 appears.

- **Memory Usage**: Means `work_mem` usage.

Bucket count calculation formula

Some of the formulas for calculating the number of buckets are:

result 1 = Min (max_pointers, INT_MAX / 2);

result 2 = Build Input rows / NTUP_PER_BUCKET

result 3 = Min (result 1, result 2)

result 4 = Max (result 3, 1024)

You can see some principles through the formula.

- The number of buckets is less than INT_MAX / 2. (INT_MAX ≑ 2^32) This is to prevent overflow problems.

- The minimum number of buckets is 1,024

- The smaller the value of NTUP_PER_BUCKET, the larger the number of buckets.

NTUP_PER_BUCKET

The value of NTUP_PER_BUCKET was changed from version 9.5 to 1. It was 10 until the previous version. The purpose of the change is to improve performance. The smaller the value, the larger the number of buckets, which leads to a shorter length of the hash chain.

Note that the NTUP_PER_BUCKET value only sets the target value. That is, you can create many hash buckets by setting it to 1, but you can't limit the length of a chain to a bucket to 1. Any hash function has a possibility of hash collision. And the values are stored in the same bucket.

Grace Hash Join and Hybrid Hash Join Overview

Suppose the size of the Build table is too large to handle the Build phase within work_mem. The easiest way to do this is to break the Build table into multiple logical partitions, then perform the Build phase several times, and run the Probe phase several times. This is called Classic Hash Join. However, there is a load that needs to read the probe table repeatedly. The solution to this problem is Grace Hash Join and Hybrid Hash Join.

The Grace hash join procedure is as follows.

1. Create N logical partitions by applying the same hash function to the Build and Probe tables.

2. As a result of (1), N (0 to N-1) build partitions and N (0 to N-1) probe partitions are created. These partitions are stored in the temporary tablespace.
3. Perform a hash join for Build partition #0 and Probe partition #0. Then, the hash join is sequentially performed up to the N-1 partition.

Grace hash joins are faster than Classic hash joins because they only access the probe table once. However, it has the disadvantage of storing all partitions in the temporary tablespace. The algorithm that supplements this problem is a hybrid hash join.

Hybrid hash joins store Build partition #0 in `work_mem` memory rather than in the temporary tablespace. This will perform a hash join without storing the probe partition #0 in the temporary tablespace.

Hybrid Hash Join Procedure

The hybrid hash join procedure is as follows.

1. Decide how to divide the Build table into several partitions. (Assuming 4 partitions)
2. Read the Build table.
   A. Perform the Build step for the record corresponding to partition #0.
   B. The records corresponding to partitions #1 to #3 are stored in the temporary tablespace.
3. Read the probe table.
   A. A. The record corresponding to the partition #0 performs the probe phase. When the probe phase is completed, the hash join for partition #0 is completed.
   B. The records corresponding to partitions #1 to #3 are stored in the temporary tablespace.
4. Perform a hash join for partitions #1~#3.
   A. Perform Build phase for Build partition #1.
   B. Perform Probe phase while reading Probe Partition #1.
   C. Repeat the above steps for partitions 2 and 3.

You can easily understand it from the picture below.

Figure 3-15 shows the situation after the build phase is complete. The h1() hash function is used to divide the Build table into 4 partitions, and the record for the #0 partition has been completed. The remaining partitions are stored in the temporary tablespace.

The h1() hash function used in the example is MOD (x, 4) and the hash function h2() is MOD (x, 2). Also, the Build Input value is 1 to 8. Therefore, 4 and 8 belong to the partition #0, and the corresponding value is placed in the 0 bucket.

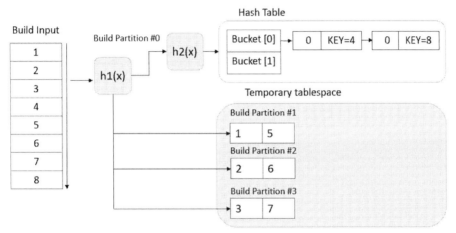

Figure 3-15. *After the Build phase is complete*

After the Build phase is completed, the Probe phase for partition #0 is performed. Then create a probe partition. The situation after these work is completed is as follows.

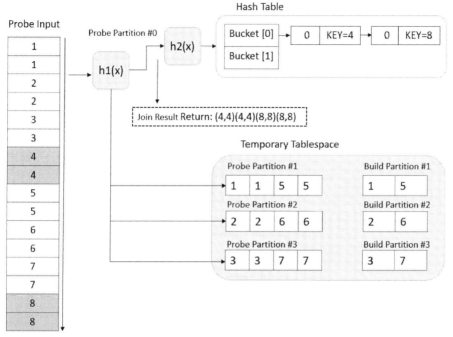

Figure 3-16. *After completion of Probe stage of partition #0 and creation of partition*

That is, the hash join for partition #0 is completed, and partitions 1 through 3 are stored in the temporary tablespace. After this operation is completed, hash joins are performed between partitions of the same number. This is called Multi-Batch.

Explain result of Multi-Batch

Let's check the explain result of Multi-Batch.

Test environment

```
drop table t1;
drop table t2;
create table t1 (c1 integer, dummy char(10));
create table t2 (c1 integer, dummy char(10));

insert into t1 select generate_series(1,100000), 'dummy';
insert into t2 select mod(generate_series(1,400000),100000)+1, 'dummy';

analyze t1;
analyze t2;
```

Analyzing Explain Results

In the following results, 32,768 buckets were created, 838 KiB of `work_mem` space was used, and 8 batches were performed in the Build phase. Also, it can be seen that Temp IO occurred in the Build phase and the Probe phase.

```
set work_mem='1MB';
explain (costs false, analyze, buffers)
select *
from   t1 a, t2 b
where  a.c1 = b.c1;
                        QUERY PLAN
----------------------------------------------------------------
Hash Join (actual time=9988.924..29263.532 rows=400000 loops=1)
  Hash Cond: (b.c1 = a.c1)
  Buffers: shared hit=2704, temp read=1889 written=1875
  ->  Seq Scan on t2 b (actual time=0.007..67.202 rows=400000 loops=1)
        Buffers: shared hit=2163
  ->  Hash (actual time=9988.600..9988.600 rows=100000 loops=1)
        Buckets: 32768  Batches: 8  Memory Usage: 838kB
        Buffers: shared hit=541, temp written=371
        ->  Seq Scan on t1 a
              (actual time=0.006..25.134 rows=100000 loops=1)
              Buffers: shared hit=541
```

Skew data optimization (Histojoin)

The examples described above were cases where the Build Input and Probe Input data were distributed evenly. However, not all of the data is evenly distributed. There are also very skewed data. Consider the following scenario.

- If the Build Input exceeds the `work_mem` size, a Multi-Batch operation is performed.

- At this time, the probe input data is very skew. For example, 1 to 9 is 90% of the total.

In this case, if 1 to 9 do not correspond to partition #0, a large amount of temp IO is generated to store the probe partitions corresponding to these values in the temporary tablespace.

The solution to this problem is called 'skew data optimization', which is called a Histojoin join. Histojoin is a hybrid hash join method using a histogram. That is, after checking the MCV (Most

Common Values) values using the histogram of the probe table, the MCV values are stored in a separate hash bucket to remove the Temp IO for the skew data. Consider the example below.

Test environment

```
drop table t1;
drop table t2;
create table t1 (c1 integer, dummy char(10));
create table t2 (c1 integer, dummy char(10));

insert into t1 select generate_series(1,100000), 'dummy';
-- Insert 1 to 9 for each 1 million.
insert into t2 select mod(generate_series(1,9000000),9)+1, 'dummy';

-- Insert a unique value from 10.
insert into t2 select generate_series(10,1000009), 'dummy';

analyze t1;
analyze t2;
```

Check the MCV (Most Common Values) and the number of blocks in the table

As a result of checking the statistics, the MCV value is 1 to 9 and the number of table blocks is 54,055.

```
select most_common_vals
from   pg_stats
where  tablename='t2' and attname='c1';
 most_common_vals
---------------------
 {9,3,4,8,6,2,5,1,7}

select relpages from pg_class where relname='t2';
 relpages
----------
    54055
```

Analyzing Explain Results

In the following results, Temp Read=4,132 and Written=4,118 blocks for the probe table. This value is less than 1/10 of the probe table size. This is the effect of skew data optimization. That is, since the MCV value is allocated to a separate bucket and the build phase is performed, it is possible to skip the probe partition creation operation for the MCV value.

```
set work_mem='1MB';
explain (costs false, analyze, buffers)
select *
from   t1 a, t2 b
where  a.c1 = b.c1;
                        QUERY PLAN
--------------------------------------------------------------------
 Hash Join (actual time=47.015..5298.413 rows=9099991 loops=1)
   Hash Cond: (b.c1 = a.c1)
   Buffers: shared hit=3 read=54596, temp read=4132 written=4118
   -> Seq Scan on t2 b
         Buffers: shared read=54055
   -> Hash (actual time=46.375..46.375 rows=100000 loops=1)
         Buckets: 32768  Batches: 8  Memory Usage: 839kB
         Buffers: shared read=541, temp written=371
         -> Seq Scan on t1 a
               Buffers: shared read=541
 Planning time: 6.944 ms
 Execution time: 6151.013 ms
```

Explain result after skew data optimization OFF

After turning off the Skew data optimization feature, the Temp IO value has increased by about 9 times. Because of this, the processing speed has also become a little slower.

```
set work_mem='1MB';
explain (costs false, analyze, buffers)
select *
from   t1 a, t2 b
where  a.c1 = b.c1;
                        QUERY PLAN
--------------------------------------------------------------------
 Hash Join (actual time=50.280..7030.957 rows=9099991 loops=1)
   Hash Cond: (b.c1 = a.c1)
   Buffers: shared hit=3 read=54596, temp read=34040 written=34026
   -> Seq Scan on t2 b
         Buffers: shared read=54055
   -> Hash (actual time=49.475..49.475 rows=100000 loops=1)
         Buckets: 32768  Batches: 8  Memory Usage: 838kB
         Buffers: shared read=541, temp written=371
         -> Seq Scan on t1 a
               Buffers: shared read=541
 Planning time: 8.576 ms
 Execution time: 7851.566 ms
```

> 🗋 **Note** To turn off skew data optimization, change the SKEW_WORK_MEM_PERCENT value in
> src/include/executor/hashjoin.h to 0 and recompile the source. This is for testing purposes only
> and should not be changed.

SKEW_WORK_MEM_PERCENT

The SKEW_WORK_MEM_PERCENT value determines the percentage of buckets to use for skew data. The default value is 2%. For example, if work_mem has space to store 100,000 buckets, 200 buckets are used for skew data. The number of MCV is set by the default_statistics_target parameter, and the default value is 100. Therefore, 2% seems to be the appropriate ratio.

Is in-memory method always faster than multi-batch method?

The in-memory method is known to be faster than the multi-batch method. However, the in-memory method is not always faster than the multi-batch method. Why? Could this happen? This is due to a hash collision.

Let's look at the picture below.

Assume that the Build Input is {1,2,3,4} and the Probe Input is {1,2,3,4}. If the most ideal hash function is used to distribute the Build Input into 4 buckets, only need to access the Build Input value once in the Probe phase. However, if a hash collision occurs and two build inputs are connected to a single bucket, the Build Input value must be accessed twice in the Probe phase.

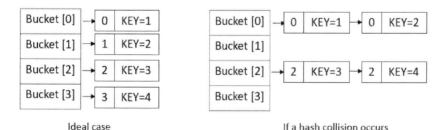

Figure 3-17. *Ideal cases vs. Cases where hash collision occur*

If the performance loss due to hash collision is greater than the benefit from eliminating Temp IO, the in-memory approach may be slower than the multi-batch approach. This happened on my system as well. Consider the example below.

In case of Multi-Batch method

```
drop table t1;
drop table t2;
create table t1 (c1 integer, dummy char(10));
create table t2 (c1 integer, dummy char(10));

insert into t1 select generate_series(1,1000000), 'dummy';
insert into t2 select mod(generate_series(1,4000000),1000000)+1, 'dummy';

analyze t1;
analyze t2;

set work_mem='1MB';
explain (costs false, analyze, buffers)
select *
from   t1 a, t2 b
where  a.c1 = b.c1;
                       QUERY PLAN
---------------------------------------------------------------
 Hash Join (actual time=331.038..2992.338 rows=4000000 loops=1)
   Hash Cond: (b.c1 = a.c1)
   Buffers: shared hit=27028, temp read=21217 written=21091
   -> Seq Scan on t2 b (actual time=0.010..504.685 ...)
         Buffers: shared hit=21622
   -> Hash (actual time=330.142..330.142 rows=1000000 loops=1)
         Buckets: 32768  Batches: 64  Memory Usage: 976kB
         Buffers: shared hit=5406, temp written=4176
         -> Seq Scan on t1 a
               Buffers: shared hit=5406
 Execution time: 3347.304 ms
```

In case of In-Memory method

```
set work_mem='100MB';
explain (costs false, analyze, buffers)
select *
from   t1 a, t2 b
where  a.c1 = b.c1;
                       QUERY PLAN
---------------------------------------------------------------
 Hash Join (actual time=417.586..3269.277 rows=4000000 loops=1)
```

```
   Hash Cond: (b.c1 = a.c1)
   Buffers: shared hit=27028
   -> Seq Scan on t2 b (actual time=0.009..517.726 ...)
      Buffers: shared hit=21622
   -> Hash (actual time=416.649..416.649 rows=1000000 loops=1)
      Buckets: 1048576 Batches: 1 Memory Usage: 54091kB
      Buffers: shared hit=5406
      -> Seq Scan on t1 a (actual time=0.011..130.632 ...)
         Buffers: shared hit=5406
 Planning time: 0.132 ms
 Execution time: 3631.746 ms
```

The above results show that the `work_mem` is set to 100 MiB and then performed with an in-memory hash join, but it is slightly slower than the Multi-Batch method. Why? Does this happen?

To solve this question, I added debugging code to the source and checked the results. As a result, it was confirmed that more hash collisions occurred in the in-memory method. (See Figure 3-18) Comparing the number of key value accesses, the in-memory method is more than 30%. (Number of key value accesses = Number of buckets * Number of keys linked)

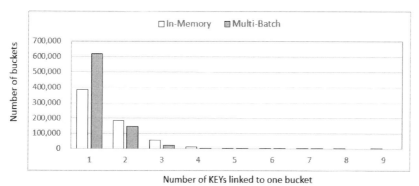

Figure 3-18. *Comparison of hash collision between In-memory and Multi-Batch*

Is this because of a hash collision? To verify this, I modified the source to change only one key value to one bucket and then test again. (This method is applicable only to the example)

As a result, the execution time of the multi-batch method was 3.162 sec and that of the in-memory method was 2.447 sec. From this result, hash join performance is most related to hash collision.

How to Identify Hash Conflicts

Here is the method I used to identify hash collisions. However, this should only be done on development or test machine.

1. Create a table.

```
create table log1 (bucketno integer, batchno integer, hashvalue bigint);
```

2. Insert debug code in source. (src/backend/executor/nodeHash.c)

```
ExecHashTableInsert(HashJoinTable hashtable,
                                TupleTableSlot *slot,
                                uint32 hashvalue)
{
...
ExecHashGetBucketAndBatch(hashtable, hashvalue, &bucketno, &batchno);

#ifdef DEBUG_HASH_COLLISION
printf("insert into log1 values(%d, %d, %u);\n",
bucketno, batchno, hashvalue);
#endif
```

3. Modify Makefile.global.

```
CFLAGS = -DDEBUG_HASH_COLLISION
```

4. Compile as root user.

```
root> # make; make install
```

5. Execute script command to save screen output.

```
postgres> $ script insert.out
```

6. After the DB is restarted, perform the hash join.

7. When done, type ^D to save the insert.out file.

8. Input into the table using the result of the insert.out file.

```
postgres> $ psql -d postgres -p 5432 -f insert.out
```

9. Check for hash collisions.

```
select cnt, count(*)
from (select count(*) cnt, bucketno
      from   log1
```

```
      group  by bucketno, batchno) a
group by cnt order by cnt;
 cnt | count
-----+--------
   1 | 385004
   2 | 183490
   3 |  58426
   4 |  14045
   5 |   2677
   6 |    444
   7 |     61
   8 |      8
   9 |      2
```

One of the advantages of open source DBMS is that you can modify the source to check for hash collisions.

Outer join

NL Outer join

NL Outer join always drives the base table first. Consider the example below.

Test environment

```
drop table t1;
drop table t2;
create table t1 (c1 integer, c2 integer, dummy char(10));
create table t2 (c1 integer, c2 integer, dummy char(10));

insert into t1 select i,i, 'dummy' from generate_series(1,1000000) a(i);
insert into t2 select i,i, 'dummy' from generate_series(1,1000000) a(i);

create index t1_idx01 on t1(c1);
create index t2_idx01 on t2(c1);

create unique index t2_uk on t2(c2);

analyze t1;
analyze t2;
```

NL join example

Before looking at the NL Outer join, let's look at an example of an NL join.

Perform the following query to access the T2 table first. This is because it is fast to join in the order of T2->T1.

```
set enable_hashjoin=off;
set enable_mergejoin=off;
set enable_bitmapscan=off;

explain (costs false, analyze, buffers)
select * from t1 a, t2 b
where   a.c1 between 1 and 10
and     a.c1 = b.c1
and     b.c2 = 1;
                           QUERY PLAN
-----------------------------------------------------------------
 Nested Loop (actual time=0.011..0.012 rows=1 loops=1)
   Buffers: shared hit=8
   ->  Index Scan using t2_uk on t2 b
         Index Cond: (c2 = 1)
         Buffers: shared hit=4
   ->  Index Scan using t1_idx01 on t1 a
         Index Cond: ((c1 = b.c1) AND (c1 >= 1) AND (c1 <= 10))
         Buffers: shared hit=4
```

NL Outer join example

If you change the above example to a LEFT OUTER join, the T1 table is accessed first. This is because the T1 table is the base table.

```
set enable_material=off;

explain (costs false, analyze, buffers)
select * from t1 a LEFT JOIN t2 b ON a.c1=b.c1 AND b.c2=1
where   a.c1 between 1 and 100;
                           QUERY PLAN
-----------------------------------------------------------------
 Nested Loop Left Join (actual time=0.017..0.221 rows=100 loops=1)
   Join Filter: (a.c1 = b.c1)
   Rows Removed by Join Filter: 99
   Buffers: shared hit=404
   ->  Index Scan using t1_idx01 on t1 a
         Index Cond: ((c1 >= 1) AND (c1 <= 100))
         Buffers: shared hit=4
   ->  Index Scan using t2_uk on t2 b
         Index Cond: (c2 = 1)
         Buffers: shared hit=400
```

What happens if you drop all indexes created in T2 table?

The results below show that the T1 table is still accessed first. As a result, the Seq Scan is repeatedly performed on the T2 table. (Of course, if the index does not exist in the T2 table, another join method is used. The example disables all other join methods to determine how NL Outer joins perform)

```
drop index t2_idx01;
drop index t2_uk;

explain (costs false, analyze, buffers)
select * from t1 a LEFT JOIN t2 b ON a.c1=b.c1 AND b.c2=1
where   a.c1 between 1 and 100;
                          QUERY PLAN
------------------------------------------------------------------
 Nested Loop Left Join (actual time=0.013..8750.334 rows=100 loops=1)
   Join Filter: (a.c1 = b.c1)
   Rows Removed by Join Filter: 99
   Buffers: shared hit=637004
   -> Index Scan using t1_idx01 on t1 a
         Index Cond: ((c1 >= 1) AND (c1 <= 100))
         Buffers: shared hit=4
   -> Seq Scan on t2 b (actual time=0.004..87.491 rows=1 loops=100)
         Filter: (c2 = 1)
         Rows Removed by Filter: 999999
         Buffers: shared hit=637000
```

Hash Outer join

Do the Hash Outer join first access the base table?

If so, this can lead to very serious performance problems. For example, suppose the base table is much larger. If the base table is selected as a build table, performance problems will occur.

To solve this problem, ORACLE swaps Build Input to Probe Input. In other words, if the build input is larger than the probe input, it changes the role of each other. PostgreSQL also provides the same functionality as ORACLE. Let's look at the example below.

Test environment

Insert 1,000 rows in the T1 table, and 10 million rows in the T2 table.

```
drop table t1;
drop table t2;

create table t1 (c1 integer, c2 integer, dummy char(10));
create table t2 (c1 integer, c2 integer, dummy char(10));

insert into t1 select i,i, 'dummy' from generate_series(1,1000) a(i);
insert into t2 select mod(i,1000)+1, i, 'dummy' from generate_series(1,10000000) a(i);

analyze t1;
analyze t2;

select relname, relpages from pg_class where relname in ('t1','t2');
 relname | relpages
---------+----------
 t1      |        7
 t2      |    63695
```

If the small table is a base set

At this time, the base set becomes the Build table. Therefore, the T1 table becomes the Build table.

```
explain (costs false, analyze, buffers)
select * from t1 a LEFT JOIN t2 b ON a.c1=b.c1;
                         QUERY PLAN
-------------------------------------------------------------------
 Hash Right Join (actual time=0.447..4736.945 rows=10000000 loops=1)
   Hash Cond: (b.c1 = a.c1)
   Buffers: shared hit=63702
   ->  Seq Scan on t2 b
         Buffers: shared hit=63695
   ->  Hash (actual time=0.431..0.431 rows=1000 loops=1)
         Buckets: 1024  Batches: 1  Memory Usage: 58kB
         Buffers: shared hit=7
         ->  Seq Scan on t1 a
               Buffers: shared hit=7
 Planning time: 0.114 ms
 Execution time: 5617.383 ms
```

If the large table is a base set

The base set becomes the probe table. That is, a small table T1 is selected as a build table. That is, the Build Input has been swapped. Because of this, query performance is similar to the previous example.

```
explain (costs false, analyze, buffers)
select * from t2 b LEFT JOIN t1 a ON a.c1=b.c1;
                        QUERY PLAN
------------------------------------------------------------------
 Hash Left Join (actual time=0.330..4798.949 rows=10000000 loops=1)
   Hash Cond: (b.c1 = a.c1)
   Buffers: shared hit=63702
   ->  Seq Scan on t2 b
         Buffers: shared hit=63695
   ->  Hash (actual time=0.313..0.313 rows=1000 loops=1)
         Buckets: 1024  Batches: 1  Memory Usage: 58kB
         Buffers: shared hit=7
         ->  Seq Scan on t1 a
               Buffers: shared hit=7
 Planning time: 0.078 ms
 Execution time: 5695.027 ms
```

Meaning of Hash Left Join and Hash Right Join in Explain Result

There is somewhat confusing part in the explain results. The first query performed a LEFT JOIN, but the explain result is a `Hash Right Join`. It's a little strange.

To understand this clearly, you need to understand the join tree and join relationships. The optimizer chooses the small table T1 as the Build table and the large table T2 as the probe table. Expressing this as a join relation, the T1 table is the RIGHT table and the T2 table is the LEFT table. (See Figure 3-19.)

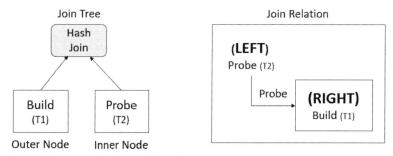

Figure 3-19. *Hash Join Tree and Join Relationship*

This can be summarized as follows.

- The `Hash Right Join` in the Explain result tells you that the base table is RIGHT, the Build table.

- The `Hash Left Join` of the Explain result tells you that that the base table is LEFT, the Probe table.

Query rewrite

Query rewrite means that the query submitted by the user is changed by the optimizer. In this section, we will discuss the sub-query Collapse, View Merging, and Join Predicate Push-Down (JPPD).

The subquery Collapse is to merge the subquery into the main query. (ORACLE calls this function a subquery unnesting)

View Merging merges views or inline views into the main query block.

JPPD pushes the join condition into the view if View Merging is not possible.

Query rewriting works based on rules. (ORACLE provides cost-based query rewriting from the 10*g* version) In general, the query rewrite improves query performance, but in some cases, performance is degraded. We'll also look at how to deal with performance problems due to unwanted query rewriting and how to derive JPPD using LATERAL joins.

Subquery

There are three ways to process subquery.

- Filter (Subplan)

- Semi join

- Subquery collapse

Let's look at an example.

Test environment

Insert 10,000 rows in the T1 table, and one million in the T2 table.

```
drop table t1;
drop table t2;

create table t1 (c1 integer, c2 integer, dummy char(100));
create table t2 (c1 integer, c2 integer, dummy char(100));

insert into t1 select i, i, 'dummy' from generate_series(1,10000) a(i);
insert into t2 select mod(i,10000), i, 'dummy' from generate_series(1,1000000) a(i);

create index t1_idx01 on t1(c1);
create index t1_idx02 on t1(c2);
create index t2_idx01 on t2(c1);

analyze t1;
analyze t2;

select relname, relpages from pg_class where relname in ('t1','t2');
relname | relpages
---------+----------
 t1      |      173
 t2      |    17242
```

Filter (Subplan)

The filter method performs a subquery for each record returned from the main query. The filter method was used before semi-join was developed. The performance is almost identical to the NL semi-join. Therefore, the optimizer prefers the semi-join instead of the filter method. If you want to filter method, you can use OFFSET. Let's look at the example below.

Derive by filter method using OFFSET 0

If you want to use filter method instead of semi-join, you can use 'OFFSET 0'.

From the results below, we can see that the NL semi-join has been changed to filter by adding 'OFFSET 0'. Of course, there is no performance difference between them. What I'm talking about here is that you can control the optimizer by adding 'OFFSET 0'.

```
explain (costs false, analyze, buffers)
select a.*
from   t1 a
where  a.c2 between 1 and 100
```

```
and      EXISTS (select 1 from t2 b where b.c1=a.c1 OFFSET 0);
                          QUERY PLAN
---------------------------------------------------------------------------
 Index Scan using t1_idx02 on t1 a (actual time=0.024..0.553 rows=100..)
   Index Cond: ((c2 >= 1) AND (c2 <= 100))
   Filter: (SubPlan 1)
   Buffers: shared hit=404
   SubPlan 1
     ->  Index Only Scan using t2_idx01 on t2 b
           Index Cond: (c1 = a.c1)
           Heap Fetches: 100
           Buffers: shared hit=400
 Planning time: 0.219 ms
 Execution time: 0.476 ms
```

> **Note** The OFFSET of a record always starts from 0. So, adding `'OFFSET  0'` does not change the query result. It only affects the optimizer's execution plan.

Semi Join

Below is an example of an NL semi-join.

```
explain (costs false, analyze, buffers)
select a.*
from    t1 a
where   a.c2 between 1 and 100
and     EXISTS (select 1 from t2 b where b.c1=a.c1);
                        QUERY PLAN
------------------------------------------------------------------
 Nested Loop Semi Join (actual time=0.018..0.588 rows=100 loops=1)
   Buffers: shared hit=404
   ->  Index Scan using t1_idx02 on t1 a
         Index Cond: ((c2 >= 1) AND (c2 <= 100))
         Buffers: shared hit=4
   ->  Index Only Scan using t2_idx01 on t2 b
         Index Cond: (c1 = a.c1)
         Heap Fetches: 100
         Buffers: shared hit=400
 Planning time: 0.289 ms
 Execution time: 0.618 ms
```

Subquery collapse

What if the subquery table does not have an index?

Will it be performed with a hash semi-join? Or will it be performed as a hash join after the subquery collapse?

In the example below, the subquery Collapse is performed. Therefore, the subquery was merged into the main query and then performed as a hash join. At this time, T2 table is a probe table, and Group By is performed internally so as not to affect the number of joining results.

```
drop index t2_idx01;
explain (costs false, analyze, buffers)
select a.*
from    t1 a
where   a.c2 between 1 and 100
and     EXISTS (select 1 from t2 b where b.c1=a.c1);
                              QUERY PLAN
--------------------------------------------------------------------
 Hash Join (actual time=445.456..449.598 rows=100 loops=1)
   Hash Cond: (b.c1 = a.c1)
   Buffers: shared hit=17246
   -> HashAggregate (actual time=445.374..448.237 rows=10000 loops=1)
         Group Key: b.c1
         Buffers: shared hit=4425
         -> Seq Scan on t2 b
               Buffers: shared hit=4425
   -> Hash (actual time=0.038..0.038 rows=100 loops=1)
         Buckets: 1024  Batches: 1  Memory Usage: 12kB
         Buffers: shared hit=3
         -> Index Scan using t1_idx02 on t1 a
               Index Cond: ((c2 >= 1) AND (c2 <= 100))
               Buffers: shared hit=3
 Planning time: 0.246 ms
 Execution time: 433.159 ms
```

Two questions arise here.

- In this case, is the hash join the best?

- Why did the optimizer choose subquery collapse instead of a hash semi-join?

Suppression of Subquery collapse with OFFSET 0

Is it really the best to have a hash join in this case? Let's take the filter method using OFFSET.

Result after suppression of subquery Collapse

In the following example, we see that the addition of `'OFFSET 0'` is performed by the filter method and that the T2 table is 100 times Seq Scan.

However, the number of buffer IO is only 142, and the execution speed is faster than before. This effect is due to the principle of semi-joining. That is, if the main query result set is small, as in this example, and the subquery result set is in the front block of the table, the filter method may be advantageous.

```
explain (costs false, analyze, buffers)
select a.*
from    t1 a
where   a.c2 between 1 and 100
and     exists (select 1 from t2 b where b.c1=a.c1 OFFSET 0);
                         QUERY PLAN
-----------------------------------------------------------------
 Index Scan using t1_idx02 on t1 a (actual time=0.018..0.864 rows=100..)
   Index Cond: ((c2 >= 1) AND (c2 <= 100))
   Filter: (SubPlan 1)
   Buffers: shared hit=146
   SubPlan 1
     -> Seq Scan on t2 b (actual time=0.008..0.008 rows=1 loops=100)
           Filter: (c1 = a.c1)
           Rows Removed by Filter: 50
           Buffers: shared hit=142
 Planning time: 0.142 ms
 Execution time: 0.899 ms
```

The criteria by which the optimizer chooses a hash semi-join

When will the optimizer choose a hash semi-join?

My analysis is performed with a hash semi-join "when the subquery result set is smaller than the main query result set". If the subquery result set is larger, it is performed as a hash join after the subquery collapse. This limitation can cause performance problems. This is because when a hash join is performed, the load on the sub-query set Group By can be large.

In the test environment, the T2 table is 100 times larger than the T1 table. Therefore, when the T2 table becomes a subquery set, it is performed as a hash join. Conversely, if a T1 table exists in a subquery, it is performed with a hash semi-join.

If the subquery set is larger

```
explain (costs false, analyze, buffers)
select a.*
from   t1 a
where  exists (select 1 from t2 b where b.c1=a.c1);
                        QUERY PLAN
--------------------------------------------------------------------------
 Hash Join (actual time=533.496..541.025 rows=9999 loops=1)
   Hash Cond: (b.c1 = a.c1)
   Buffers: shared hit=17415
   -> HashAggregate (actual time=529.186..532.122 rows=10000 loops=1)
        Group Key: b.c1
        Buffers: shared hit=17242
        -> Seq Scan on t2 b
             Buffers: shared hit=17242
   -> Hash (actual time=4.289..4.289 rows=10000 loops=1)
        Buckets: 16384  Batches: 1  Memory Usage: 1505kB
        Buffers: shared hit=173
        -> Seq Scan on t1 a
             Buffers: shared hit=173
 Planning time: 0.204 ms
 Execution time: 541.976 ms
```

If the subquery set is smaller

```
explain (costs false, analyze, buffers)
select b.*
from   t2 b
where  exists (select 1 from t1 a where a.c1=b.c1);
                        QUERY PLAN
-------------------------------------------------------------------
 Hash Semi Join (actual time=4.598..660.089 rows=999900 loops=1)
   Hash Cond: (b.c1 = a.c1)
   Buffers: shared hit=17415
   -> Seq Scan on t2 b
        Buffers: shared hit=17242
   -> Hash (actual time=4.573..4.573 rows=10000 loops=1)
        Buckets: 16384  Batches: 1  Memory Usage: 480kB
        Buffers: shared hit=173
        -> Seq Scan on t1 a
             Buffers: shared hit=173
 Planning time: 0.155 ms
 Execution time: 765.458 ms
```

View Merging and JPPD (Join Predicate Push-Down)

View Merging and JPPD have a big impact on performance. First, let's look at the concepts of View Merging and JPPD.

What is View Merging?

View Merging merges views or inline views into the main query. By viewing merging, the optimizer can choose from various join sequences and join methods. View can be classified into two types.

- **Simple View**: View without Aggregate function (E.g., Group by, Distinct)

- **Complex View**: View with Aggregate function (E.g., Group by, Distinct)

Simple View always succeeds in View Merging.

Consider the example below. The reason for this is that you want to improve readability, or you know that it is more efficient to process inline views first.

```
SELECT *
FROM   (SELECT A.C1, B.C2
        FROM    A, B
        WHERE   A.C1 = B.C1
        AND     A.C2 BETWEEN 1 AND 10) V1, C
WHERE  V1.C1 = C.C1
AND    C.C2  = 1;
```

However, the above query may or may not process the inline view first. This is because Simple View is always successful in View Merging.

```
SELECT *
FROM   A, B, C
WHERE  A.C1 = B.C1
AND    A.C1 = C.C1
AND    A.C2 BETWEEN 1 AND 10
AND    C.C2 = 1;
```

Complex View always fails View Merging.

PostgreSQL does not provide Complex View Merging. Since GROUP BY exists in the inline view of the query below, this view is a complex view. If Complex View Merging is supported, then GROUP BY will be performed at the last step after joins between A and B tables. However, PostgreSQL does not provide this functionality.

```
SELECT  *
FROM    A, (SELECT C1, SUM(C2) C2
            FROM    B
            GROUP BY C1) V1
WHERE   A.C1 = V1.C1
AND     A.C1 = 1;
```

However, if View Merging is not performed in this case, very serious performance degradation may occur. This is because GROUP BY is performed on the B table. Therefore, try JPPD in this case.

What is JPPD?

JPPD pushes join conditions into view when View Merging fails. At this time, the join condition is pushed down to a constant, which makes it possible to use an index.

Simple View Merging example

Test environment

```
drop table t1;
drop table t2;
drop table t3;

create table t1 (c1 integer, dummy char(100));
create table t2 (c2 integer, c1 integer, dummy char(100));
create table t3 (c2 integer, c1 integer, dummy char(100));

insert into t1 select i, 'dummy'
from    generate_series(1,1000000) a(i);
insert into t2 select i, mod(i,1000000), 'dummy'
from    generate_series(1,2000000) a(i);
insert into t3 select i, mod(i,2000000), 'dummy'
from    generate_series(1,4000000) a(i);
```

```
create unique index t1_uk on t1(c1);
create unique index t2_uk on t2(c2);
create unique index t3_uk on t3(c2);

create index t2_c1_indx on t2(c1);
create index t3_c1_indx on t3(c1);

analyze t1;
analyze t2;
analyze t3;
```

Let's look at the example below. As View Merging occurs, the T1 and T2 tables are performed with a hash join. The result and the T3 table are then performed with an NL join.

```
set enable_bitmapscan=off;

explain (costs false)
select *
from   t1 a, (select b.c1, c.c2
              from   t2 b, t3 c
              where  b.c2=c.c2
              and    b.c2 between 1 and 100) v1
where  a.c1 = v1.c1
and    a.c1 between 1 and 10;
                    QUERY PLAN
-----------------------------------------------------------
 Nested Loop
   -> Hash Join
        Hash Cond: (b.c1 = a.c1)
        -> Index Scan using t2_uk on t2 b
             Index Cond: ((c2 >= 1) AND (c2 <= 100))
        -> Hash
             -> Index Scan using t1_uk on t1 a
                  Index Cond: ((c1 >= 1) AND (c1 <= 10))
   -> Index Only Scan using t3_uk on t3 c
        Index Cond: (c2 = b.c2)
```

How to Suppress View Merging in Simple View

To suppress View Merging in Simple View, use the 'OFFSET 0'. As a result, the hash build phase for the T1 table is performed first. Then, the probe phase is performed using the result of inline view.

```
explain (costs false)
select *
from   t1 a, (select b.c1, c.c2
```

```
            from    t2 b, t3 c
            where   b.c2=c.c2
            and     b.c2 between 1 and 100
                         OFFSET 0) v1
where   a.c1 = v1.c1
and     a.c1 between 1 and 10;
                    QUERY PLAN
-----------------------------------------------------------

Hash Join
  Hash Cond: (b.c1 = a.c1)
   -> Nested Loop
         -> Index Scan using t2_uk on t2 b
               Index Cond: ((c2 >= 1) AND (c2 <= 100))
         -> Index Only Scan using t3_uk on t3 c
               Index Cond: (c2 = b.c2)
   -> Hash
         -> Index Scan using t1_uk on t1 a
               Index Cond: ((c1 >= 1) AND (c1 <= 10))
```

When will JPPD succeed?

JPPD succeeds only in very limited cases. For JPPD to succeed, a constant must be entered as an Equal condition in the join column. That is, as in the example below, a constant ('10') must be entered as an equality condition in the join column, the C1 column.

```
explain (costs false, timing false, analyze)
select *
from    t2 a, (select    c1, max(c2) c2
              from      t3
              group by c1) v1
where   a.c1 = v1.c1
and     a.c1 = 10;
                    QUERY PLAN
-----------------------------------------------------------

 Nested Loop (actual rows=2 loops=1)
   -> Index Scan using t2_c1_indx on t2 a (actual rows=2 loops=1)
         Index Cond: (c1 = 10)
   -> Materialize (actual rows=1 loops=2)
         -> GroupAggregate (actual rows=1 loops=1)
               Group Key: t3.c1
               -> Index Scan using t3_c1_indx on t3
                     Index Cond: (c1 = 10)
 Planning time: 0.107 ms
 Execution time: 0.154 ms
```

If you change the constant condition to A.C2 instead of A.C1, JPPD fails. A.C2 column is not a join column. Let's look at the example below. JPPD failed and query performance is very slow.

```
explain (costs false, timing false, analyze)
select *
from   t2 a, (select   c1, max(c2) c2
                from     t3
                group by c1) v1
where  a.c1 = v1.c1
and    a.c2 = 10;
                        QUERY PLAN
-----------------------------------------------------------------
Hash Join (actual rows=1 loops=1)
   Hash Cond: (t3.c1 = a.c1)
   -> GroupAggregate (actual rows=2000000 loops=1)
        Group Key: t3.c1
        -> Index Scan using t3_c1_indx on t3
   -> Hash (actual rows=1 loops=1)
        Buckets: 1024  Batches: 1  Memory Usage: 9kB
        -> Index Scan using t2_uk on t2 a (actual rows=1 loops=1)
             Index Cond: (c2 = 10)
 Planning time: 0.125 ms
 Execution time: 2476.803 ms
```

BETWEEN and IN conditions also fail JPPD. Let's look at the example below. A constant condition is entered in C1, which is a join column. However, since it is an IN condition, JPPD fails.

```
explain (costs false, timing false, analyze)
select *
from   t2 a, (select   c1, max(c2) c2
                from     t3
                group by c1) v1
where  a.c1 = v1.c1
and    a.c1 IN (10,20);
                        QUERY PLAN
-----------------------------------------------------------------
Hash Join (actual rows=4 loops=1)
   Hash Cond: (t3.c1 = a.c1)
   -> GroupAggregate (actual rows=2000000 loops=1)
        Group Key: t3.c1
        -> Index Scan using t3_c1_indx on t3
   -> Hash (actual rows=4 loops=1)
        Buckets: 1024  Batches: 1  Memory Usage: 9kB
        -> Index Scan using t2_c1_indx on t2 a (actual rows=4 loops=1)
             Index Cond: (c1 = ANY ('{10,20}'::integer[]))
 Planning time: 0.199 ms
 Execution time: 2318.751 ms
```

In fact, queries of the type in which JPPD failed are used more frequently than those in which JPPD succeeds. So how can we solve this problem? Fortunately, PostgreSQL provides LATERAL inline view.

LATERAL inline view

LATERAL inline views are available starting with PostgreSQL 9.3.

LATERAL Inline view syntax

Add the `LATERAL` keyword and move the join condition into the side view.

```
select  *
from    t1 a,
        LATERAL (select    c1, max(c2) c2
                 from      t3
                 where     t3.c1=a.c1
                 group by c1) v1
where   a.c1 between 1 and 10;
```

Performance improvement of LATERAL inline view

Let's look at the performance improvement after changing two queries that previously failed JPPD to LATERAL inline view respectively. In the Explain results below, after changing to LATERAL inline view, both queries succeeded in JPPD, which greatly improved query performance.

Query #1

```
explain (costs false, timing false, analyze)
select  *
from    t2 a,
        LATERAL (select    c1, max(c2) c2
                 from      t3
                 where     t3.c1 = a.c1
                 group by c1) v1
where   a.c2 = 10;
                          QUERY PLAN
---------------------------------------------------------------
Nested Loop (actual rows=1 loops=1)
  ->  Index Scan using t2_uk on t2 a (actual rows=1 loops=1)
        Index Cond: (c2 = 10)
  ->  GroupAggregate (actual rows=1 loops=1)
        Group Key: t3.c1
        ->  Index Scan using t3_c1_indx on t3 (actual rows=2 loops=1)
              Index Cond: (c1 = a.c1)
Planning time: 0.154 ms
Execution time: 0.189 ms
```

Query #2

```
explain (costs false, timing false, analyze)
select *
from    t2 a,
        LATERAL (select    c1, max(c2) c2
                 from      t3
                 where     t3.c1 = a.c1
                 group by c1) v1
where   a.c1 IN (10,20);
                        QUERY PLAN
-----------------------------------------------------------------
 Nested Loop (actual rows=4 loops=1)
   ->  Index Scan using t2_c1_indx on t2 a (actual rows=4 loops=1)
         Index Cond: (c1 = ANY ('{10,20}'::integer[]))
   ->  GroupAggregate (actual rows=1 loops=4)
         Group Key: t3.c1
         ->  Index Scan using t3_c1_indx on t3 (actual rows=2 loops=4)
               Index Cond: (c1 = a.c1)
 Planning time: 0.164 ms
 Execution time: 0.200 ms
```

As you can see from the above results, dramatic performance improvements are possible with LATERAL inline views. However, changing existing queries to LATERAL inline view is a lot of work. So, it is better to use LATERAL inline view from the beginning of development. In addition, we look forward to enhancing View Merging and JPPD functionality in future versions of PostgreSQL.

LATERAL inline view of ORACLE
ORACLE can also use LATERAL inline view directly from version 12c. Up to the previous version, the optimizer used internally only at JPPD.

LEFT JOIN with LATERAL inline view

When performing LEFT JOIN using LATERAL inline view, use ON TRUE keyword.

```
explain (costs false)
select *
from    t1 a
        LEFT JOIN
        LATERAL (select    c1, max(c2) c2
                 from      t3
```

```
            where     t3.c1=a.c1
                    group by c1) v1 ON TRUE
where   a.c1 between 1 and 10;
                  QUERY PLAN
--------------------------------------------------
Nested Loop Left Join
  ->  Index Scan using t1_c1_indx on t1 a
        Index Cond: ((c1 >= 1) AND (c1 <= 10))
  ->  GroupAggregate
        Group Key: t3.c1
        ->  Index Scan using t3_c2_indx on t3
              Index Cond: (c1 = a.c1)
```

Tuning method using PG_HINT_PLAN

There are cases where you can't achieve the desired performance by simply turning on and off the access method and the join method. What you need is a hint. However, PostgreSQL does not officially provide hint.

But a hint to the tuner is a very necessary feature. This is because, for example, operations such as specifying a join order, using a specific index, or specifying a join method occur very frequently at the time of tuning. You can do this with PG_HINT_PLAN.

This section will explain some of the hints PG_HINT_PLAN provides.

Installing PG_HINT_PLAN

PG_HINT_PLAN Installation process is as follows.

Download PG_HINT_PLAN

You can download the installation files for each version of PostgreSQL from the following site.

```
https://osdn.net/projects/pghintplan/
```

Compile the source

Compile and install the source as root user.

```
# gunzip pg_hint_plan96-1.1.3.tar.gz
```

```
# tar xvf pg_hint_plan96-1.1.3.tar
# make PG_CONFIG=/usr/local/pgsql/bin/pg_config
# make PG_CONFIG=/usr/local/pgsql/bin/pg_config install
```

How to apply PG_HINT_PLAN

There are two ways to apply `PG_HINT_PLAN`: register in `postgresql.conf` file and use `LOAD`.
Registering in the `postgresql.conf` file affects all sessions, and the `LOAD` method affects only
that session. The usage of each is as follows.

How to register in the postgresql.conf file

```
shared_preload_libraries = 'pg_hint_plan'
```

How to use LOAD

```
postgres=# LOAD 'pg_hint_plan';
LOAD
```

PG_HINT_PLAN How it works and hints list

`PG_HINT_PLAN` controls the execution plan in a very powerful way. `PG_HINT_PLAN` is a way to
directly change the Plan Tree, rather than provide a mechanism to instruct the optimizer like the
ORACLE hints. In other words, the hint of ORACLE can be ignored in some situations, but the
way of directly changing the Plan Tree is reflected in the execution plan under any circumstances
(even slower). Therefore, before using `PG_HINT_PLAN`, you need to check the mechanism.

The list of hints provided by `PG_HINT_PLAN` is as follows.

Table 3-7. *List of hints provided by PG_HINT_PLAN*

Type	Usage	Description
Access method	`SeqScan (table)`	Forces Seq Scan.
	`IndexScan (table index)`	Forces Index Scan.
	`IndexOnlyScan (table index)`	Forces Index Only Scan. Index Only. If can't force Index Only Scan, it forces the Index Scan.
	`BitmapScan (table index)`	Forces Bitmap Scan.
	`NoIndexScan (table)`	Do not use Index Scan and Index Only

		Scan.
	NoIndexOnlyScan (table)	Do not use Index Only Scan.
	NoBitmapScan (table)	Do not use Bitmap Scan.
Join method	NestLoop (table table)	Forces NL join.
	HashJoin (table table)	Forces Hash join.
	MergeJoin (table table)	Forces Merge join.
	NoNestLoop (table table)	Do not use NL join.
	NoHashJoin (table table)	Do not use Hash join.
	NoMergeJoin (table table)	Do not use Merge join.
Join order	Leading (table table [table...])	Forces Join order. However, the joining direction is not controlled.
	Leading ((table table))	Forces Jon order and direction. The left table is the Driving or Outer table.

PG_HINT_PLAN example

Let's take a look at some of the hints provided by PG_HINT_PLAN.

Test environment

```
drop table t1;
drop table t2;
drop table t3;
drop table t4;

create table t1 (c1 int, c2 int, c3 int, dummy char(100));
create index t1_idx1 on t1 (c1, c2, c3);
create index t1_idx2 on t1 (c2, c3);
create index t1_idx3 on t1 (c3);

create table t2 (c1 int, c2 int, c3 int, dummy char(100));
create index t2_idx1 on t2 (c1, c2, c3);
create index t2_idx2 on t2 (c2, c3);
create index t2_idx3 on t2 (c3);

create table t3 (c1 int, c2 int, c3 int, dummy char(100));
create index t3_idx1 on t3 (c1, c2, c3);
create index t3_idx2 on t3 (c2, c3);
create index t3_idx3 on t3 (c3);
```

```
create table t4 (c1 int, c2 int, c3 int, dummy char(100));
create index t4_idx1 on t4 (c1, c2, c3);
create index t4_idx2 on t4 (c2, c3);
create index t4_idx3 on t4 (c3);

insert into t1 select 1, mod(i,100), mod(i,1000), 'dummy'
from generate_series(1,100000) a(i);

insert into t2 select 1, mod(i,100), mod(i,1000), 'dummy'
from generate_series(1,10000) a(i);

insert into t3 select 1, mod(i,100), i, 'dummy'
from generate_series(1,100) a(i);

insert into t4 select 1, mod(i,100), i, 'dummy'
from generate_series(1,100) a(i);

analyze t1;
analyze t2;
analyze t3;
analyze t4;

select relname, reltuples, relpages
from   pg_class where relname in ('t1','t2','t3','t4');
 relname | reltuples | relpages
---------+-----------+----------
 t1      |    100000 |     1819
 t2      |     10000 |      182
 t3      |       100 |        2
 t4      |       100 |        2
```

IndexScan hint example

First, let's look at the `IndexScan` hint. If you look at the Explain results before applying the hint, you can see that it uses the `T1_IDX02` index.

```
explain (costs false, analyze, buffers)
select a.*
from   t1 a
where  a.c1=1
and    a.c2 between 1 and 10
and    a.c3=1;
                            QUERY PLAN
-------------------------------------------------------------------------
 Index Scan using t1_idx2 on t1 a
   Index Cond: ((c2 >= 1) AND (c2 <= 10) AND (c3 = 1))
   Filter: (c1 = 1)
   Buffers: shared hit=140
```

```
Planning time: 0.149 ms
Execution time: 0.466 ms
```

The above example would be better to use the T1_IDX03 index. The result of using IndexScan hint is as follows. It can be seen that the number of buffer IO and the execution time are improved by using the T1_IDX03 index.

```
load 'pg_hint_plan';

/*+ IndexScan(a t1_idx3) */
explain (costs false, analyze, buffers)
select a.*
from    t1 a
where   a.c1=1
and     a.c2 between 1 and 10
and     a.c3=1;
                         QUERY PLAN
-------------------------------------------------------------------------
 Index Scan using t1_idx3 on t1 a
   Index Cond: (c3 = 1)
   Filter: ((c2 >= 1) AND (c2 <= 10) AND (c1 = 1))
   Buffers: shared hit=102
 Planning time: 0.092 ms
 Execution time: 0.154 ms
```

So, what happens if you hint to use the most inefficient T1_IDX01 index? Since PG_HINT_PLAN is a method of directly changing the plan tree, it uses the T1_IDX01 index specified in the hint.

```
/*+ IndexScan(a t1_idx1) */
explain (costs false, analyze, buffers)
select a.*
from    t1 a
where   a.c1=1
and     a.c2 between 1 and 10
and     a.c3=1;
                         QUERY PLAN
-------------------------------------------------------------------------
 Index Scan using t1_idx1 on t1 a
   Index Cond: ((c1 = 1) AND (c2 >= 1) AND (c2 <= 10) AND (c3 = 1))
   Buffers: shared hit=145
 Planning time: 0.116 ms
 Execution time: 0.674 ms
```

Example of joining two tables

This time, let's look at a join example between two tables. The result of Explain before applying the hint is as follows. This is currently the best join method and join order.

```
explain (costs false, analyze)
select a.*, b.*
from    t1 a, t2 b
where   a.c1=b.c1
and     a.c2=b.c2
and     a.c3=b.c3;
                          QUERY PLAN
--------------------------------------------------------------------------
 Hash Join (actual time=4.348..369.166 rows=1000000 loops=1)
   Hash Cond: ((a.c1 = b.c1) AND (a.c2 = b.c2) AND (a.c3 = b.c3))
     -> Seq Scan on t1 a (actual time=0.006..17.766 rows=100000 loops=1)
     -> Hash (actual time=4.316..4.316 rows=10000 loops=1)
         Buckets: 16384  Batches: 1  Memory Usage: 1545kB
           -> Seq Scan on t2 b (actual time=0.004..1.765 rows=10000 loops=1)
 Planning time: 1.582 ms
 Execution time: 454.325 ms
```

Let's use a hint to change the join between tables to an NL join. As a result of applying the hint, it can be seen that the NL join is performed, T2 is the driving table, and T1 is the inner table.

```
/*+ NestLoop(a b) */
explain (costs false, analyze)
select a.*, b.*
from    t1 a, t2 b
where   a.c1=b.c1
and     a.c2=b.c2
and     a.c3=b.c3;
                        QUERY PLAN
--------------------------------------------------------------------------
 Nested Loop (actual time=0.022..869.603 rows=1000000 loops=1)
   -> Seq Scan on t2 b (actual time=0.007..2.035 rows=10000 loops=1)
   -> Index Scan using t1_idx2 on t1 a
       Index Cond: ((c2 = b.c2) AND (c3 = b.c3))
         Filter: (b.c1 = c1)
 Planning time: 0.282 ms
 Execution time: 958.431 ms
```

Why are there two leading hints?

If so, how do you specify the T1 table as the driving table at this time? The results below show that adding a Leading hint does not change the join direction.

```
/*+ Leading(a b) NestLoop(a b) */
explain (costs false, analyze)
select a.*, b.*
from   t1 a, t2 b
where  a.c1=b.c1
and    a.c2=b.c2
and    a.c3=b.c3;
                            QUERY PLAN
-----------------------------------------------------------------------------
 Nested Loop (actual time=0.022..858.288 rows=1000000 loops=1)
   -> Seq Scan on t2 b (actual time=0.007..2.222 rows=10000 loops=1)
   -> Index Scan using t1_idx2 on t1 a
        Index Cond: ((c2 = b.c2) AND (c3 = b.c3))
        Filter: (b.c1 = c1)
 Planning time: 0.422 ms
 Execution time: 950.195 ms
```

This is because the Leading hint only determines the join order and does not specify the join direction. For example, 'Leading(a b c)' means to join a and b first, then join c. At this time, the joining direction between (a b) is determined by the optimizer.

If you want to specify the join direction yourself, you can use the Leading() hint instead of the Leading hint. Let's look at the example below. As a result of applying Leading((a b)), the T1 table became a driving table.

```
/*+ Leading((a b)) NestLoop(a b) */
explain (costs false, analyze)
select a.*, b.*
from   t1 a, t2 b
where  a.c1=b.c1
and    a.c2=b.c2
and    a.c3=b.c3;
                            QUERY PLAN
-----------------------------------------------------------------------------
 Nested Loop (actual time=0.030..944.609 rows=1000000 loops=1)
   -> Seq Scan on t1 a (actual time=0.013..17.301 rows=100000 loops=1)
   -> Index Scan using t2_idx2 on t2 b
        Index Cond: ((c2 = a.c2) AND (c3 = a.c3))
        Filter: (a.c1 = c1)
 Planning time: 0.435 ms
 Execution time: 1032.679 ms
```

That is, the table to the left of the Leading () hint is the Driving or Outer table. For example, at the time of NL join, the table located to the left of the Leading () hint is the driving table. At the time of hash join, the table located to the left of the Leading () hint becomes the probe table.

Example of joining three tables

Let's look at an example of a join between three tables. In the following results, it is seen that the join order is T2->T1->T3, the join between T1 and T2 is performed by hash join, and the join is performed by NL join with T3.

```
/*+ Leading(a b c) HashJoin(a b) NestLoop(a b c) */
explain (costs false, analyze)
select a.*, b.*, c.*
from    t1 a, t2 b, t3 c
where   a.c1=b.c1
and     a.c2=b.c2
and     a.c3=b.c3
and     b.c1=c.c1
and     b.c2=c.c2
and     b.c3=c.c3;
                        QUERY PLAN
-------------------------------------------------------------------------
 Nested Loop (actual time=4.753..1178.641 rows=100000 loops=1)
   -> Hash Join (actual time=4.739..370.122 rows=1000000 loops=1)
        Hash Cond: ((a.c1 = b.c1) AND (a.c2 = b.c2) AND (a.c3 = b.c3))
        -> Seq Scan on t1 a
        -> Hash (actual time=4.708..4.708 rows=10000 loops=1)
            Buckets: 16384  Batches: 1  Memory Usage: 1545kB
            -> Seq Scan on t2 b
   -> Index Scan using t3_idx3 on t3 c
        Index Cond: (c3 = a.c3)
        Filter: ((a.c1 = c1) AND (a.c2 = c2))
 Planning time: 0.948 ms
 Execution time: 1187.221 ms
```

Change the hint so that the join order is T1->T2->T3 and the join method is NL join. To do this, use the Leading() hint and the NestLoop hint. That is, use the Leading() hint to enclose the parentheses, as shown below. Note that the inner parentheses are performed first, and the table to the left is the driving table. The NestLoop hint is specified as follows.

```
/*+ Leading(((a b) c)) NestLoop(a b) NestLoop(a b c) */
explain (costs false, analyze)
select a.*, b.*, c.*
from    t1 a, t2 b, t3 c
where   a.c1=b.c1
and     a.c2=b.c2
and     a.c3=b.c3
and     b.c1=c.c1
and     b.c2=c.c2
and     b.c3=c.c3;
```

```
                    QUERY PLAN
-------------------------------------------------------------------
Nested Loop (actual time=0.040..1802.490 rows=100000 loops=1)
   -> Nested Loop (actual time=0.034..954.774 rows=1000000 loops=1)
        -> Seq Scan on t1 a
        -> Index Scan using t2_idx2 on t2 b
            Index Cond: ((c2 = a.c2) AND (c3 = a.c3))
            Filter: (a.c1 = c1)
   -> Index Scan using t3_idx3 on t3 c
        Index Cond: (c3 = a.c3)
        Filter: ((a.c1 = c1) AND (a.c2 = c2))
Planning time: 1.148 ms
Execution time: 1811.314 ms
```

Example of joining four tables

Let's use a more complex example to learn how to use hints. The following explains the result before applying the hint. That is, it can be seen that the join order is T4->T3->T2->T1, the hash joins between T4 and T3, and the NL join with the remaining tables.

```
explain (costs false, analyze)
select a.*, b.*, c.*
from   t1 a, t2 b, t3 c, t4 d
where  a.c1=b.c1 and a.c2=b.c2 and a.c3=b.c3
and    a.c1=c.c1 and a.c2=c.c2 and a.c3=c.c3
and    a.c1=d.c1 and a.c2=d.c2 and a.c3=d.c3;
                    QUERY PLAN
-------------------------------------------------------------------
Nested Loop (actual time=0.069..86.474 rows=100000 loops=1)
   -> Nested Loop (actual time=0.062..1.849 rows=1000 loops=1)
        -> Hash Join (actual time=0.054..0.280 rows=100 loops=1)
             -> Seq Scan on t3 c
             -> Hash (actual time=0.039..0.039 rows=100 loops=1)
                    Buckets: 1024  Batches: 1  Memory Usage: 13kB
                 -> Seq Scan on t4 d
        -> Index Scan using t2_idx2 on t2 b
             Index Cond: ((c2 = c.c2) AND (c3 = c.c3))
             Filter: (c.c1 = c1)
   -> Index Scan using t1_idx2 on t1 a
        Index Cond: ((c2 = b.c2) AND (c3 = b.c3))
        Filter: (b.c1 = c1)
Planning time: 2.119 ms
Execution time: 95.453 ms
```

NL join example (The Join order is T1->T2->T3->T4)

`Leading()` hint is performed from inside parentheses. In case of NL join, since left is driving table, use `'(a b)'` to set `T1` as driving table and `T2` as inner table. And thereafter in order of c->d.

```
/*+
  Leading((((a b) c) d)) NestLoop(a b) NestLoop(a b c) NestLoop(a b c d)
*/
explain (costs false, analyze)
select a.*, b.*, c.*
from    t1 a, t2 b, t3 c, t4 d
where   a.c1=b.c1 and a.c2=b.c2 and a.c3=b.c3
and     a.c1=c.c1 and a.c2=c.c2 and a.c3=c.c3
and     a.c1=d.c1 and a.c2=d.c2 and a.c3=d.c3;
                          QUERY PLAN
------------------------------------------------------------------------
 Nested Loop (actual time=0.071..4370.725 rows=100000 loops=1)
   Join Filter: ((a.c1 = d.c1) AND (a.c2 = d.c2) AND (a.c3 = d.c3))
   Rows Removed by Join Filter: 9900000
   ->  Nested Loop (actual time=0.063..1753.210 rows=100000 loops=1)
         ->  Nested Loop (actual time=0.058..928.410 rows=1000000 loops=1)
               ->  Seq Scan on t1 a
               ->  Index Scan using t2_idx2 on t2 b
                     Index Cond: ((c2 = a.c2) AND (c3 = a.c3))
                     Filter: (a.c1 = c1)
         ->  Index Scan using t3_idx3 on t3 c
               Index Cond: (c3 = a.c3)
               Filter: ((a.c1 = c1) AND (a.c2 = c2))
   ->  Materialize
         ->  Seq Scan on t4 d
 Planning time: 1.240 ms
 Execution time: 4381.032 ms
```

Hash Join Example # 1

If the hint is applied as shown below, the join order is `T4->T3->T2->T1`.

The processing method is as follows.

1. Perform `'(c d)'` in the innermost parentheses first. Therefore, a hash build operation is performed on the `T4` table.
2. Perform a hash join while scanning the `T3` table.
3. Perform a hash build operation using the result of step 2.
4. Perform a hash join while scanning the `T2` table.

5. Perform a hash build operation using the result of step 4.

6. Perform a hash join while scanning the T1 table.

```
/*+
 Leading((a (b (c d)))) HashJoin(c d) HashJoin(b c d) HashJoin(a b c d)
*/
explain (costs false, analyze)
select a.*, b.*, c.*
from    t1 a, t2 b, t3 c, t4 d
where   a.c1=b.c1 and a.c2=b.c2 and a.c3=b.c3
and     a.c1=c.c1 and a.c2=c.c2 and a.c3=c.c3
and     a.c1=d.c1 and a.c2=d.c2 and a.c3=d.c3;
                          QUERY PLAN
----------------------------------------------------------------------
 Hash Join (actual time=4.127..84.745 rows=100000 loops=1)
   ->  Seq Scan on t1 a (actual time=0.032..17.478 rows=100000 loops=1)
   ->  Hash (actual time=4.047..4.047 rows=1000 loops=1)
         Buckets: 1024  Batches: 1  Memory Usage: 278kB
         ->  Hash Join (actual time=0.133..3.756 rows=1000 loops=1)
               ->  Seq Scan on t2 b
               ->  Hash (actual time=0.125..0.125 rows=100 loops=1)
                     Buckets: 1024  Batches: 1  Memory Usage: 24kB
                     ->  Hash Join
                           ->  Seq Scan on t3 c
                           ->  Hash
                                 Buckets: 1024  Batches: 1
                                 ->  Seq Scan on t4 d
 Planning time: 1.364 ms
 Execution time: 96.287 ms
```

Hash Join Example # 2

If the hint is applied as shown below, the join order is T4->T3->T2->T1. That is, the join order is the same as the above result, but the processing method is different. The processing method is as follows.

1. Perform ' (c d) ' in the innermost parentheses first. Therefore, the build operation for the T4 table is performed.

2. Perform a hash join while scanning the T3 table. (This is the same as the previous example)

3. Perform a hash build operation on the T2 table.

4. Perform the hash join using the result of step 2.

5. Perform a hash build operation on the `T1` table.

6. Perform the hash join using the results from step 4.

```
/*+
  Leading((((c d) b) a)) HashJoin(c d) HashJoin(c d b) HashJoin(c d b a)
*/
explain (costs false, analyze)
select a.*, b.*, c.*
from   t1 a, t2 b, t3 c, t4 d
where  a.c1=b.c1 and a.c2=b.c2 and a.c3=b.c3
and    a.c1=c.c1 and a.c2=c.c2 and a.c3=c.c3
and    a.c1=d.c1 and a.c2=d.c2 and a.c3=d.c3;
                         QUERY PLAN
------------------------------------------------------------------------
 Hash Join (actual time=52.546..111.230 rows=100000 loops=1)
   -> Hash Join (actual time=3.716..4.309 rows=1000 loops=1)
       -> Hash Join (actual time=0.052..0.179 rows=100 loops=1)
           -> Seq Scan on t3 c
           -> Hash (actual time=0.039..0.039 rows=100 loops=1)
               Buckets: 1024  Batches: 1  Memory Usage: 13kB
               -> Seq Scan on t4 d
       -> Hash (actual time=3.650..3.650 rows=10000 loops=1)
           Buckets: 16384  Batches: 1  Memory Usage: 1545kB
           -> Seq Scan on t2 b
   -> Hash (actual time=48.461..48.461 rows=100000 loops=1)
       Buckets: 32768 (originally 32768)  Batches: 8
       -> Seq Scan on t1 a
 Planning time: 1.189 ms
 Execution time: 119.939 ms
```

Hash Join Example # 3

Applying the hint as shown below, the inline view `(a c)` is performed with a hash join, and the inline view `(b d)` is also performed with a hash join. Then, the hash join is performed again using the result.

```
/*+
  Leading(((a c) (b d))) HashJoin(a c) HashJoin(b d) HashJoin(a c b d)
*/
explain (costs false, analyze)
select a.*, b.*, c.*
from   t1 a, t2 b, t3 c, t4 d
where  a.c1=b.c1 and a.c2=b.c2 and a.c3=b.c3
and    a.c1=c.c1 and a.c2=c.c2 and a.c3=c.c3
and    a.c1=d.c1 and a.c2=d.c2 and a.c3=d.c3;
                         QUERY PLAN
```

```
------------------------------------------------------------------------------
Hash Join (actual time=10.570..74.836 rows=100000 loops=1)
  Hash Cond: ((a.c1 = b.c1) AND (a.c2 = b.c2) AND (a.c3 = b.c3))
  -> Hash Join (actual time=0.065..36.195 rows=10000 loops=1)
       Hash Cond: ((a.c1 = c.c1) AND (a.c2 = c.c2) AND (a.c3 = c.c3))
       -> Seq Scan on t1 a
       -> Hash (actual time=0.051..0.051 rows=100 loops=1)
            Buckets: 1024  Batches: 1  Memory Usage: 23kB
            -> Seq Scan on t3 c
  -> Hash (actual time=10.497..10.497 rows=1000 loops=1)
       Buckets: 1024  Batches: 1  Memory Usage: 165kB
       -> Hash Join (actual time=0.045..10.197 rows=1000 loops=1)
            -> Seq Scan on t2 b
            -> Hash (actual time=0.039..0.039 rows=100 loops=1)
                 Buckets: 1024  Batches: 1  Memory Usage: 13kB
                 -> Seq Scan on t4 d
Planning time: 1.104 ms
Execution time: 83.348 ms
```

Thus, using the hints provided by PG_HINT_PLAN, it can be seen that the execution plan can be derived in various ways. Again, remember that an inappropriate hint is very dangerous.

Risk of Leading hint when using subquery

When using the Leading hint, you need to make sure that the subquery exists. For example, a subquery condition may be added dynamically to a query. In this case, the query performance may be significantly degraded due to the Leading hint. Consider the example below.

If there is no subquery

When the following hint is applied, the NL join is performed. The T1 table is the driving table and the T2 table is the inner table. Until then, there is no problem.

```
/*+ Leading((a b)) NestLoop(a b) */
explain (costs false, analyze)
select  a.*, b.*
from    t1 a, t2 b
where   a.c1 = b.c1
and     a.c2 = b.c2
and     a.c2 between 1 and 5;
                    QUERY PLAN
-----------------------------------------------------------------
Nested Loop (actual time=0.647..411.298 rows=500000 loops=1)
  -> Bitmap Heap Scan on t1 a (actual time=0.633..3.453 rows=5000 loops=1)
       Recheck Cond: ((c2 >= 1) AND (c2 <= 5))
```

```
              Heap Blocks: exact=1000
                 ->  Bitmap Index Scan on t1_idx2
                       Index Cond: ((c2 >= 1) AND (c2 <= 5))
      ->  Index Scan using t2_idx2 on t2 b
             Index Cond: (c2 = a.c2)
             Filter: (a.c1 = c1)
   Planning time: 0.409 ms
   Execution time: 461.528 ms
```

If the subquery is dynamically added

Suppose, however, that an IN subquery has been added as certain conditions are added. The IN subquery is performed as a join by the subquery collapse, but it can be seen that the join order is performed by T1->T2->T3 by the Leading() hint. As a result, 'Rows Removed by Join Filter' was performed for 400,000 rows. This is a very inefficient execution plan. Therefore, you should consider whether subqueries can be added when using the Leading hint.

```
/*+ Leading((a b)) NestLoop(a b) */
explain (costs false, analyze)
select  a.*, b.*
from    t1 a, t2 b
where   a.c1 = b.c1
and     a.c2 = b.c2
and     b.c2 in (select c2 from t3 c where c.c3=1)
and     a.c2 between 1 and 5;
                               QUERY PLAN
------------------------------------------------------------------------
 Nested Loop (actual time=0.630..449.454 rows=100000 loops=1)
   Join Filter: (a.c2 = c.c2)
   Rows Removed by Join Filter: 400000
   ->  HashAggregate (actual time=0.020..0.020 rows=1 loops=1)
         Group Key: c.c2
         ->  Seq Scan on t3 c (actual time=0.008..0.017 rows=1 loops=1)
               Filter: (c3 = 1)
               Rows Removed by Filter: 99
   ->  Nested Loop (actual time=0.608..367.197 rows=500000 loops=1)
         ->  Bitmap Heap Scan on t1 a
               Recheck Cond: ((c2 >= 1) AND (c2 <= 5))
               Heap Blocks: exact=1000
               ->  Bitmap Index Scan on t1_idx2
                     Index Cond: ((c2 >= 1) AND (c2 <= 5))
         ->  Index Scan using t2_idx2 on t2 b
               Index Cond: (c2 = a.c2)
               Filter: (a.c1 = c1)
 Planning time: 0.576 ms
 Execution time: 458.418 ms
```

⌐ **Note** For some hints and additional caveats not explained in this section,

Please refer to http://pghintplan.osdn.jp/pg_hint_plan.html.

Histogram

The histogram is the most important statistics for the optimizer in that it provides the distribution of the column values. The optimizer determines the access method and the join method according to the Cardinality. And the Cardinality is calculated by using the histogram.

Skewed data must generate a histogram. This allows you to choose the appropriate access method based on the column value. Not only that, but even data, a histogram is needed for BETWEEN processing.

In this section, we will learn the basics of histograms and the histograms provided by PostgreSQL.

Histogram Overview

Let's look at an overview of the histogram. There are two general types of histogram.

- Frequency histogram

- Height-Balance histogram

Frequency histogram

Frequency histogram provides the number of occurrences for each column value. Thus, there is an advantage of providing a very accurate distribution. However, because the number of buckets to store the column values is limited, it is applied only when the NDV (Number of Distinct Value) of the column is small. For example, suppose you have four buckets capable of storing histograms, and NDV is 4. In this case, a frequency histogram can be applied. (See Figure 3-20)

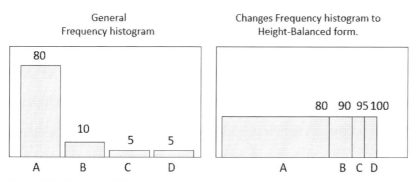

General
Frequency histogram

Changes Frequency histogram to
Height-Balanced form.

Figure 3-20. *Frequency histogram representation method*

The left figure in Figure 3-20 is a general representation of the Frequency histogram. It is very intuitive and it is very easy to calculate the frequency and occurrence rate of each value. PostgreSQL uses this method.

The figure on the right in Figure 3-20 shows the frequency histogram by right-clicking it. The shape is the same as the Height-Balanced histogram. In this case, the number of occurrences is calculated as 'the endpoint value of the current bucket - the endpoint value of the previous bucket'. It is less intuitive than the left method, but has the advantage of being able to unify the representation with a Height-Balanced histogram. ORACLE uses this method.

Height-Balanced histogram

Height-Balanced histograms are used when the NDV of a column is greater than the number of buckets. Consider the following situation.

- Number of buckets: 4

- NDV: 8 (1 to 8)

- Input value (total 20): [**1**,1,1,1,1] [**2**,3,3,3,3] [**3**,3,3,4,5] [**6**,7,7,8,8]

The Height-Balanced histogram at this time is shown in Figure 3-21. The Height-Balanced histogram has the advantage of being able to represent the distribution of NDV more than the number of buckets, but it has a disadvantage that it is difficult to confirm the exact distribution of skew data. For example, '3' is a very frequent value, but it is hard to see the exact distribution with the histogram. PostgreSQL handles this problem very efficiently. This section will be explained in the 'Hybrid Histogram' section.

Height-Balanced Histogram

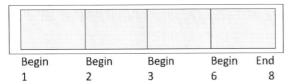

Begin	Begin	Begin	Begin	End
1	2	3	6	8

Figure 3-21. *Height-Balanced Histogram Example*

PostgreSQL vs. ORACLE

PostgreSQL provides a hybrid histogram that combines the advantages of both Frequency and Height-Balanced histograms. ORACLE provided only a Frequency histogram and a Height-Balanced histogram until 12c, but provides a Top-N frequency and Hybrid histogram from 12c.

Create histogram

The histogram is generated using the `ANALYZE` command.

The number of buckets is set by the `default_statistics_target` parameter, and the default value is 100. That is, allocate 100 buckets per column. The minimum value is 1 and the maximum value is 10,000. You can also set the number of buckets per table column. The setting method is as follows.

How to change the number of buckets in a column

```
alter table t4 alter column c1 set statistics 200;
```

How to check after change

```
select attname, attstattarget
from   pg_attribute
where  attrelid = (select oid from pg_class where relname='t4')
and    attname='c1';
 attname | attstattarget
---------+---------------
 c1      |           200
```

Height-Balanced histogram

PostgreSQL provides three types of histogram:

- **Height-Balanced histogram**: Used when the NDV is greater than the number of buckets and the values are evenly distributed.

- **Frequency histogram**: Used when NDV is less than the number of buckets

- **Hybrid histogram**: Used when NDV is greater than the number of buckets and the values are skewed.

First, let's look at the Height-Balanced histogram.

Test environment

Configure the test environment for the Height-Balanced histogram.

```
# of buckets: 10 (Change default_statistics_target parameter value to 10)
NDV: 20
Distribution of values: evenly distributed
```

What we want to check is how the optimizer uses the histogram to calculate the 'Estimated Rows'. Therefore, in order to easily check the explain result, we will proceed without creating the index.

Insert test data

Insert 20 values evenly.

```
drop table t1;
create table t1 (c1 integer, dummy char(100));
insert into t1 select mod(i,20)+1, 'dummy' from generate_series(1,1000000) a(i);
```

Check the number of records and histogram after ANALYZE

```
analyze t1;
select reltuples::integer from pg_class where relname='t1';
 reltuples
-----------
```

```
    1000036
select n_distinct, most_common_vals,most_common_freqs,
      histogram_bounds
from  pg_stats where tablename='t1' and attname='c1';
-[ RECORD 1 ]-----+------------------------------
n_distinct        | 20
most_common_vals  |
most_common_freqs |
histogram_bounds  | {1,2,5,7,9,11,13,14,16,19,20}
```

The above results are as follows.

- **n_distinct**: NDV is 20.

- **most_common_vals**: {NULL}, so no frequency histogram was created.

- **histogram_bounds**: 1 to 19 are the starting values of each bucket and 20 are the end values of the 10th bucket.

How the optimizer computes the Estimated Rows

How does the optimizer calculate the Estimated Rows? For example, let's check.

Equal condition

If '1' is entered, the Estimated Rows is 50,002. This is very close to the Actual Rows of 50,000. That is, when the Height-Balanced histogram is used, the Estimated Rows is calculated as follows.

```
Eistimated Rows = PG_CLASS.reltuples / NDV
=> 50,002 = 1,000,036 / 20
```

```
explain (analyze) select * from t1 where c1=1;
                    QUERY PLAN
----------------------------------------------------------
 Seq Scan on t1  (cost=0.00..29742.45 rows=50002 width=105)
          (actual time=0.010..135.153 rows=50000 loops=1)
   Filter: (c1 = 1)
```

IN condition

The IN condition is calculated by the following formula.

```
Eistimated Rows = Total number / NDV * (# of input values)
=> 250,009 = 1,000,036 / 20 * 5
```

```
explain (analyze) select * from t1 where c1 in (1,2,3,4,5);
                    QUERY PLAN
---------------------------------------------------------------
 Seq Scan on t1   (cost=0.00..33492.58 rows=250009 width=105)
          (actual time=0.012..171.738 rows=250000 loops=1)
   Filter: (c1 = ANY ('{1,2,3,4,5}'::integer[]))
```

Between condition

Since NDV is 20 and there are 10 buckets, it is ideal to assign two values per bucket. However, the `histogram_bounds` above shows that the first bucket manages one value (1), and the second bucket manages three values (2,3,4). At this time, let's check the `Estimated Rows` after performing the BETWEEN condition corresponding to each bucket range.

```
-- BETWEEN condition for first bucket scope
explain (analyze) select * from t1 where c1 >= 1 and c1 < 2;
                    QUERY PLAN
---------------------------------------------------------------
 Seq Scan on t1   (cost=0.00..32242.54 rows=49902 width=105)
          (actual time=0.013..149.177 rows=50000 loops=1)
   Filter: ((c1 >= 2) AND (c1 < 5))

-- BETWEEN condition for the second bucket
explain (analyze) select * from t1 where c1 >= 2 and c1 < 5;
                    QUERY PLAN
---------------------------------------------------------------
 Seq Scan on t1   (cost=0.00..32242.54 rows=150005 width=105)
          (actual time=0.011..179.225 rows=150000 loops=1)
   Filter: ((c1 >= 2) AND (c1 < 5))
```

From the above results, it can be seen that the `Estimated Rows` for the first bucket is 49,902 and the `Estimated Rows` for the second bucket is 15,0005. This number is very close to the `Actual Rows`. From this result, it can be inferred that the buckets are not evenly cut and that the range (and ratio) of the values managed by each bucket is internally stored.

Frequency histogram

Test environment

Configure the test environment for the Frequency histogram.

```
# of buckets: 10 (Change default_statistics_target parameter value to 10)
NDV: 5
Distribution of values: Skew
```

Insert test data

One value should be 60% of the total, and the four values should be 10% each.

```
drop table t2;
create table t2 (c1 integer, dummy char(100));
insert into t2 select 1, 'dummy' from generate_series(1,600000);
insert into t2 select mod(i,4)+2, 'dummy' from generate_series(1,400000) a(i);

select c1, count(*) from t2 group by c1 order by 1;
 c1 | count
----+---------
  1 | 600000
  2 | 100000
  3 | 100000
  4 | 100000
  5 | 100000
```

Check the number of records and histogram after ANALYZE

```
analyze t2;
select reltuples::integer from pg_class where relname='t2';
 reltuples
-----------
   1000036
```

```
select n_distinct, most_common_vals,most_common_freqs, histogram_bounds from   pg_stats
where tablename='t2' and attname='c1';
-[ RECORD 1 ]-----+--------------------------------
n_distinct        | 5
most_common_vals  | {1,2,3,4,5}
most_common_freqs | {0.593667,0.104,0.103667,0.101,0.0976667}
histogram_bounds  |
```

The above results are as follows.

- **n_distinct**: NDV is 5.

- **most_common_vals**: MCV (Most Common Value) value.

- **most_common_freqs**: The ratio of the MCV value to the total number.

- **histogram_bounds**: Since it is {NULL}, a Height-Balanced histogram is not created.

How the optimizer computes the Estimated Rows

The method of calculating the Estimated Rows with the Frequency histogram is very intuitive. Consider the example below.

Equal condition

If '1' is entered, the Estimated Rows is 59,3688. This value is calculated as follows.

```
Estimated Rows = PG_CLASS.reltuples*{FREQ ratio of the value}
=> 593,688 = 1,000,036 * 0.593667
```

```
explain (analyze) select * from t1 where c1=1;
                  QUERY PLAN
-----------------------------------------------------------
 Seq Scan on t2  (cost=0.00..29742.45 rows=593688 width=105)
         (actual time=0.010..168.480 rows=600000 loops=1)
   Filter: (c1 = 1)
```

IN and BETWEEN condition

Both the IN and BETWEEN conditions use the following formula.

```
Estimated Rows
= Total number * (FREQ ratio of values corresponding to IN or BETWEEN)
=> 308,678 = 1,000,036 * ( 0.104+0.103667+0.101)
```

```
-- IN condition
explain (analyze) select * from t2 where c1 in (2,3,4);
                      QUERY PLAN
-----------------------------------------------------------
 Seq Scan on t2  (cost=0.00..30992.50 rows=308678 width=105)
        (actual time=88.026..183.651 rows=300000 loops=1)
   Filter: (c1 = ANY ('{2,3,4}'::integer[]))

-- BETWEEN condition
explain (analyze) select * from t2 where c1 between 2 and 4;
                      QUERY PLAN
-----------------------------------------------------------
 Seq Scan on t2  (cost=0.00..32242.54 rows=308678 width=105)
        (actual time=95.094..202.220 rows=300000 loops=1))
   Filter: ((c1 >= 2) AND (c1 <= 4))
```

Thus, the Frequency histogram has the advantage of being able to calculate the `Estimated Rows` very intuitively and accurately.

Hybrid histogram

Hybrid histograms combine the advantages of Frequency histogram and Height-Balanced histogram. (The term Hybrid histogram is not an official term used in PostgreSQL. It's just a term I've used for convenience)

For example, suppose NDV is more than the number of buckets and there is a lot of data skewed. In this case, if the Height-Balanced histogram is used, it is highly possible to calculate the `Estimated Rows` of skewed data very inaccurately. The Hybrid histogram is a way to overcome this problem.

Test environment

Configure the test environment for the Hybrid histogram.

```
# of buckets: 10 (Change default_statistics_target parameter value to 10)
NDV: 100
Distribution of values: Skew
```

Insert test data

Insert 20 values for 80% of the total, and 100 values for 20% of the total.

```
drop table t3;
create table t3 (c1 integer, dummy char(100));
insert into t3 select mod(i,20)+1,  'dummy' from generate_series(1,800000) a(i);
insert into t3 select mod(i,100)+21, 'dummy' from generate_series(1,200000) a(i);
select min(c1), max(c1), cnt as avg_rows, cnt*count(*) as total_rows
from  (select c1, count(*) cnt from t3 group by c1) a
group by cnt order by 1;
 min | max | avg_rows | total_rows
-----+-----+----------+------------
   1 |  20 |    40000 |     800000
  21 | 120 |     2000 |     200000
```

Check the number of records and histogram after ANALYZE

```
analyze t3;
select reltuples::integer from pg_class where relname='t3';
 reltuples
-----------
   1000036
select n_distinct, most_common_vals,most_common_freqs, histogram_bounds from   pg_stats
where tablename='t3' and attname='c1';
-[ RECORD 1 ]-----+-----------------------------
n_distinct        | 120
most_common_vals  | {5,1,18,13,20,16,9,11,12,14}
most_common_freqs | {0.0463333,0.046,0.0443333,0.0436667,0.0436667,
0.0433333,0.0423333,0.0423333,0.0403333,0.0403333}
histogram_bounds  | {2,3,6,7,10,15,19,31,60,94,120}
```

The above results are as follows.

- **n_distinct**: NDV is 120.

- **most_common_vals**: 10 MCV values are shown from 20 MCV values.

- **most_common_freqs**: It represents the ratio to 10 MCV values.

- **histogram_bounds**: 2 through 94 are the start values of each bucket, and 120 is the end of the 10th bucket.

Thus, if the `default_statistics_target` parameter is set to 10, 10 buckets for the Frequency histogram and 10 buckets for the Height-Balanced histogram are created, respectively.

How the optimizer computes the Estimated Rows

The values registered as MCV in the Hybrid histogram are the same as those in the Frequency histogram. However, the Height-Balance histogram method is used when the MCV value is not actually registered as the MCV due to the shortage of the number of buckets or is not the MCV value.

Let's take an example.

If you entered the value registered as MCV

If 5 is entered, the `Estimated Rows` is 46,335. This is calculated in the same way as the Frequency histogram.

```
Estimated Rows = PG_CLASS.reltuples*{FREQ ratio of the value}
=> 46,335 = 1,000,036 * 0.0463333
```

```
explain (analyze) select * from t3 where c1=5;
                  QUERY PLAN
-----------------------------------------------------------
 Seq Scan on t3  (cost=0.00..29742.45 rows=46335 width=105)
          (actual time=0.009..141.253 rows=40000 loops=1)
```

Calculation formula when a value not registered as MCV

Values not registered in MCV use the following formula.

In fact, you do not need to know all of the formulas below. It is only necessary to know that the `Estimated Rows` and the `Actual Rows` can be significantly different because of the use of such formulas.

Step 1: Add all the ratios of the MCV values.

```
Result value: 0.4326665
```

Step 2: Calculate the number of non-MCV values.

The total number of non-MCV values not registered in MCV is 567,354.

```
(1 - {The value of step 1}) * PG_CLASS.reltuples
   =>   (1 - 0.4326665) * 1000036)
   =>   567,354
```

Step 3: Calculate the distribution per Height-Balanced histogram bucket.

The distribution per bucket is 56,735.

```
{The value of step 2} / Number of buckets
   => 567,354 / 10
   => 56,735
```

Step 4: Calculate the distribution of non-MCV values.

It is 5,158 per Non-MCV.

```
{The value of step 3} / (Total NDV - NDV of MCV)
=> 56,734 / (120 - 10)
=> 5,158
```

Example of non-MCV value

After entering a non-MCV value of 99, let's check the Estimated Rows. In this case, it is estimated to be 5,158, which is more than twice as high as the actual number of 2,000. This result is the result of the above formula.

```
explain (analyze) select * from t3 where c1=99;
                  QUERY PLAN
-----------------------------------------------------------
 Seq Scan on t3  (cost=0.00..29742.45 rows=5158 width=105)
        (actual time=91.134..114.105 rows=2000 loops=1)
   Filter: (c1 = 99)
```

Example of MCV value but not registered in MCV

Enter '3', which is actually the MCV value but is not registered in the MCV. In this case, it is estimated to be 5,158. This value is very small compared to the actual number of 40,000.

```
explain (analyze) select * from t3 where c1=3;
                    QUERY PLAN
---------------------------------------------------------------
 Seq Scan on t3  (cost=0.00..29742.45 rows=5158  width=105)
         (actual time=0.008..130.834 rows=40000 loops=1)
   Filter: (c1 = 3)
```

If it is a range condition

Let's enter the range of the second bucket: C1> = 3 AND C1 <6. The MCV value '5' is also present in this range. In this case, use the following formula.

```
Rows per bucket + (The ratio of MCV value * Number of Records)
=> 56,735+(0.0463333*1,000,036)
=> 103,070
```

```
explain (analyze) select * from t3 where c1 >= 3 and c1 < 6;
                    QUERY PLAN
---------------------------------------------------------------
 Seq Scan on t3  (cost=0.00..32242.54 rows=103070 width=105)
         (actual time=0.007..150.626 rows=120000 loops=1)
   Filter: ((c1 >= 3) AND (c1 < 6))
```

As mentioned earlier, there is no need to memorize these formulas. However, as we apply these formulas, it is understandable that the Estimated Rows may be inaccurate if the number of buckets is insufficient. In this case, it is necessary to increase the number of buckets. The NDV for the example is 120. Let's look at the results after increasing the number of buckets in the T3 table to 120.

Results after increasing the number of histogram buckets

After increasing the number of buckets in the T3 table, check the statistical information in the PG_STATS view.

```
alter table t3 alter column c1 set statistics 120;
analyze t3;

select n_distinct, most_common_vals,most_common_freqs, histogram_bounds from pg_stats
where tablename='t3' and attname='c1';
-[ RECORD 1 -----------------------------------
n_distinct      | 120
most_common_vals | {17,5,20,6,19,13,2,3,15,16,4,14,8,12,18,1,10,11,9,7,82,53,22,31,93,...
Omitted below }
```

```
most_common_freqs | {0.0415,0.0414722,0.0411111,0.0410556,0.0409167,0.04075,0.0401667,...
Omitted below}
histogram_bounds  |
```

If you increase the number of buckets by NDV, a Frequency histogram is used.

Thus, the optimizer computes the `Estimated Rows` based on the histogram information, which is the most important information when generating the execution plan. So, if the optimizer's execution plan is not what you want, you must make sure of the difference between the `Estimated Rows` and `Actual Rows`.

Summary

In this chapter, we have learned a lot about the optimizer's operating principles. First, we learned about COST. Understanding COST and understanding how COST is calculated will help you understand query performance issues.

In the statistics section, we learned that the index scan method changes according to the correlation value.

Explain is an essential tool for query tuning. Therefore, you need the ability to analyze the results of the Explain as well as how to use Explain. To do this, we learned the meaning of the keywords provided by Explain and the order of reading the Explain. In particular, you will remember that reading the hash join execution order is different from ORACLE.

In the query parsing section, we learned about the Plan Caching feature. This is a feature of the PostgreSQL architecture. Through Plan Caching, Bind SQL can always refer to the histogram.

In the Access Methods section, we learned a variety of access methods. Understanding the access method is the basis of tuning. Among the various access methods, we have described the Bitmap Index Scan method very deeply. In this way, we can understand the correct operation principle of Bitmap Index Scan method.

Also, note that because of the MVCC nature of PostgreSQL, `Vacuum` must be preceded for index only scan performance.

In the Join Methods section, we learned about NL joins and hash joins. Especially hash joins explained very detailed operation principle.

You will also remember the Skew data optimization technique (Histojoin) to optimize the probe work on the skew data. And we have learned that in-memory hash joins are not always faster than Multi-Batch methods.

In the Outer join section, we learned about NL outer join and hash outer join. You will also remember that the hash outer join provides the ability to select a small set as the Build table.

In the query rewrite section, we learned the subquery Collapse, View Merging, and JPPD.

In the PG_HINT_PLAN section, we learned how to use hints to control access methods, join methods, and join order.

In the histogram section, we learned the Frequency histogram and the Height-Balanced histogram. And remember that PostgreSQL provides a hybrid histogram that combines the features of both methods.

As the optimizer generated execution plan, it learned that the `Estimated Rows` is the most important factor and how to use the histogram information when estimating the `Estimated Rows`. Finally, we have seen how to generate more accurate histogram information by increasing the number of buckets.

chapter **4**.

Understanding Vacuum

chapter 4.

Understanding Vacuum

In this chapter, we will learn Vacuum.

Vacuum performs the task of organizing unnecessary garbage data and compressing (vacuuming) the organized space to increase the efficiency of disk space. It will also clean up old transaction IDs. This is everything Vacuum does.

But it is very difficult to understand Vacuum accurately. This is probably due to the difficulty of understanding the PostgreSQL MVCC model. In particular, the Age concept is a confusing concept for the first-time learning Vacuum.

So, in this chapter, we will first look at the characteristics of the PostgreSQL MVCC model. We will look at the need for Vacuum, how it works, how Autovacuum works, and the performance improvements of Vacuum since 9.6.

PostgreSQL MVCC Model

What is MVCC?

MVCC seems to be understood as 'a technique that can provide multiple versions of data at the same time'. Here, 'version' means time-specific data. That is, the latest data is regarded as the 'current version', and the data before the change is regarded as the 'before version'.

MVCC provides the ability to read the data version at the time the query was performed. In this case, the criterion of 'performed point' is the transaction ID. The transaction ID is incremented by 1 for each transaction. The MVCC operation principle will be easy to understand from the picture below. (See Figure 4-1)

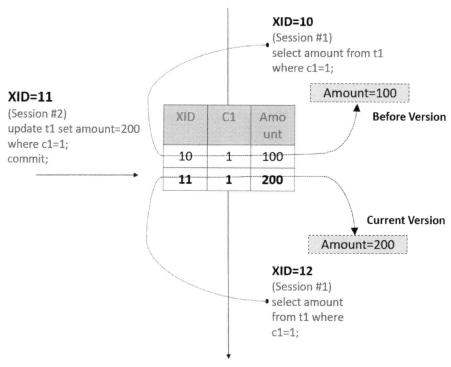

Figure 4-1. *How MVCC works*

Reading the data version that is equal to or smaller than the XID at the start of the query is the core principle of MVCC. This is a very important concept. This ensures that concurrency can be increased by completely eliminating blocking between READ and WRITE operations. If it is not Multi-Version, the concurrency is very low because the READ operation blocks the WRITE operation and the WRITE operation can block the READ operation.

Features of PostgreSQL MVCC

As you can see in Figure 4-1, in order to implement MVCC, keep the 'before data'. PostgreSQL keeps before data in table blocks. This is a feature of PostgreSQL MVCC, and it is why we need Vacuum.

Let's take a closer look at the features of PostgreSQL MVCC and why we need Vacuum.

Feature-1. Store the before data in a table block.

This feature has the advantage that MVCC can be implemented very simply. Consider the case of using undo segments like ORACLE. The complexity of the MVCC increases for the following reasons:

- A session must be assigned an undo segment for each transaction.

- Because undo segments are limited resources, contention for undo segments can occur if concurrent transactions are spiked.

- Applying MVCC requires accessing the undo segment, and requires a CR copy operation to apply the contents of the undo segment to the CR block.

PostgreSQL does not use undo segments, so there is no such complexity. However, keeping before data and current data in the table causes inconvenience of management and inefficiency of table use.

For example, suppose a very old 'before data' exists in the table that is not accessed by any transaction. The more such data, the lower the space utilization efficiency of the table. There are two ways to solve this problem.

1. Delete before data.
2. Delete before data and compress space.

The first method is performed with the Vacuum (or Vacuum Freeze) command, and the second method is executed with the Vacuum Full command.

Feature-2. Manages the transaction ID (XID) for each record.

The reason for managing XID by record is 'Feature-1'. Since the before data and the current data are stored in the table, the XID is required for each record in order to extract data at a specific point in time.

Managing XID by record is very inefficient in terms of space usage. The larger the XID size, the greater the inefficiency. Concerned about this, the PostgreSQL development team decided to use XID as a 4-byte integer. This decision leads to the problem that `Vacuum` must be performed.

Problem with XID of 4-byte integer

What's problem with using XID as 4-byte integer?

The XID is incremented by 1 for every transaction. The maximum value that can be expressed as a 4-byte integer is approximately 4.3 billion. Thus, if the TPS of the system is 1000, then 4.3 billion will be exhausted after 50 days. (49.7 days = 4.3 billion / (86,400 sec * 1,000 TPS))

After exhausting 4.3 billion, it starts from 1 again. Generally, the clock is used when describing. That is, using a 4-byte integer type is the same principle as using a clock with 4.3 billion ticks. However, using a clock to illustrate this was somewhat confusing. (In my case, it was) So I use the following method instead of the clock. (See Figure 4-2)

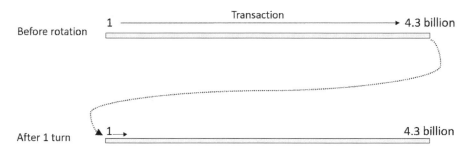

Figure 4-2. *XID initialization routine*

What happens after one wheel rotation?

This problem is clearly shown in Figure 4-2. Compare 1 after 1 turn and 4.3 billion before turn. Compared with the value, 4.3 billion is greater. However, in practice, the 1 is greater. In other words, if one wheel is rotated without any action, the XID order is ruined.

There are two ways to solve this problem.

- Increase the Wrap number after one turn.

- Change the previous XID to a specific value or flag it before one turn.

In fact, the first approach is more convenient and intuitive.

ORACLE uses this approach. ORACLE uses two bytes for the wrap number and four bytes for the SCN. Therefore, in the case of 1,000 TPS, SCN overflow occurs after approximately 9,000 years. (2^16 * 50 days = 8,977 years) In other words, you do not have to worry about SCN overflow issues.

The disadvantage of this approach is that it requires space to store the wrap number. However, since ORACLE stores SCN on a block-by-block basis, 2 bytes for storing wrap numbers are not a problem at all.

However, PostgreSQL needs to store the wrap number per record, so there is a burden on additional space allocation. To be more precise, it manages XMIN (minimum XID) and XMAX (maximum XID) per record, so additional 4 bytes per record is required to store the wrap number. Because of this, PostgreSQL uses the second method.

What is Frozen XID?

To understand exactly how PostgreSQL is used, you need to know Frozen XID. There are three types of XID in PostgreSQL:

- **Bootstrap XID**: Assigned at `initdb()`. The value is 1

- **Frozen XID**: XID for `Anti-Wraparound Vacuum`. The value is 2.

- **Normal XID**: XID for the transaction. Start with 3.

The Frozen XID is 2 and the XID of the generic transaction is 3, so Frozen XID is smaller than any XID. In other words, applying Frozen XID will always be visible. (See Figure 4-3)

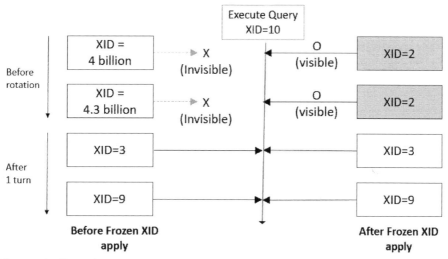

Figure 4-3. *Effects of Frozen XID*

The MVCC principle is to read a version of a record that is less than or equal to the XID at the start of the query. Therefore, if you do not apply Frozen XID as shown on the left in Figure 4-3, records with XID greater than 10 are invisible. If this works, the result of the query is messed up. To solve this problem, PostgreSQL changes the old XID to the Frozen XID before one rotation.

This operation is called 'Anti-wraparound Vacuum'.

🗋 **Note** Prior to PostgreSQL 9.4, when Anti-Wraparound Vacuum was performed, the XMIN (Minimal XID) value was actually changed to Frozen XID 2. However, since version 9.4, the 10th bit of the Flag (t_infomask) column is set to 1 without changing the XMIN value to 2. (This will be discussed later)

Vacuum

In this section, we will learn the basic knowledge to understand the operation principle of Vacuum. Beginning with the question, "Do you need a vacuum?", I will explain the relationship between Vacuum and lock, the amount of redo generated by Vacuum type, and the concept of Age.

In addition, we will also look at the `vacuum_freeze_min_age` parameter, which controls XID Frozen operation.

Vacuum Basics

Let's take a few questions to the basics of Vacuum.

- Question-1. What is the purpose of Vacuum?

- Question-2. Is Vacuum Essential?

Question-1. What is the purpose of Vacuum?

`Vacuum has two main purposes.`

1. Space reuse
2. XID Frozen

Space reuse is divided into two.

1. Delete before data
2. Delete before data and compress space

The first method is performed with the `Vacuum` (or `Vacuum Freeze`) command, and the second method is executed with the `Vacuum Full` command. The XID Frozen operation is performed when the `Vacuum`, `Vacuum Freeze`, and `Vacuum Full` commands are executed. Vacuum for XID Frozen operation is called anti-wraparound vacuum.

Question-2. Is Vacuum Essential?

Vacuum for space reuse is not a requirement. However, anti-wraparound vacuum for XID Frozen must be performed.

Effect of Vacuum

Let's check the effect of Vacuum through `Vacuum` and `Vacuum Full` commands.

Vacuum command

The usage of `Vacuum` command is as follows.

```
vacuum <table name>
```

> ☐ **Note**   There is no `Vacuum` command for Index. The `Vacuum` command performs a vacuum operation on the indexes created on the table and table.

Insert test data and verify current XID

```
drop table t1;
create table t1 (c1 integer);
select txid_current();
 txid_current
--------------
      2006822
```

Check XID value after insert 1 row

A value one greater than the previous XID is assigned to XMIN.

```
insert into t1 values(1);
select lp, t_xmin, t_xmax from heap_page_items(get_raw_page('t1',0));
 lp | t_xmin  | t_xmax
----+---------+--------
  1 | 2006823 |      0
```

Check the status of the block after UPDATE

From the results below, it can be seen that after UPDATE, the current record and the previous record are all in one block. The XID value of the current record is larger than the previous XID, and the XMAX value of the previous record is changed to the current XID value. That is, the XMAX value of the previous record is changed to the XID value of the change point.

```
update t1 set c1=10 where c1=1;
select lp, t_xmin, t_xmax from heap_page_items(get_raw_page('t1',0));
```

```
lp | t_xmin  | t_xmax
----+---------+---------
  1 | 2006823 | 2006824
  2 | 2006824 |       0
```

Check for block changes after Vacuum

The Vacuum command deletes the previous record. Therefore, there is space in the table that can be reuse.

```
vacuum t1;
select lp, t_xmin, t_xmax from heap_page_items(get_raw_page('t1',0));
 lp | t_xmin  | t_xmax
----+---------+---------
  1 |         |
  2 | 2006824 |       0
```

Vacuum Full command

The Vacuum Full command recreates the table compactly.

```
vacuum full t1;
select lp, t_xmin, t_xmax from heap_page_items(get_raw_page('t1',0));
 lp | t_xmin  | t_xmax
----+---------+---------
  1 | 2006824 |       0
```

Vacuum and Lock

In this section, we look at the lock waiting issues that can occur during Vacuum execution.

Lock compatibility of Vacuum command

The Vacuum command is lock compatible with SELECT, DML (DELETE, UPDATE, INSERT). You can perform Vacuum during SELECT and DML, and perform SELECT and DML during Vacuum. Consider the example below.

Session # 1: Perform DML

When DML is executed, ROW EXCLUSIVE lock is acquired. Therefore, it is simulated using the LOCK TABLE command.

```
postgres=# begin;
postgres=# lock table t1 in row exclusive mode;
```

Session # 2: Vacuum command execution

Vacuum command is executed.

```
postgres=# vacuum t1;
VACUUM
```

Lock compatibility of Vacuum Full command

The Vacuum Full command is not lock compatible with DML. In addition, there is no compatibility with SELECT. That is, if the Vacuum Full command is executed on the table being Selected, it waits for a lock. A more serious problem is that a session that performs a SELECT on the table in this state also waits for a lock. (This is the same problem as the CLUSTER command described above)

Session # 1: Perform a SELECT

When SELECT is executed, ACCESS SHARE lock is acquired. Therefore, it is simulated using the LOCK TABLE command

```
postgres=# begin;
postgres=# lock table t1 in access share mode;
```

Session # 2: Vacuum Full command execution

Wait for the lock.

```
postgres=# vacuum full t1;
-- lock waiting
```

Lock monitoring

A lock holder for a session that performs Vacuum Full is the session that performed the LOCK TABLE command.

```
select pid, wait_event_type||'-'||wait_event wait,
       pg_blocking_pids(pid) holder, query
```

```
from   pg_stat_activity;
  pid  |     wait      | holder  |             query
-------+---------------+---------+------------------------------------
 19309 |               | {}      | lock table t1 in access share mode;
 20674 | Lock-relation | {19309} | vacuum full t1;
```

📄 **Note**   Beginning with version 9.6, a wait event column is provided for ease of session monitoring. Although the number provided is not very large, it is encouraging that waiting events are provided. Also, `pg_blocking_pid()` function is provided for convenience of lock monitoring. This function makes it easy to check the PID of a lock holder session.

Session #3

At this time, when another session performs a SELECT on the T1 table, it waits for a lock.

```
postgres=# select * from t1;
-- Lock waiting
```

Lock monitoring

A lock holder for a session that performs SELECT is the session that performed the Vacuum Full command.

```
select pid, wait_event_type||'-'||wait_event wait,
       pg_blocking_pids(pid) holder, query
from   pg_stat_activity;
  pid  |     wait      | holder  |             query
-------+---------------+---------+------------------------------------
 19309 |               | {}      | lock table t1 in access share mode;
 20674 | Lock-relation | {19309} | vacuum full t1;
 20888 | Lock-relation | {20674} | select * from t1;
```

This lock waiting problem can cause very serious performance problems. Therefore, the Vacuum Full command should be performed very carefully.

📄 **Note**   If you need to execute the Vacuum Full command, it is also possible to use the PG_REPACK extension introduced earlier in the CLUSTER command section. If DML does not occur, CTAS (Create Table As Select) may also be considered.

Vacuum and Redo

In this section, let's look at the amount of redo that occurs in `Vacuum`.

If a large amount of redo occurs during a vacuum, there is a possibility of an IO bottleneck. If archive log mode is enabled, the amount of archive logs can also increase. Consider the example below.

Test environment

```
drop table t1;
create table t1 (c1 integer, dummy char(500));
insert into t1 select generate_series(1,1000000), 'dummy';
analyze t1;

select relpages, round(relpages*8/1024,0) "size(MiB)"
from    pg_class where relname='t1';
 relpages | size(MiB)
----------+-----------
    66667 |       520
```

Perform UPDATE

As you can see, after Updating all the records in the table (1 million), you can see that the size of the table is twice as big as the previous size. Because the before record is stored in the table, DELETE & INSERT is used even if UPDATE is performed.

```
update t1 set c1=c1*10;
analyze t1;

select relpages, round(relpages*8/1024,0) "size(MiB)"
from    pg_class where relname='t1';
 relpages | size(MiB)
----------+-----------
   133334 |      1041
```

So how much redo will be generated at this time? Surprisingly, the amount of Redo is 1,248 MiB. (1,248 MiB = 78 WAL logs * 16 MiB) The reason why so many Redo occur is related to PostgreSQL's recovery mechanism.

The first change after the checkpoint is written to the WAL log at the block level. And writes to the WAL log at record level until the next checkpoint occurs. This mechanism can cause much more Redo than ORACLE. (ORACLE uses this mechanism only during HOT Backup.)

> 📄 **Note**   This mechanism is controlled by the `full_page_writes` parameter. The default value is on. If set to off, complete recovery after a disk failure may not be possible. Therefore, it must be set to on in the operating environment. However, when migrating, it is necessary to consider setting the parameter to off in order to improve the performance. As a result of performing an UPDATE with the parameter set to off on my system, the size of the Redo was reduced to 672 MiB, which caused the UPDATE to run about 30% faster.

Amount of Redo generated by Vacuum

How much redo will occur when performing a `vacuum` after UPDATE?

In the following results, 1 million "before records" were deleted during the `Vacuum`. However, the `Vacuum` at this time does not generate Redo.

```
vacuum verbose t1;
INFO:  vacuuming "public.t1"
INFO:  "t1": removed 1000000 row versions in 66667 pages
INFO:  "t1": found 1000000 removable, 1000000 nonremovable row versions
       in 133334 out of 133334 pages
DETAIL: 0 dead row versions can't be removed yet.
There were 0 unused item pointers.
Skipped 0 pages due to buffer pins.
0 pages are entirely empty.
CPU 0.00s/0.49u sec elapsed 0.60 sec.
```

Amount of Redo generated by Vacuum Freeze

Let's do the `Vacuum Freeze` command.

The result of the following operation shows that the number of data to be deleted is zero. This is a natural result because we have already done `Vacuum`. Strangely, it took 11.77 seconds to run. Even more surprising is the amount of redo caused by `Vacuum Freeze` is 528 MiB. Why is this happening?

Let's clarify the cause of the problem.

```
vacuum freeze verbose t1;
INFO:  vacuuming "public.t1"
INFO:  "t1": found 0 removable, 1000000 nonremovable row versions
       in 66668 out of 133334 pages
DETAIL: 0 dead row versions can't be removed yet.
```

```
There were 10 unused item pointers.
Skipped 0 pages due to buffer pins.
0 pages are entirely empty.
CPU 0.41s/0.45u sec elapsed 11.77 sec.
```

Why Vacuum Freeze causes a lot of redo

A large amount of redo occurred during Vacuum Freeze because the processing logic of Vacuum Freeze is different from Vacuum. Let's check the definition of Vacuum Freeze in the manual.

```
Selects aggressive "freezing" of tuples. Specifying FREEZE is equivalent to performing
VACUUM with the vacuum_freeze_min_age and vacuum_freeze_table_age parameters set to
zero.
```

Readers who are new to PostgreSQL will find it hard to tell the difference. In a nutshell, Vacuum Freeze makes the XID Frozen work very aggressive by setting the vacuum_freeze_min_age parameter to zero. In other words, the lot of redo caused by Vacuum Freeze is due to the XID Frozen operation. The XID Frozen operation is to set the FROZEN bit in the t_infomask column for each record. (Up to version 9.3, the XMIN value was changed to 2). The XID Frozen operation caused a change in the record, and only one bit changed, but a block level redo was created due to the full_page_writes feature.

Let's look at an example.

Check t_infomask value before Vacuum

The t_infomask value before the Vacuum is 10242.

```
select lp, t_xmin, t_xmax, t_infomask
from   heap_page_items(get_raw_page('t1',66667)) limit 3;
 lp | t_xmin  | t_xmax | t_infomask
----+---------+--------+------------
  1 | 2006893 |      0 |      10242
  2 | 2006893 |      0 |      10242
  3 | 2006893 |      0 |      10242
```

Check t_infomask value after Vacuum

The t_infomask value after the Vacuum is 10498.

```
select lp, t_xmin, t_xmax, t_infomask
from    heap_page_items(get_raw_page('t1', 66667)) limit 3;
 lp | t_xmin  | t_xmax | t_infomask
----+---------+--------+------------
  1 | 2006893 |      0 |      10498
  2 | 2006893 |      0 |      10498
  3 | 2006893 |      0 |      10498
```

Check t_infomask value after Vacuum Freeze

The value of `t_infomask` after performing `Vacuum Freeze` is 11010.

```
select lp, t_xmin, t_xmax, t_infomask
from    heap_page_items(get_raw_page('t1', 66667)) limit 3;
 lp | t_xmin  | t_xmax | t_infomask
----+---------+--------+------------
  1 | 2006893 |      0 |      11010
  2 | 2006893 |      0 |      11010
  3 | 2006893 |      0 |      11010
```

Results analysis

If you convert the t_infomask value to binary and compare it, you can see that the 9th bit is set to 1 after `Vacuum` and the 10th bit is set to 1 after `Vacuum Freeze`. (See Figure 4-4.) If you perform a `Vacuum Freeze` without performing `Vacuum`, the 9th and 10th bits are set to 1 at the same time.

Bit#	14	13	12	11	10	9	8	7	6	5	4	3	2	1
Before Vacuum	1	0	1	0	0	0	0	0	0	0	0	0	1	0
After Vacuum	1	0	1	0	0	1	0	0	0	0	0	0	1	0
After Vacuum Freeze	1	0	1	0	1	1	0	0	0	0	0	0	1	0

Figure 4-4. *Comparison of t_infomask values before / after Vacuum*

So, what does the 10th bit mean? Let's check through the source.

Src 4-1. *src/include/access/htup_details.h*

```
#define HEAP_XMIN_COMMITTED 0x0100 /* t_xmin committed */
#define HEAP_XMIN_INVALID   0x0200 /* t_xmin invalid/aborted */
#define HEAP_XMIN_FROZEN(HEAP_XMIN_COMMITTED|HEAP_XMIN_INVALID)
```

The result of the source check is as follows.

- HEAP_XMIN_COMMITTED is used to set the ninth bit to 1. (0x100 is **1**00,000,000 in binary)

- HEAP_XMIN_INVALID is used to set the 10th bit to 1. (0x200 is a binary number of **1**,000,000,000)

- HEAP_XMIN_FROZEN is used to set both the ninth and tenth bits to 1. (The HEAP_XMIN_FROZEN value is **1,1**00,000,000)

That is, the tenth bit is used to FROZEN the XMIN value.

Why? Would not Redo be generated during previous Vacuum?

Looking at the changes in t_infomask, we can see that the 9th bit of t_infomask is changed to 1 when Vacuum is executed. But why? Would not Redo occur during the previous Vacuum? I did not find any official documents for this. Perhaps Vacuum for space cleaning seems to be because there is no need for recovery. In other words, there is no problem in recovering the transaction even if there is no redo associated with Vacuum for space cleaning. However, the Vacuum for XMIN FROZEN must be recovered. Otherwise, there will be problems in MVCC operation. Therefore, redo occurs at this time.

Amount of Redo in Vacuum Full

How much redo is generated in Vacuum Full?

Vacuum Full creates a new table internally. Therefore, you can assume that as many redo occur as you enter a new million rows. Consider the example below. Due to the Vacuum Full, the size of the T1 table is reduced to half, and the amount of redo generated is 528 MiB. (This size is about the size of the newly created T1 table)

```
vacuum full verbose t1;
INFO:  vacuuming "public.t1"
INFO:  "t1": found 123801 removable, 1000000 nonremovable row versions in 133334 pages
DETAIL:  0 dead row versions can't be removed yet.
CPU 0.71s/0.85u sec elapsed 12.55 sec.

analyze t1;
select relpages, round(relpages*8/1024,0) "size(MiB)"
from   pg_class where relname='t1';
```

```
relpages | size(MiB)
-----------+-------------
   66667 |       520
```

What is age?

To understand precisely the principle of operation of Vacuum, it is necessary to understand Age concept. The 'age' of PostgreSQL has the following characteristics:

- Manage age by database, table, and record

- The age at which the user database is created is equal to the age of the template1 database. This is because it is cloned using the template1 database.

- When the table is created, it is one year old.

- When the record is inserted, it is one year old.

- Each transaction increases the age of the database, table, and record by one year.

- In other words, age is calculated as 'current XID - creation XID'.

- Older tables and records are subject to Vacuum.

- After performing a Vacuum, the age of the table and record will be younger.

The reason for managing age is entirely due to the XID Frozen work. Let's look at an example.

Database creation and age

When you create a user database, all the objects in the template1 database are cloned. Therefore, the age of the user database at this point is equal to the age of the template1 database.

```
create database mydb;
select datname, datfrozenxid, age(datfrozenxid)
```

```
from    pg_database where datname in ('mydb', 'template1');
  datname  | datfrozenxid |  age
-----------+--------------+-------
 mydb      |      3407909 | 41905
 template1 |      3407909 | 41905
```

Table creation and age

When you create a table, the age of the table is one year. At this time, the age of the database also increases by one year.

```
create table t1 (c1 integer, dummy char(100));
select 'DATABASE '||datname as name, age(datfrozenxid)
from    pg_database where datname = 'mydb'
union    all
select 'TABLE    '||relname as name, age(relfrozenxid )
from    pg_class where relname='t1';
     name         |  age
------------------+-------
 DATABASE mydb    | 41906
 TABLE    t1      |     1
```

Record insert and age

When a record is entered, the age of the record is one year. At this time, the age of the table and the database also increases by one.

```
insert into t1 values(1,'dummy');
select 'DATABASE '||datname as name, age(datfrozenxid)
from    pg_database where datname = 'mydb'
union    all
select 'TABLE    '||relname as name, age(relfrozenxid )
from    pg_class where relname='t1'
union    all
select 'REC(t1)  '||c1      as name, age(xmin)  from t1;
     name         |  age
------------------+-------
 DATABASE mydb    | 41907
 TABLE    t1      |     2
 REC(t1)  1       |     1
```

Additional table creation and age

If you create one more table, the database, table, and record will grow by one.

```
create table t2 (c1 integer, dummy char(100));
select 'DATABASE '||datname as name, age(datfrozenxid)
from    pg_database where datname = 'mydb'
union   all
select 'TABLE   '||relname as name, age(relfrozenxid )
from    pg_class where relname in ('t1','t2')
union   all
select 'REC(t1) '||c1      as name, age(xmin)  from t1;
     name      |  age
---------------+-------
 DATABASE mydb |  41908
 TABLE     t1  |     3
 TABLE     t2  |     1
 REC(t1)   1   |     2
```

Additional data insert and age

This is the last example. If you insert one record in the T2 table, the database, table, and record will grow by one.

```
insert into t2 values(1,'dummy');
select 'DATABASE '||datname as name, age(datfrozenxid)
from    pg_database where datname = 'mydb'
union   all
select 'TABLE   '||relname as name, age(relfrozenxid )
from    pg_class where relname in ('t1','t2')
union   all
select 'REC(t1) '||c1      as name, age(xmin)  from t1
union   all
select 'REC(t2) '||c1      as name, age(xmin)  from t2;
     name      |  age
---------------+-------
 DATABASE mydb |  41909
 TABLE     t1  |     4
 TABLE     t2  |     2
 REC(t1)   1   |     3
 REC(t2)   1   |     1
```

What we have explained so far is all of the 'age' we should know. Here we can identify important principles.

- Principle-1. The age of the database is greater than the age of any table in the database.

- Principle-2. The age of the table is greater than the age of any records in the table.

vacuum_freeze_min_age parameter

Check the parameters related to the vacuum using the `pg_setttings` view.

Of these, `vacuum_freeze_min_age` is the parameter you should look at. This parameter is used to select the XID Frozen target record during the vacuum operation.

```
select name, setting from pg_settings where name like 'vacuum%';
             name                   | setting
------------------------------------+----------
 vacuum_cost_delay                  | 0
 vacuum_cost_limit                  | 200
 vacuum_cost_page_dirty             | 20
 vacuum_cost_page_hit               | 1
 vacuum_cost_page_miss              | 10
 vacuum_defer_cleanup_age           | 0
 vacuum_freeze_min_age              | 50000000
 vacuum_freeze_table_age            | 150000000
 vacuum_multixact_freeze_min_age    | 5000000
 vacuum_multixact_freeze_table_age  | 150000000
```

The definition of the parameter is as follows. That is, records older than the value of the parameter are subject to XID Frozen.

```
Specifies the cutoff age (in transactions) that VACUUM should use to decide whether to
freeze row versions while scanning a table.
```

Principles of Vacuum to understand through Quiz

I will explain some of the key elements needed to understand Vacuum through some quizzes.

Test scenarios

The test scenarios for the quiz are:

1. Change the `vacuum_freeze_min_age` parameter to 50,000.
2. Insert one record in the `T1` table.
3. Increase the XID by 30,000.
4. Insert one record in the `T1` table.
5. Increase the XID by 30,000.

6. Perform `Vacuum` on the `T1` table.

7. Perform `Vacuum Freeze` on the `T1` table.

This can be expressed as follows.

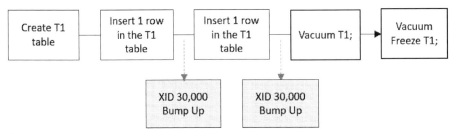

Figure 4-5. *Test scenarios*

Preparing for testing

Create DBLINK Extension and procedures

Create a procedure using the `dblink` extension and DB link to easily bump up the XID.

```
create extension dblink;
drop table txid_bump_t;
create table txid_bump_t (c1 integer);

CREATE OR REPLACE FUNCTION insert_txid_bump_t(v1 integer) RETURNS VOID AS $$
BEGIN
    PERFORM dblink('myconn','INSERT INTO txid_bump_t SELECT ' || '''' || v1 || '''');
END;
$$ LANGUAGE plpgsql;

CREATE or replace FUNCTION loop_insert_txid_bump_t(v_begin integer, v_end integer)
RETURNS VOID AS $$
BEGIN
    FOR i in v_begin..v_end LOOP
        PERFORM insert_txid_bump_t(i);
    END LOOP;
END;
$$ LANGUAGE plpgsql;
```

Create PAGEINSPECT Extension

Install the `pageinspect` extension to see the contents of the block.

```
create extension pageinspect;
```

Insert test data

```
drop table t1;
create table t1 (c1 integer, dummy char(100));

-- DBLINK connection
select dblink_connect('myconn','dbname=mydb port=5436 user=postgres password=postgres');

-- Insert one record in table T1
insert into t1 values(1,'dummy');

-- Increased XID by 30,000
select loop_insert_txid_bump_t (1,30000);

-- Insert one record in table T1
insert into t1 values(2,'dummy');

-- Increased XID by 30,000
select loop_insert_txid_bump_t (1,30000);
```

Quiz

Take a total of eight quizzes.

Quiz-1) What is the age of the T1 table?

1. 3
2. 60,003

Quiz-2) What is the age of the first record inserted in the T1 table?

1. 2
2. 60,002

Quiz-3) After Vacuum, what is the age of the T1 table?

1. 1
2. 50,000

Quiz-4) After Vacuum, what is the age of the first record inserted in table T1?

1. 1
2. 60,002

Quiz - 5) How many records are Frozen after Vacuum?

1. 0
2. 1
3. 2

Quiz-6) After Vacuum Freeze, what is the age of the T1 table?

1. 0
2. 1
3. 50,000

Quiz-7) After Vacuum Freeze, what is the age of the first record inserted in table T1?

1. 0
2. 1
3. 60,002

Quiz-8) What is the number of additional Frozen records after Vacuum Freeze?

1. 0
2. 1
3. 2

answer: 1)2 2)2 3)2 4)2 5)2 6)1 7)3 8)2

If all eight have been matched, you can jump to the Autovacuum section.

Problem solving

Quiz-1) What is the age of the T1 table?

1. 3
2. 60,003

Answer: 2) 60,003

After the creation of the T1 table, 60,002 transactions occurred. Therefore, the age of T1 is 1 + 60,002.

Quiz-2) What is the age of the first record inserted in the T1 table?

1. 2
2. 60,002

Answer: 2) 60,002

After the record was inserted, 60,001 transactions occurred. Therefore, the age of the record is 1 + 60,001.

Check the result

```
select 'TABLE    '||relname as name, age(relfrozenxid )
from    pg_class where relname='t1'
union    all
select 'REC(t1)  '||c1     as name, age(xmin)  from t1;
    name      |  age
--------------+-------
  TABLE     t1 | 60003
  REC(t1)   1  | 60002
  REC(t1)   2  | 30001
```

Quiz-3) After Vacuum, what is the age of the T1 table?

1. 1
2. 50,000

Answer: 2) 50,000

After vacuuming, the age of the table is set to `vacuum_freeze_min_age`.

Records older than this parameter value are frozen. Therefore, after Vacuum, all records older than 50,000 years are frozen. On the other hand, records less than 50,000 years old are not frozen.

Quiz-4) After Vacuum, what is the age of the first record inserted in table T1?

1. 1
2. 60,002

Answer: 2) 60,002

As of version 9.4, you will remember that the XMIN value does not change to 2 during the XID Frozen operation. The record age is calculated using XMIN, so the age of the record does not change even if the `Vacuum` is performed. However, since records of 50,000 years old or older are frozen, only the 10th bit of `t_infomask` is set to '1'. The age of a frozen record is internally considered to be two years old.

Quiz - 5) How many records are Frozen after Vacuum?

1. 0
2. 1
3. 2

Answer: 2) 1

Since the `vacuum_freeze_min_age` is 50,000, the record of 50,000 years old or more is frozen. Therefore, only the first record is frozen.

Check the result

```
vacuum t1;
select 'TABLE    '||relname as name, age(relfrozenxid )
from     pg_class where relname='t1'
union    all
select 'REC(t1)  '||c1     as name, age(xmin)   from t1;
```

```
    name    |  age
------------+-------
TABLE    t1 | 50000
REC(t1)  1  | 60002
REC(t1)  2  | 30001


select lp, t_xmin, t_xmax, t_infomask, t_infomask::bit(16)
from   heap_page_items(get_raw_page('t1', 0));
 lp | t_xmin   | t_xmax | t_infomask |    t_infomask
----+----------+--------+------------+-------------------
  1 | 3569833  |    0   |    2818    | 0000101100000010
  2 | 3599834  |    0   |    2306    | 0000100100000010
```

Quiz-6) After Vacuum Freeze, what is the age of the T1 table?

1. 0
2. 1
3. 50,000

Answer: 1) 0

Vacuum Freeze sets vacuum_freeze_min_age to zero. Therefore, after Vacuum Freeze, the table age is 0 years old.

Quiz-7) After Vacuum Freeze, what is the age of the first record inserted in table T1?

1. 0
2. 1
3. 60,002

Answer: 3) 60,002

We have confirmed earlier that the Vacuum does not change the XMIN of the record. Vacuum Freeze is the same.

Quiz-8) What is the number of additional Frozen records after Vacuum Freeze?

1. 0

2.   1

3.   2

Answer: 2) 1

Because `Vacuum Freeze` causes the table age to be 0, all records in the table are frozen. Therefore, one additional record is frozen.

Check the result

```
vacuum freeze t1;
select 'TABLE    '||relname as name, age(relfrozenxid )
from   pg_class where relname='t1'
union  all
select 'REC(t1)  '||c1     as name, age(xmin)  from t1;
    name    |  age
------------+-------
 TABLE    t1 |      0
 REC(t1)  1  | 60002
 REC(t1)  2  | 30001

select lp, t_xmin, t_xmax, t_infomask, t_infomask::bit(16)
from   heap_page_items(get_raw_page('t1', 0));
 lp | t_xmin   | t_xmax | t_infomask |    t_infomask
----+----------+--------+------------+------------------
  1 | 3569833 |      0 |       2818 | 0000101100000010
  2 | 3599834 |      0 |       2818 | 0000101100000010
```

The next explanation is Autovacuum. Autovacuum is a bit more complicated than Vacuum.

Autovacuum

Autovacuum automatically performs `Vacuum`.

In this section, we will look at how Autovacuum works. In addition, we will review the problems that Anti-Wraparound Vacuum has repeatedly performed in versions prior to 9.6, and we will look at how effectively this problem has been improved since version 9.6.

How to set Auovacuum

Autovacuum is set with the `autovacuum` parameter.

Can I turn off Autovacuum completely?

none. If set to off, Anti-wraparound autovacuum will still work. If the XID Frozen operation can't be performed at an appropriate time, it will cause serious problems that the DB can't use. This is a very troublesome problem for system administrators. If an Autovacuum operation is performed on a large table during business hours, business applications may be slowed down due to IO contention.

Fortunately, this problem has been fixed since 9.6.

autovacuum_freeze_max_age parameter

To understand Autovacuum's core operating principles correctly, we need to know only one `autovacuum_freeze_max_age` parameter.

The definition of the parameter is as follows. In summary, if the age of the table is greater than the value of the corresponding parameter, an Anti-wraparound autovacuum is performed. This is done even if the autovacuum parameter is off.

```
Specifies the maximum age (in transactions) that a table's pg_class.relfrozenxid field
can attain before a VACUUM operation is forced to prevent transaction ID wraparound
within the table. Note that the system will launch autovacuum processes to prevent
wraparound even when autovacuum is otherwise disabled.
```

As a result of my testing, the Anti-wraparound autovacuum is performed even if the autovacuum parameter is off. However, there is a slight delay in calling the autovacuum process. So, the test below will proceed with keeping the `autovacuum` parameter on.

The principle of Autovacuum to understand through Quiz

A description of how Autovacuum works will also use quizzes.

Test scenarios

The test scenarios for the quiz are:

1. Set the `autovacuum_freeze_max_age` parameter to 200,000.
2. Keep the `vacuum_freeze_min_age` parameter at 50,000.
3. Insert 200,000 rows in the `T1` table. At this time, COMMIT every record.
4. Increase the XID by 150,000.
5. Increase the XID by 150,001.

This can be expressed as follows.

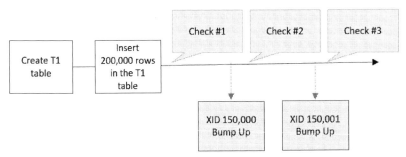

Figure 4-6. *Test scenarios*

Preparing for testing

Procedure Creation

Create a procedure that performs a COMMIT for every record.

```
CREATE OR REPLACE FUNCTION insert_t1(v1 integer) RETURNS VOID AS $$
BEGIN
    PERFORM dblink('myconn','INSERT INTO t1 SELECT ' || '''' || v1 || '''');
END;
$$ LANGUAGE plpgsql;

CREATE or replace FUNCTION loop_insert_t1(v_begin integer, v_end integer) RETURNS VOID AS
$$
BEGIN
    FOR i in v_begin..v_end LOOP
        PERFORM insert_t1(i);
    END LOOP;
END;
```

```
$$ LANGUAGE plpgsql;
```

Create PG_VISIBILITY Extension

Create an extension to view the Visibility Map.

```
create extension pg_visibility;
```

Insert test data

```
drop table txid_bump_t;
create table txid_bump_t (c1 integer);

drop table t1;
create table t1 (c1 integer, dummy char(1000));

-- DBLINK connection
select dblink_connect('myconn','dbname=mydb port=5436 user=postgres password=postgres');

-- Insert 200,000 rows
select loop_insert_t1(1,200000);
```

Step 1 - Quiz

Let's solve the following quiz.

Quiz -1) If you insert for each commit 200,000 rows in the T1 table, the age increases by 200,000. At this time, the T1 table age is 200,001. This value is larger than the value of the `autovacuum_freeze_max_age` parameter, so the Anti-wraparound autovacuum is performed. What is the age of the table after performing autovacuum?

1. 0
2. 50,000

Quiz-2) At this time, what is the number of frozen records in the T1 table?

1. 200,000
2. 150,000

Quiz - 3) At this time, is redo generated?

1. Yes.
2. No.

Step 1 - Problem Solving

Quiz -1) If you insert for each commit 200,000 rows in the T1 table, the age increases by 200,000. At this time, the `T1` table age is 200,001. This value is larger than the value of the `autovacuum_freeze_max_age` parameter, so the Anti-wraparound autovacuum is performed. What is the age of the table after performing autovacuum?

1. 0
2. 50,000

Answer: 2) 50,000

After vacuum, the table age is set to the `vacuum_freeze_min_age` parameter value. Therefore, it is 50,000 years old.

Quiz-2) At this time, what is the number of frozen records in the `T1` table?

1. 200,000
2. 150,000

Answer: 2) 150,000

Since the `vacuum_freeze_min_age` parameter value is 50,000, 150,000 records will be frozen from 50,001 to 200,000 years old.

Quiz - 3) At this time, is redo generated?

1. Yes
2. No

Answer: 1) Yes

The XID Frozen operation changes the record. Therefore, redo is generated.

Step 1 - Detailed Description

Let's take a closer look.

Age of table and record before Vacuum

The age of the table just before Vacuum was 200,001 years old. The records are 200,000 years old and 199,999 years old respectively.

```
select 'TABLE    '||relname as name, age(relfrozenxid )
from    pg_class where relname='t1'
union   all
select 'REC(t1)  '||c1      as name, age(xmin)  from t1 limit 3;
    name      |  age
------------+--------
 TABLE    t1 | 200001
 REC(t1)  1  | 200000
 REC(t1)  2  | 199999
```

Age of table and record after Vacuum

After Vacuum, the table age is 50,000. However, the age of the record does not change.

```
select 'TABLE    '||relname as name, age(relfrozenxid ) from pg_class where relname='t1'
union all
select 'REC(t1)  '||c1      as name, age(xmin)  from t1
limit 3;
    name      |  age
------------+--------
 TABLE    t1 | 50000
 REC(t1)  1  | 200000
 REC(t1)  2  | 199999
```

Autovacuum monitoring

You can monitor autovacuum activity using the pg_stat_activity view.

```
select pid, query from pg_stat_activity;
  pid  |                    query
-------+-------------------------------------------------------
 15254 | autovacuum: VACUUM public.t1 (to prevent wraparound)
```

Autovacuum log

Looking at the activity of Autovacuum in the log file, all `T1` table blocks (28,572 blocks) were scanned, which took 31 seconds. Since the first Autovacuum is performed, there is no block skipped during Frozen operation.

```
LOG:   automatic vacuum of table "mydb.public.t1": index scans: 0
       pages: 0 removed, 28572 remain, 0 skipped due to pins,
       0 skipped frozen
       tuples: 0 removed, 201774 remain, 0 are dead but not yet removable
       buffer usage: 57670 hits, 2 misses, 9540 dirtied
       avg read rate: 0.000 MB/s, avg write rate: 2.371 MB/s
       system usage: CPU 0.08s/0.20u sec elapsed 31.42 sec
```

Check the frozen status of a record

Let's check the frozen status of each record using LATERAL inline view. After extracting only the tenth bit of `t_infomask` and grouping it, you can see that 150,001 rows have been frozen.

```
select substr(cast(b.t_infomask::bit(16) as text),7,1) frozen_flag,
       count(*)
from   (select i from generate_series(0,28571) a(i)) a,
       LATERAL (select * from heap_page_items(get_raw_page('t1', a.i))) b
group by substr(cast(b.t_infomask::bit(16) as text),7,1);
 frozen_flag | count
-------------+--------
     0       |  49999
     1       | 150001
```

Step 2 - Quiz

After generating 151,000 transactions in the table created for XID Bump up, let's solve the following quiz.

```
select dblink_connect('myconn','dbname=postgres port=5436 user=postgres
password=postgres');

-- Insert 150,001 rows
select loop_insert_txid_bump_t(1,150001);
```

Quiz -1) What is the age of the T1 table after 150,001 transactions have occurred?

1. 50,000
2. 200,001

Quiz-2) At this point, is the T1 table the target of the Anti-wraparound autovacuum?

1. Yes
2. No

Quiz-3) If the T1 table is the target of an Anti-wraparound autovacuum, how many rows are Frozen?

1. 0
2. 49,999

Quiz-4) At this time, is redo generated?

1. Yes
2. No

Answer: 1)2 2)1 3)2 4)1

Step 2 - Problem Solving

If you understand the concept of age exactly, the second stage will be very easy.

Quiz -1) What is the age of the T1 table after 150,001 transactions have occurred?

1. 50,000
2. 200,001

Answer: 2) 200,001

The age of the table grows by one every time a transaction occurs, so it is 200,001 years old. This is repeated several times. If you are wrong with this quiz, please read the previous explanation again.

Quiz-2) At this point, is the T1 table the target of the Anti-wraparound autovacuum?

1. Yes
2. No

Answer: 1) Yes

The table is older than 200,000 years old. Therefore, the T1 table is the target of Vacuum.

Quiz-3) If the T1 table is the target of an Anti-wraparound autovacuum, how many rows are Frozen?

1. 0
2. 49,999

Answer: 2) 49,999

Of the records in the T1 table, 49,999 were not Frozen records. After 150,001 transactions have occurred, all of these records are larger than the `vacuum_freeze_min_age parameter` value of 5,000. So, it becomes all Frozen.

Quiz-4) At this time, is redo generated?

1. Yes
2. No

Answer: 1) Yes

Redo is generated for frozen 49,999 rows.

Step 2 - Detailed Description

Let's take a closer look at Autovacuum logs and Frozen.

Autovacuum log

The important point here is that 21,428 blocks previously frozen were skipped. This is a new feature provided since 9.6. This is described in the Visibility Map section.

```
LOG:   automatic vacuum of table "mydb.public.t1": index scans: 0
       pages: 0 removed, 28572 remain, 0 skipped due to pins,
       21428 skipped frozen
       tuples: 0 removed, 199997 remain, 0 are dead but not yet removable
       buffer usage: 7153 hits, 7155 misses, 7145 dirtied
       system usage: CPU 0.07s/0.11u sec elapsed 25.45 sec
```

Check the frozen status of a record

All records (200,000) have been frozen.

```
select substr(cast(b.t_infomask::bit(16) as text),7,1) frozen_flag,
       count(*)
from  (select i from generate_series(0,28571) a(i)) a,
      LATERAL (select * from heap_page_items(get_raw_page('t1', a.i))) b
group by substr(cast(b.t_infomask::bit(16) as text),7,1);
  frozen_flag | count
-------------+--------
  1          |  200000
```

Step 3

At this point, when you issue 150,001 transactions, the age of the T1 table grows to 200,001. Therefore, it is again target to Anti-wraparound autovacuum. But since all the records have already been frozen, all blocks are skipped. Let's look at the log below. All frozen blocks have been skipped and the execution time is 0 seconds.

```
LOG:   automatic vacuum of table "mydb.public.t1": index scans: 0
       pages: 0 removed, 28572 remain, 0 skipped due to pins,
       28571 skipped frozen
       tuples: 0 removed, 199993 remain, 0 are dead but not yet removable
       buffer usage: 10 hits, 12 misses, 0 dirtied
       avg read rate: 105.574 MB/s, avg write rate: 0.000 MB/s
       system usage: CPU 0.00s/0.00u sec elapsed 0.00 sec
```

This is the effect of 9.6 new features. Until the previous version, all blocks were always scanned, regardless of Frozen. A detailed description of this will be given in the next section.

Visibility Map

The Visibility Map (VM) is also needed because of the PostgreSQL MVCC.

In this section, we will look at a brief description of the VM and the improvements available since version 9.6.

What is Visibility Map?

The VM consists of two bits per table block. (Up to 9.6 was 1 bit per block.) The purpose of each bit is as follows.

ALL_VISIBLE bit

If all records in the block are 'Visible', which is visible in all transactions, it is 1. Otherwise, it is zero. Immediately after the Vacuum, the ALL_VISIBLE bit is changed to 1. If the record is changed, it is changed to 0. Among the above, it will be remembered that the ALL_VISIBLE bit of all blocks must be 1 in order to perform Index Only Scan method.

ALL_FROZEN bit

If all records in the block have been frozen, this is 1. Otherwise, it is zero. Therefore, only the block with ALL_FROZEN bit 0 should be processed in the next Frozen operation. The ALL_FROZEN bit is provided from 9.6. This has drastically improved the Vacuum problem.

Improved Vacuum performance due to ALL_FROZEN bits

It is a case of dramatic tuning success with a very simple idea. Let's review the problems up to 9.6 and look at the tuning effect caused by the ALL_FROZEN bit.

Issues with Vacuum up to 9.6

To simplify the discussion, set the parameter values as follows:

```
vacuum_freeze_min_age      = 0          (The default value is 50 million)
autovacuum_freeze_max_age = 200,000,000 (default value)
```

With the above settings, an Anti-wraparound autovacuum will be performed every 200 million transactions. Consider the example below.

Step-1) After 200 million transactions

If 200 million transactions occur after the creation of the T1 table, a Frozen operation is performed. At this time, a change is made in the table, so the same amount of redo as the table block is generated.

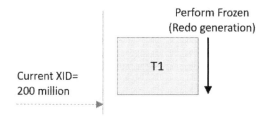

Step-2) After another 200 million transactions

If there are 200 million transactions after the T2 table creation, the Frozen operation is performed. Problems arise from this point on. The T1 table is also included in the target of the Anti-wraparound autovacuum because it has been increased by 200 million years. At this time, there is no way to verify that all the records in the T1 table are frozen. Therefore, it is checked whether or not frozen while performing Seq Scan. The larger the T1 table, the greater the load of Seq Scan.

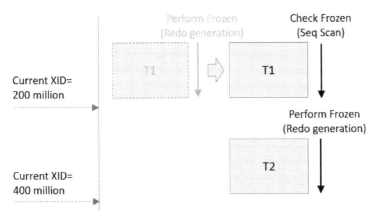

Step-3) After another 200 million transactions

Consider the case where 200 million transactions occurred after the creation of the T3 table. In this case, not only the T3 table but also the T1 and T2 tables are targets of the Anti-wraparound autovacuum. Because of this method, the target of the Anti-wraparound autovacuum increases with time, and the processing time for this increases gradually. This is a problem that can cause very serious performance degradation.

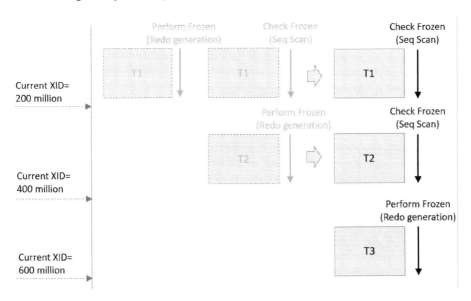

Performance improvement using 9.6 version of ALL_FROZEN bit

When the ALL_FROZEN bit is applied, the following changes are made.

- After performing Step-1, all records in table T1 are frozen. At this time, the ALL_FROZEN bit in the VM associated with the T1 table is changed to 1.

- After performing Step-2, all records in table T2 are frozen. At this time, the ALL_FROZEN bit in the VM associated with the T2 table is changed to 1.

- In Step-3, check the VM of each table for frozen operations on T1 and T2 tables.

- As a result of the VM check, the ALL_FROZEN bit is all 1, so the frozen operation is skipped. (See Figure 4-7)

This is very simple and provides excellent performance improvements.

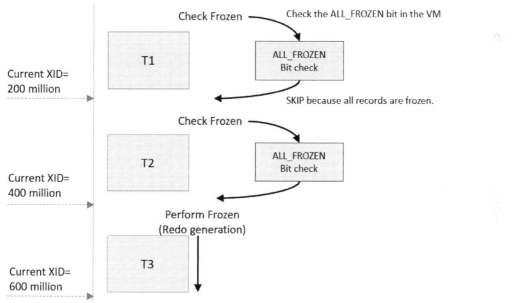

Figure 4-7. *Performance improvement of ALL_FROZEN bit*

HOT (Heap Only Tuple)

In the PostgreSQL documentation, the term HOT sometimes appears.

HOT is also one of the tuning techniques to overcome the weaknesses of the PostgreSQL MVCC model. If HOT is interpreted literally, it is 'record that exists only in table'. Readers who are new to PostgreSQL do not know what this means. Therefore, in this section, I want to improve the understanding of HOT by dealing with the reason why HOT is necessary, the background, the principle of operation, and how to reduce the size of the table and index through HOT.

Why do I need HOT?

HOT is a feature provided since PostgreSQL 8.3.

To understand the need for HOT, you need to understand the characteristics of the PostgreSQL MVCC model. One of the features of PostgreSQL MVCC is that before records are stored in table blocks. To accomplish this, UPDATE is handled by DELETE & INSERT. This is because the before record can be kept in a table block. However, this method has a problem that not only the table size but also the index size is increased. Even if the value of the index key is not changed, the index size is increased because it is processed by the DELETE & INSERT method. (See Figure 4-10) This is a serious problem not only in performance but also in capacity management. The feature introduced to solve this problem is HOT.

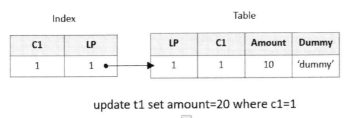

update t1 set amount=20 where c1=1

Figure 4-8. *Problems before introduction of HOT*

HOT Concept

HOT will only change the table record (DELETE & INSERT) if the column being changed is not an index column. The picture below will help you understand.

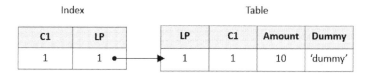

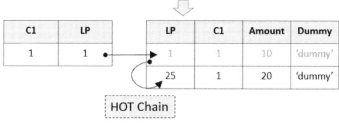

Figure 4-9. *After applying HOT*

That is, HOT does not change the index. Instead, make sure that the before record in the table points to the current record. At this time, the connection between the before record and the current record is called 'HOT Chain'.

HOT Chain Pruning

If you change the same record several times, the HOT Chain becomes longer, which can cause performance problems. Therefore, the length of the HOT chain is kept short by the pruning operation. This will be discussed in the section "HOT Operation Principle".

Limitation of HOT

HOT works only when the changed record is stored in the same block as the before record.

Conceptually, it is also possible to create a HOT chain over several blocks, but there is a problem of reading two or more blocks to access one record. HOT works only when modified records are stored in the same block to avoid this problem. Therefore, tables with frequent changes should have a smaller FILLFACTOR. (The correlation between FILLFACTOR and table and index sizes will be discussed in later)

HOT operation principle

Let's analyze the HOT operation principle by using a block dump.

Test environment

Set FILLFACTOR very small for testing.

```
drop table t1;
create table t1 (c1 integer, c2 integer) with (fillfactor=10);

insert into t1 values(1,1);
insert into t1 select i,i from generate_series(100,200) a(i);

create index t1_indx on t2(c1);
analyze t1;

select relname, relpages
from   pg_class where relname = 't1';
 relname | relpages
---------+----------
 t1      |        5
```

Block status before UPDATE

The block status before UPDATE is as follows. (See Figure 4-12)

```
-- 테이블
select lp, lp_off, t_xmin, t_xmax, t_ctid, t_data
from   heap_page_items(get_raw_page('t1', 0))
where  lp=1;
 lp | lp_off | t_xmin  | t_xmax | t_ctid |        t_data
----+--------+---------+--------+--------+--------------------
  1 |   8160 | 6893509 |      0 | (0,1)  | \x0100000001000000

-- 인덱스
select lp, lp_off, t_xmin, t_xmax, t_ctid, t_data
from   heap_page_items(get_raw_page('t1_indx', 1))
where  lp=1;
 lp | lp_off | t_xmin | t_xmax | t_ctid | t_data
----+--------+--------+--------+--------+--------
  1 |   8160 |        |        |        |
```

C1	LP
1	1

LP	Offset	T_CTID	C1	C2
1	8160	(0,1)	1	1

Figure 4-10. *Block status before change*

Block state after first UPDATE

Let's check the table block after changing the `C2` value to 2. The first record points to the 23rd record. At this time, the index still points to the first LP (Line Pointer) of the table. (See Figure 4-11.)

```
update t1 set c2=2 where c1=1;

-- Table
select lp, lp_off, t_xmin, t_xmax, t_ctid, t_data
from   heap_page_items(get_raw_page('t1', 0))
where  lp in (1,23);
 lp | lp_off | t_xmin  | t_xmax  | t_ctid |       t_data
----+--------+---------+---------+--------+--------------------
  1 |   8160 | 6893509 | 6893512 | (0,23) | \x0100000001000000
 23 |   7456 | 6893512 |       0 | (0,23) | \x0100000002000000

-- Index
select lp, lp_off, t_xmin, t_xmax, t_ctid, t_data
from   heap_page_items(get_raw_page('t1_indx', 1))
where  lp=1;
 lp | lp_off | t_xmin | t_xmax | t_ctid | t_data
----+--------+--------+--------+--------+--------
  1 |   8160 |        |        |        |
```

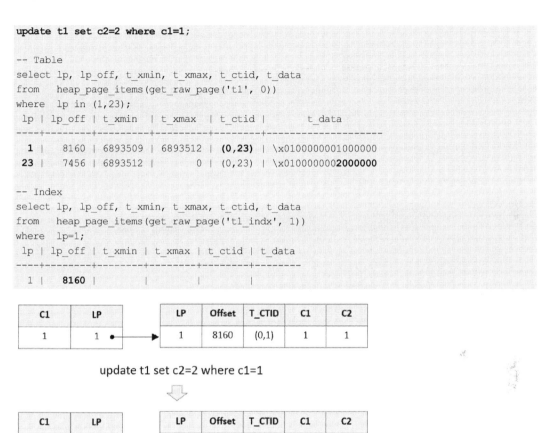

Figure 4-11. *Block status after first change*

Block status after secondary UPDATE

After changing the `C2` value to 3, the HOT Chain is `LP(1)->LP(23)->LP(24)`. (See Figure 4-12)

At this time, the first record, `LP(1)`, points to `LP(23)` using the Offset column, and all the rest of the `LP(1)` record is changed to NULL. In this way, it can be assumed that the HOT chain is kept short.

```
update t1 set c2=3 where c1=1;

-- Table
select lp, lp_off, t_xmin, t_xmax, t_ctid, t_data
from   heap_page_items(get_raw_page('t1', 0))
where  lp in (1,23,24);
 lp | lp_off | t_xmin  | t_xmax  | t_ctid |        t_data
----+--------+---------+---------+--------+--------------------
  1 |     23 |         |         |        |
 23 |   7488 | 6893512 | 6893513 | (0,24) | \x0100000002000000
 24 |   7456 | 6893513 |       0 | (0,24) | \x0100000003000000
```

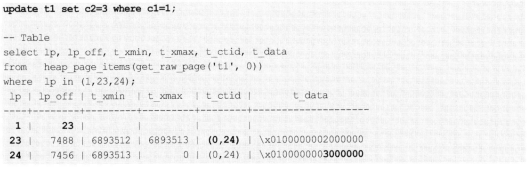

update t1 set c2=3 where c1=1

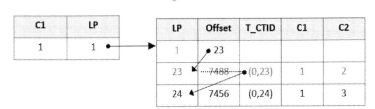

Figure 4-12. *Block state after secondary change*

Block state after third UPDATE

After changing the `C2` value to 4, the HOT Chain is `LP(1)->LP(24)->LP(23)`. (See Figure 4-13)

That is, HOT Chain did not become long. Another important fact is that the previously used record slots are reused alternately. Through this, it can be assumed that, when HOT is applied, the size of the table will remain constant even if very frequent changes occur. This will be covered in the "HOT Performance Test" section.

```
update t1 set c2=4 where c1=1;
```

```
-- Table
select lp, lp_off, t_xmin, t_xmax, t_ctid, t_data
from   heap_page_items(get_raw_page('t1', 0))
where  lp in (1,23,24);
 lp | lp_off | t_xmin  | t_xmax  | t_ctid |        t_data
----+--------+---------+---------+--------+--------------------
  1 |     24 |         |         |        |
 23 |   7456 | 6893514 |       0 | (0,23) | \x0100000004000000
 24 |   7488 | 6893513 | 6893514 | (0,23) | \x0100000003000000
```

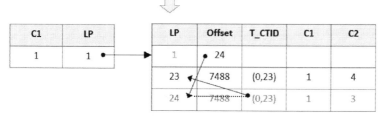

update t1 set c2=4 where c1=1

Figure 4-13. *Block state after third UPDATE*

Singe Page Vacuum

At this time, what happens when you scan a T1 table?

When the scan is performed, the HOT Chain becomes as short as possible. Let's look at the example below. As a result of the scan, the HOT Chain is changed to LP(1) ->LP(23) and the LP(24) slot is returned. This operation is called 'Single Page Vacuum'. (See Figure 4-14)

```
select count(*) from t1;

-- Table
select lp, lp_off, t_xmin, t_xmax, t_ctid, t_data
from   heap_page_items(get_raw_page('t1', 0))
where  lp in (1,23,24);
 lp | lp_off | t_xmin  | t_xmax | t_ctid |        t_data
----+--------+---------+--------+--------+--------------------
  1 |     23 |         |        |        |
```

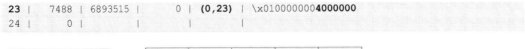

```
23 |    7488 | 6893515 |        0 | (0,23) | \x0100000004000000
24 |       0 |         |          |        |
```

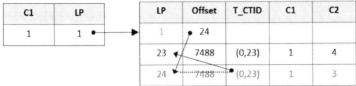

select count(*) from t1;

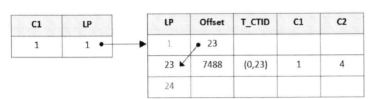

Figure 4-14. *Block status before and after scan*

Does Single Page Vacuum work for tables that do not have indexes?

Yes. The technique of pruning the chain seems to have been introduced before HOT. This is because it is not necessary to keep the chain long at a certain point in time.

HOT performance test

So far, we have learned how HOT works. From now on, let's do tests to determine the impact of HOT on the actual operating environment.

Test Overview

- FILLFACTOR of T1 table is the default (100%)

- Set FILLFACTOR of T2 table to 50%.

- Insert 500,000 in each table.

- After that, change all the 500,000 cases repeatedly seven times.

- Compare the table size, index size, execution speed, and WAL log count for each test.

Test environment

```
drop table t1;
drop table t2;

create table t1 (c1 integer, amount integer, dummy char(100));
create table t2 (c1 integer, amount integer, dummy char(100))
with (fillfactor=50);

insert into t1 select i,i,'dummy' from generate_series(1,500000) a(i);
insert into t2 select i,i,'dummy' from generate_series(1,500000) a(i);

analyze t1;
analyze t2;

select relname, relpages, round(500000/relpages,0) rec_per_page,
       round(relpages*8/1024,0) "size(MiB)", reloptions
from   pg_class where relname in ('t1','t2');
 relname | relpages | rec_per_page | size(MiB) |    reloptions
---------+----------+--------------+-----------+------------------
 t1      |     8621 |           57 |        67 |
 t2      |    17242 |           28 |       134 | {fillfactor=50}

create index t1_indx on t1(c1);
create index t2_indx on t2(c1);

select relname, relpages, round(relpages*8/1024,0) "size(MiB)"
from   pg_class where relname in ('t1_indx','t2_indx');
 relname  | relpages | size(MiB)
----------+----------+-----------
 t1_indx  |     1374 |        10
 t2_indx  |     1374 |        10
```

Since the FILLFACTOR of the T2 table is set to 50%, immediately after the initial loading, the T2 table is twice as large as the T1 table. At this time, the index size is the same.

Table size comparison

The T1 table grows each time a change is made. On the other hand, the T2 table maintains a constant size. Why is this happening?

UPDATE is performed internally by DELETE & INSERT. Therefore, the size of the T1 table increases because the new record is Inserted every time UPDATE is performed. However, the size of the T2 table did not increase. This is the effect of the Single Page Vacuum described above. This shows that the tables with frequent changes need to adjust the FILLFACTOR ratio accordingly. To reduce the size of large tables due to frequent changes, you should perform the Vacuum Full command.

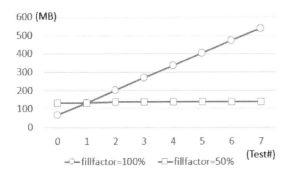

Index size comparison

The index size of the T1 table grows steadily. On the other hand, the index size of the T2 table does not increase. To reduce the size of large tables due to frequent changes, you should perform the REINDEX or Vacuum Full command.

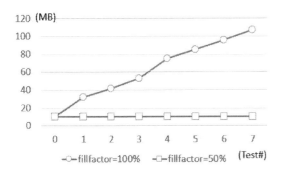

WAL log count comparison

At the time of changing the T1 table, more than twice as much redo is generated as compared with the T2 table. This is because not only the T1 table but also the index of the T1 table are changed. On the other hand, the index of the T2 table is not changed.

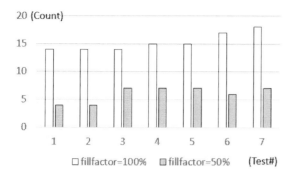

Performance comparison

The UPDATE performance for the T2 table is at least twice as fast. This is due to the difference in table scan range and redo generation.

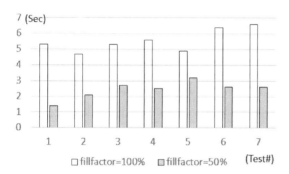

Summary

In this chapter, we have learned in detail the fundamental principles of Vacuum. Vacuum is a part of the MVCC that is the basis of PostgreSQL transaction processing, so it is very complicated to look at in detail. However, if you understand what you have learned so far, it will help you learn the details that were not covered in this book.

chapter **5**.

Partial Index and BRIN

Partial Index and BRIN

In this chapter, we will learn Partial Indexes and Block Range Index (BRIN).

Partial Index

PostgreSQL supports a WHERE clause for index creation syntax. In other words, it provides the ability to index only records that satisfy the WHERE clause. The index created by applying the WHERE clause is called a partial index.

Purpose of partial index

Partial indexes are well suited for processing skew data.

Of course, PostgreSQL can refer to histogram information not only in Literal SQL but also in BIND SQL, thus making access to skew data efficient. For example, data with large distribution can be processed by Seq Scan, and data with small distribution can be processed by Index Scan. However, it is very inefficient for the index to grow by indexing the data to be processed by Seq Scan. Let's take an example.

Example of partial index

Test environment

Insert data that is extremely skewed.

```
drop table t1;
create table t1 (c1 integer, flag char(1), dummy char(100));
```

```
insert into t1 select i, 'Y', 'dummy'
from generate_series(1,9999000) a(i);

insert into t1 select i, 'N', 'dummy'
from generate_series(9999001,10000000) a(i);

select flag, count(*) from t1 group by flag;
 c1 |   count
----+----------
 Y  | 9999000
 N  |    1000

-- Creating an index on the C1 column
create index t1_c1_indx on t1(c1);
```

Create regular index on the Flag column

Generate a regular index first for comparison with partial index. The index size is 27,422 blocks.

```
create index t1_flag_indx on t1(flag);
analyze t1;

select relpages from pg_class where relname='t1_flag_indx';
 relpages
----------
    27422
```

Perform a query

Let's execute the query that counts the value of 'Y' and the query that counts 'N' respectively. In case of 'Y', the index created in the C1 column is used, and in the case of 'N', the index created in the Flag column is used. This is a very good choice with a histogram.

```
-- If flag = 'Y' condition
explain (costs false)
select count(*)
from t1 where c1 >= 9000000 and flag='Y' and dummy='dummy';
                             QUERY PLAN
-------------------------------------------------------------------
 Aggregate
   ->  Index Scan using t1_c1_indx on t1
         Index Cond: (c1 >= 9000000)
         Filter: ((flag = 'Y'::bpchar) AND (dummy = 'dummy'::bpchar))

-- If flag = 'N' condition
explain (costs false)
```

```
select count(*)
from t1 where c1 >= 9000000 and flag='N' and dummy='dummy';
                          QUERY PLAN
-------------------------------------------------------------------
Aggregate
  -> Index Scan using t1_flag_indx on t1
        Index Cond: (flag = 'N'::bpchar)
        Filter: ((c1 >= 9000000) AND (dummy = 'dummy'::bpchar))
```

Partial index creation

Create a partial index after dropping the existing index. At this time, the size of the index is 5 blocks. Since the index contains only records with a flag value of 'N', the size of the index is very small.

```
drop index t1_flag_indx;
create index t1_flag_indx on t1(flag) where flag='N';
analyze t1;

select relpages from pg_class where relname='t1_flag_indx';
 relpages
----------
        5
```

Perform a query

The partial index also establishes the same execution plan as the regular index.

```
-- If flag = 'Y' condition
explain (costs false)
select count(*)
from t1 where c1 >= 9000000 and flag='Y' and dummy='dummy';
                          QUERY PLAN
-------------------------------------------------------------------
Aggregate
   -> Index Scan using t1_c1_indx on t1
        Index Cond: (c1 >= 9000000)
        Filter: ((flag = 'Y'::bpchar) AND (dummy = 'dummy'::bpchar))

-- If flag = 'N' condition
explain (costs false)
select count(*)
from t1 where c1 >= 9000000 and flag='N' and dummy='dummy';
                          QUERY PLAN
-------------------------------------------------------------------
Aggregate
   -> Index Scan using t1_flag_indx on t1
```

```
    Index Cond: (flag = 'N'::bpchar)
       Filter: ((c1 >= 9000000) AND (dummy = 'dummy'::bpchar))
```

If you create an index without a WHERE clause, NULL values are also included in the index. It can be seen that the 'IS NULL' condition is also performed by the index scan as shown below.

```
insert into t1 select NULL, 'Y', 'dummy' from generate_series(1,100) a(i);

explain (costs false)
select * from t1 where c1 IS NULL;
                      QUERY PLAN
----------------------------------------------------------------
 Index Scan using t1_c1_indx on t1
   Index Cond: (c1 IS NULL)
```

BRIN (Block Range Index)

BRIN is the index type provided since PostgreSQL 9.5. BRIN is also called Block Range Index. BRIN is indexed using MIN / MAX values for a range of records, rather than indexed by records. This has the advantage that the index size is very small. Because of these advantages, BRIN is chosen when there is insufficient disk space. However, if you do not understand the operation principle of BRIN correctly, there is a possibility of performance degradation.

So, in this section we will look at how BRIN works.

BRIN vs. EXADATA Storage Index
The storage indexes of BRIN and EXADATA are very similar. However, BRIN can be created by the user, but the storage index can't be created by the user. Also, BRIN is stored on disk, while Storage index is stored in daemon memory. That is, the storage index disappears when the storage server is shut down.

BRIN concept

The following figure shows the concept of BRIN very easily.

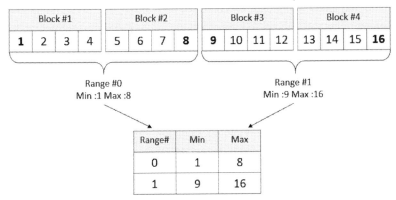

Figure 5-1. *BRIN concept (BRIN when table is sorted well)*

BRIN stores the minimum and maximum values for each block range in the index as shown in the figure above. The default value of the block range is 128. Therefore, in the case of 8 KiB blocks, the block range is 1 MiB. From this fact, we can infer some facts.

- BRIN is advantageous only when performing a wide range of index scans. This is because even if only one row is searched, it accesses 128 table blocks.

- It is advantageous that the table is sorted by the BRIN column. This is because access targets are reduced when sorted by BRIN column.

The second part can be easily understood by looking at Figure 5-1 and 5-2. For example, assume that the condition 'BETWEEN 10 AND 15' is entered. In Figure 5-1, only range # 1 is accessed. However, in Figure 5-2, all ranges are accessed.

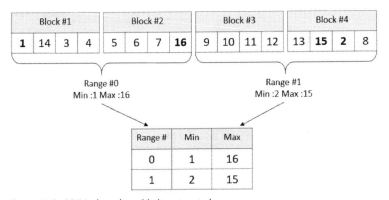

Figure 5-2. *BRIN when the table is not sorted*

Questions about BRIN

The concept of BRIN is very simple. However, to apply BRIN in practice, you need to understand BRIN correctly. This is because you can make the most of the benefits of BRIN and compensate for the drawbacks.

My questions about BRIN was as follows. Let's take a look at each of the questions below and see how BRIN works.

1. When should I use BRIN?
2. How small is BRIN?
3. Does BRIN access 128 blocks when reading 1 row?
4. Is BRIN faster than Index Only Scan?
5. Is BRIN faster than Index Scan?
6. Will record sorting affect BRIN performance?
7. How will the records that are inserted after the creation of the BRIN be accessed?
8. Will BRIN use low-level lock?
9. Can large table be effectively accessed using the BITAND operation?
10. Can I get a partition-like effect with BRIN?

When should I use BRIN?

My conclusion is as follows.

- BRIN is useful for a wide range of index scan. This is particularly useful when there is insufficient disk space.

- A dramatic performance improvement can be expected when searching for various conditions on the FACT table. Because BRIN is capable of BITAND operation.

- You can create a logical sub partition with BRIN. As with the second reason, this is also possible with the BITAND operation.

The following is a series of test procedures to get this conclusion. Let 's take one step at a time.

How small is BRIN?

It is too small.

BRIN stores the minimum and maximum values in units of 128 blocks. In other words, there is one index key per 1MiB of the table. For example, in the case of 1 GiB table, the size of the BRIN is 6 blocks. Consider the example below.

```
drop table t1;
create table t1 (c1 integer, c2 integer, dummy char(100));
insert into t1 select i, i, 'dummy' from generate_series(1,10000000) a(i);

create index t1_c1_indx on t1(c1);
Time: 6678.988 ms

create index t1_c2_brin on t1 using brin (c2);
Time: 2094.280 ms

analyze t1;

select relname, relpages, round(relpages*8/1024,0) "size(MiB)"
from   pg_class where relname in ('t1','t1_c1_indx','t1_c2_brin');
   relname    | relpages | size(MiB)
--------------+----------+----------
 t1           |   172414 |      1346
 t1_c1_indx   |    27422 |       214
 t1_c2_brin   |        6 |         0
```

▭ **Note**   In the test case, BRIN creation time is about 1/3 of the b*tree index. The difference in the creation time is not large compared to the difference in the index size. This is because table scans are required for indexing.

Does BRIN access 128 blocks when reading 1 row?

Yes.

BRIN accesses 128 table blocks even if 1 row is read. Therefore, accessing a very narrow range is slower than a b*tree index. Consider the example below.

B*tree Index

explain (costs false, analyze, buffers)

```
select * from t1 where c1=1;
                        QUERY PLAN
-----------------------------------------------------------------
 Index Scan using t1_c1_indx on t1
   Index Cond: (c1 = 1)
   Buffers: shared hit=4
 Planning time: 0.077 ms
 Execution time: 0.033 ms
```

BRIN

```
explain (costs false, analyze, buffers)
select * from t1 where c2=1;
                        QUERY PLAN
-----------------------------------------------------------------
 Bitmap Heap Scan on t1
    Recheck Cond: (c2 = 1)
(4) Rows Removed by Index Recheck: 7423
(3) Heap Blocks: lossy=128
         Buffers: shared hit=133
(2) ->  Bitmap Index Scan on t1_c2_brin
           Index Cond: (c2 = 1)
(1)         Buffers: shared hit=5
 Planning time: 0.041 ms
 Execution time: 1.236 ms
```

Explain results of BRIN are very similar to those of Bitmap Index Scan. BRIN uses Bitmap Index Scan method internally. Among the above results, let's analyze the important parts to understand the characteristics of BRIN.

(1) Buffers: shared hit=5

BRIN scans all index blocks regardless of what condition is entered.

That is, all index key values must be checked to see if the input value is between the minimum value and the maximum value. This is true even if the data is perfectly sorted. However, since all index blocks are only 5 blocks, there is no performance problem caused by index scan.

BRIN metadata

BRIN metadata is stored in index #0 block. It can be seen that one key value manages 128 blocks.

```
select * from brin_metapage_info(get_raw_page('t1_c2_brin', 0));
```

```
  magic     | version | pagesperrange | lastrevmappage
------------+---------+---------------+------------------
0xA8109CFA  |       1 |           128 |                1
```

Index key value of BRIN

BRIN stores the index key in the format {minimum, maximum}.

```
-- The first block
select itemoffset, blknum, value
from   brin_page_items(get_raw_page('t1_c2_brin',2), 't1_c2_brin')
limit  3;
 itemoffset | blknum |       value
------------+--------+-------------------
          1 |      0 | {1 .. 7424}
          2 |    128 | {7425 .. 14848}
          3 |    256 | {14849 .. 22272}

-- The last block
select itemoffset, blknum, value
from   brin_page_items(get_raw_page('t1_c2_brin', 5), 't1_c2_brin')
order  by 1 desc limit 3;
 itemoffset | blknum |         value
------------+--------+----------------------
        123 | 172288 | {9992705 .. 10000000}
        122 | 172160 | {9985281 .. 9992704}
        121 | 172032 | {9977857 .. 9985280}
```

(2) Bitmap Index Scan

BRIN uses the Bitmap Index Scan method.

(3) Heap Blocks: lossy=128

BRIN always operates in lossy mode.

As described in the bitmap index scan method, the lossy mode uses a block-level bitmap. Since BRIN stores only the minimum and maximum values without storing actual records, lossy mode is used.

(4) Rows Removed by Index Recheck: 7423

Since it uses `lossy` mode, it always needs a Recheck. The `T1` table in the example stores 58 records per block. Therefore, 7,423 rows are discarded after a recheck of 128 blocks. (58 rows * 128 blocks - 1 = 7,423 rows)

Will increasing the default value of BRIN be good for performance?

The default value of BRIN is 128 blocks (1 MiB). This value can be modified with the `pages_per_range` parameter and can be modified at the table level. As a result of my testing, it would not be desirable to increase this value. For example, assume that it increases by 10 times. In this case, the number of index keys will be reduced to 1/10, but the range to be rechecked will increase. It is also disadvantageous to the BITAND operation described later. Therefore, increasing this value does not seem to be a performance benefit.

Is BRIN faster than Index Only Scan?

No.

Index Only Scan is a method of scanning only index. However, BRIN must access the table. Therefore, BRIN is slower than Index Only Scan method. Consider the example below.

Index Only Scan

```
explain (costs false, analyze, buffers)
select count(*) from t1 where c1 between 7000001 and 10000000;
                        QUERY PLAN
--------------------------------------------------------------
 Aggregate (actual time=1280.480..1280.480 rows=1 loops=1)
   Buffers: shared hit=59925
   ->  Index Only Scan using t1_c1_indx on t1
         Index Cond: ((c1 >= 7000001) AND (c1 <= 10000000))
         Heap Fetches: 3000000
         Buffers: shared hit=59925
 Planning time: 0.096 ms
 Execution time: 1280.508 ms
```

BRIN

```
explain (costs false, analyze, buffers)
select count(*) from t1 where c2 between 7000001 and 10000000;
```

```
                          QUERY PLAN
-----------------------------------------------------------------
Aggregate (actual time=1149.551..1149.551 rows=1 loops=1)
  Buffers: shared hit=51843
  ->  Bitmap Heap Scan on t1
        Recheck Cond: ((c2 >= 7000001) AND (c2 <= 10000000))
        Rows Removed by Index Recheck: 6592
        Heap Blocks: lossy=51838
        Buffers: shared hit=51843
        ->  Bitmap Index Scan on t1_c2_brin
              Index Cond: ((c2 >= 7000001) AND (c2 <= 10000000))
              Buffers: shared hit=5
Planning time: 0.078 ms
Execution time: 1149.590 ms
```

The above results show that BRIN is slightly faster. However, the number of buffer IO of Index Only Scan is 59,925. This is larger than the index size (27,422 blocks).

We learned earlier that we need to perform Vacuum to use Index Only Scan. After Vacuum, Index Only Scan is faster than BRIN.

Index Only Scan after Vacuum

```
vacuum t1;
explain (costs false, analyze, buffers)
select count(*) from t1 where c1 between 7000001 and 10000000;
                          QUERY PLAN
-----------------------------------------------------------------
Aggregate (actual time=929.133..929.134 rows=1 loops=1)
  Buffers: shared hit=8203
  ->  Index Only Scan using t1_c1_indx on t1
        Index Cond: ((c1 >= 7000001) AND (c1 <= 10000000))
        Heap Fetches: 0
        Buffers: shared hit=8203
Planning time: 0.094 ms
Execution time: 929.160 ms
```


Is BRIN faster than Index Scan?

When all blocks are processed as memory IO, the BRIN is slightly faster.

Both the BRIN and Index Scan methods access the same table block. However, BRIN has very few IO for index blocks than b*tree index. For this reason, BRIN is slightly faster when all blocks are processed in memory IO.

However, when DISK IO occurs, there is a case that it is seriously slow.

This was a different result than I expected. Since BRIN is a method of scanning contiguous table blocks, the effect of OS Prefetch was expected to be great, but the results were different. Therefore, readers who want to use BRIN in this case should always test their environment.

Let's first check if all blocks are processed as memory IO.

B*tree index - In case of memory IO

```
explain (costs false, analyze, buffers)
select count(*) from t1 where c1 between 7000001 and 10000000 and dummy='dummy';
                        QUERY PLAN
------------------------------------------------------------------
 Aggregate (actual time=1724.788..1724.788 rows=1 loops=1)
   Buffers: shared hit=59925
   ->  Index Scan using t1_c1_indx on t1
         Index Cond: ((c1 >= 7000001) AND (c1 <= 10000000))
         Filter: (dummy = 'dummy'::bpchar)
         Buffers: shared hit=59925
 Planning time: 0.102 ms
 Execution time: 1724.814 ms
```

BRIN - In case of memory IO

```
explain (costs false, analyze, buffers)
select count(*) from t1 where c2 between 7000001 and 10000000 and dummy='dummy';
                        QUERY PLAN
------------------------------------------------------------------
 Aggregate (actual time=1614.410..1614.411 rows=1 loops=1)
   Buffers: shared hit=51843
   ->  Bitmap Heap Scan on t1
         Recheck Cond: ((c2 >= 7000001) AND (c2 <= 10000000))
         Rows Removed by Index Recheck: 6592
         Filter: (dummy = 'dummy'::bpchar)
         Heap Blocks: lossy=51838
         Buffers: shared hit=51843
         ->  Bitmap Index Scan on t1_c2_brin
               Index Cond: ((c2 >= 7000001) AND (c2 <= 10000000))
               Buffers: shared hit=5
 Planning time: 0.084 ms
 Execution time: 1614.448 ms
```

The above results show that BRIN is slightly faster. But the difference is minimal. Therefore, in this case, disk use efficiency is more important than performance improvement purpose.

B*tree index - In case of DISK IO (3 million in front)

```
explain (costs false, analyze, buffers)
select count(*) from t1 where c1 between 1 and 3000000 and dummy='dummy';
                          QUERY PLAN
--------------------------------------------------------------------
Aggregate (actual time=2517.360..2517.360 rows=1 loops=1)
  Buffers: shared hit=4 read=59920
  ->  Index Scan using t1_c1_indx on t1
          Index Cond: ((c1 >= 1) AND (c1 <= 3000000))
          Filter: (dummy = 'dummy'::bpchar)
          Buffers: shared hit=4 read=59920
Planning time: 12.158 ms
Execution time: 2518.058 ms
```

B*tree index - In case of DISK IO (3 million in back)

```
explain (costs false, analyze, buffers)
select count(*) from t1 where c1 between 7000001 and 10000000 and dummy='dummy';
                          QUERY PLAN
--------------------------------------------------------------------
Aggregate (actual time=2471.412..2471.412 rows=1 loops=1)
  Buffers: shared hit=3 read=59922
  ->  Index Scan using t1_c1_indx on t1
          Index Cond: ((c1 >= 7000001) AND (c1 <= 10000000))
          Filter: (dummy = 'dummy'::bpchar)
          Buffers: shared hit=3 read=59922
Planning time: 12.872 ms
Execution time: 2472.048 ms
```

From the above results, it can be seen that the Index Scan method is performed in approximately 2.5 seconds under any circumstance. However, the following results show that BRIN has a speed of 2.4 milliseconds to retrieve 3 million from the front, and 8.7 seconds to retrieve 3 million from the back.

What's even worse is that it's slower to search for 'one million to three million' than to search 'one to three million'. In other words, it is slower when it is inquired from the middle. I have not found the exact cause of these anomalies. Therefore, it is advisable to perform sufficient pre-tests when using BRIN in this case.

BRIN - In case of DISK IO (3 million in front)

```
explain (costs false, analyze, buffers)
select count(*) from t1 where c2 between 1 and 3000000 and dummy='dummy';
                            QUERY PLAN
------------------------------------------------------------------
 Aggregate (actual time=2388.949..2388.949 rows=1 loops=1)
   Buffers: shared hit=4 read=51848
   -> Bitmap Heap Scan on t1
         Recheck Cond: ((c2 >= 1) AND (c2 <= 3000000))
         Rows Removed by Index Recheck: 6720
         Filter: (dummy = 'dummy'::bpchar)
         Heap Blocks: lossy=51840
         Buffers: shared hit=4 read=51848
         -> Bitmap Index Scan on t1_c2_brin
               Index Cond: ((c2 >= 1) AND (c2 <= 3000000))
               Buffers: shared hit=4 read=8
 Planning time: 7.333 ms
 Execution time: 2391.453 ms
```

BRIN - In case of DISK IO (3 million in back)

```
explain (costs false, analyze, buffers)
select count(*) from t1 where c2 between 7000001 and 10000000 and dummy='dummy';
                            QUERY PLAN
------------------------------------------------------------------
 Aggregate (actual time=8730.656..8730.656 rows=1 loops=1)
   Buffers: shared hit=4 read=51846
   -> Bitmap Heap Scan on t1
         Recheck Cond: ((c2 >= 7000001) AND (c2 <= 10000000))
         Rows Removed by Index Recheck: 6592
         Filter: (dummy = 'dummy'::bpchar)
         Heap Blocks: lossy=51838
         Buffers: shared hit=4 read=51846
         -> Bitmap Index Scan on t1_c2_brin
               Index Cond: ((c2 >= 7000001) AND (c2 <= 10000000))
               Buffers: shared hit=4 read=8
 Planning time: 7.475 ms
 Execution time: 8731.884 ms
```

BRIN - In case of DISK IO (2 million in the middle)

```
explain (costs false, analyze, buffers)
select count(*) from t1 where c2 between 1000001 and 3000000 and dummy='dummy';
                            QUERY PLAN
------------------------------------------------------------------
 Aggregate (actual time=6029.354..6029.354 rows=1 loops=1)
   Buffers: shared hit=4 read=34696
   -> Bitmap Heap Scan on t1
         Recheck Cond: ((c2 >= 1000001) AND (c2 <= 3000000))
```

```
        Rows Removed by Index Recheck: 11904
        Filter: (dummy = 'dummy'::bpchar)
        Heap Blocks: lossy=34688
        Buffers: shared hit=4 read=34696
        -> Bitmap Index Scan on t1_c2_brin
                Index Cond: ((c2 >= 1000001) AND (c2 <= 3000000))
                Buffers: shared hit=4 read=8
Planning time: 8.353 ms
Execution time: 6030.610 ms
```

Will record sorting affect BRIN performance?

There is no significant effect on memory IO. However, there is a big impact on DISK IO. This is the same problem in the Index Scan method as well as the BRIN. This is because, if the table sorting status is bad, the number of table blocks to be accessed increases.

Test environment

```
drop table t2;
create table t2 (c1 integer, c2 integer, dummy char(100));

-- Insert data in an unordered form.
do $$
begin
  for i in 1..200000 loop
    for j in 0..49 loop
        insert into t2 values (i+(j*200000), i+(j*200000),'dummy');
    end loop;
  end loop;
end$$;

create index t2_c1_indx on t2 (c1);
create index t2_c2_brin on t2 using brin (c2);
analyze t2;

select relname, relpages, round(relpages*8/1024,0) "size(MiB)"
from   pg_class where relname in ('t2','t2_c1_indx','t2_c2_brin');
  relname    | relpages | size(MiB)
-------------+----------+----------
 t2          |   172414 |    1346
 t2_c1_indx  |    27422 |     214
 t2_c2_brin  |        6 |       0
```

B*tree index − In case of memory IO

Since the table sort status is bad, the optimizer chooses the Bitmap Index Scan method. However, since the sorting status is bad, the number of block accesses increases as compared to when the sorting status is good. (when sorting status is good: 59,925 blocks) This is slower than when sorting is status good. (when sorting status is good: 1.72 sec)

```
explain (costs false, analyze, buffers)
select count(*) from t2 where c1 between 7000001 and 10000000 and dummy='dummy';
                              QUERY PLAN
-----------------------------------------------------------------------
Aggregate (actual time=2913.683..2913.684 rows=1 loops=1)
  Buffers: shared hit=180614
  ->  Bitmap Heap Scan on t2
        Recheck Cond: ((c1 >= 7000001) AND (c1 <= 10000000))
        Rows Removed by Index Recheck: 5346698
        Filter: (dummy = 'dummy'::bpchar)
        Heap Blocks: exact=40724 lossy=131690
        Buffers: shared hit=180614
        ->  Bitmap Index Scan on t2_c1_indx
              Index Cond: ((c1 >= 7000001) AND (c1 <= 10000000))
              Buffers: shared hit=8200
Planning time: 0.161 ms
Execution time: 2913.718 ms
```

BRIN – In case of memory IO

BRIN has also increased the number of IO. (when sorting status is good: 51,843 blocks) This is slower than when sorting status is good (when sorting status is good: 1.61 sec)

```
explain (costs false, analyze, buffers)
select count(*) from t2 where c2 between 7000001 and 10000000 and dummy='dummy';
                              QUERY PLAN
-----------------------------------------------------------------------
Aggregate (actual time=2711.648..2711.648 rows=1 loops=1)
  Buffers: shared hit=172419
  ->  Bitmap Heap Scan on t2
        Recheck Cond: ((c2 >= 7000001) AND (c2 <= 10000000))
        Rows Removed by Index Recheck: 7000000
        Filter: (dummy = 'dummy'::bpchar)
        Heap Blocks: lossy=172414
        Buffers: shared hit=172419
        ->  Bitmap Index Scan on t2_c2_brin
              Index Cond: ((c2 >= 7000001) AND (c2 <= 10000000))
              Buffers: shared hit=5
Planning time: 0.092 ms
Execution time: 2711.682 ms
```

B*tree index – In case of DISK IO (3 million in front)

The results below show a significant performance degradation compared to sorting status is good. (when sorting status is good: 59,920 blocks, 2.52 sec)

```
explain (costs false, analyze, buffers)
select count(*) from t2 where c1 between 1 and 3000000 and dummy='dummy';
                        QUERY PLAN
------------------------------------------------------------------
 Aggregate (actual time=11474.854..11474.854 rows=1 loops=1)
   Buffers: shared hit=4 read=180609
   -> Bitmap Heap Scan on t2
         Recheck Cond: ((c1 >= 1) AND (c1 <= 3000000))
         Rows Removed by Index Recheck: 5346766
         Filter: (dummy = 'dummy'::bpchar)
         Heap Blocks: exact=40724 lossy=131690
         Buffers: shared hit=4 read=180609
         -> Bitmap Index Scan on t2_c1_indx
               Index Cond: ((c1 >= 1) AND (c1 <= 3000000))
               Buffers: shared hit=3 read=8196
 Planning time: 9.383 ms
 Execution time: 11475.983 ms
```

BRIN – In case of DISK IO (3 million in front)

BRIN also has serious performance degradation when sorting status is bad, like B*tree index.

(when sorting status is good: 51,848 blocks, 2.39 sec)

```
explain (costs false, analyze, buffers)
select count(*) from t2 where c2 between 1 and 3000000 and dummy='dummy';
                        QUERY PLAN
------------------------------------------------------------------
 Aggregate (actual time=12496.175..12496.175 rows=1 loops=1)
   Buffers: shared hit=4 read=172422
   -> Bitmap Heap Scan on t2
         Recheck Cond: ((c2 >= 1) AND (c2 <= 3000000))
         Rows Removed by Index Recheck: 7000000
         Filter: (dummy = 'dummy'::bpchar)
         Heap Blocks: lossy=172414
         Buffers: shared hit=4 read=172422
         -> Bitmap Index Scan on t2_c2_brin
               Index Cond: ((c2 >= 1) AND (c2 <= 3000000))
               Buffers: shared hit=4 read=8
 Planning time: 9.259 ms
 Execution time: 12498.610 ms
```

Summary of results

Let's summarize the test results in a table. Table 5-1 shows that BRIN is slightly faster at memory IO. However, according to Table 5-2, BRIN is always slow when DISK IO occurs. Because the test case caused 100% DISK IO, the test result may be different depending on the ratio of DISK IO.

Table 5-1. *Index Scan vs. BRIN in case of memory IO*

Item	Sorting status is good	Sorting status is bad
Index Scan	1.7 sec	2.9 sec
BRIN	1.6 sec	2.7 sec

Table 5-2. *Index Scan vs. BRIN in case of DISK IO*

Item	Sorting status is good	Sorting status is bad
Index Scan	Within 2.5 sec	11.5 sec
BRIN	2.4~8.7 sec	12.5 sec

How will the records that are inserted after the creation of the BRIN be accessed?

Read all new blocks until Vacuum is performed. This is because it is necessary to perform a Vacuum to update the BRIN. Consider the example below.

Insert 5 million rows

```
insert into t1 select i, i, 'dummy' from generate_series(10010001,15000000) a(i);
```

Access 1,000 rows from new insert records

From the results below, it can be seen that buffer access is 86,210 times even when only 1,000 of 5 million new entries are read.

```
explain (costs false, analyze, buffers)
select count(*) from t1 where c2 between 14999001 and 15000000;
                       QUERY PLAN
-------------------------------------------------------------------
 Aggregate (actual time=655.187..655.187 rows=1 loops=1)
   Buffers: shared hit=86210
   -> Bitmap Heap Scan on t1
        Recheck Cond: ((c2 >= 14999001) AND (c2 <= 15000000))
        Rows Removed by Index Recheck: 4998872
```

```
            Heap Blocks: lossy=86205
            Buffers: shared hit=86210
            ->  Bitmap Index Scan on t1_c2_brin
                  Index Cond: ((c2 >= 14999001) AND (c2 <= 15000000))
                  Buffers: shared hit=5
 Planning time: 0.066 ms
 Execution time: 655.224 ms
```

Results after Vacuum

`Vacuum` will update the BRIN. This reduces the number of buffer accesses and speeds up the execution.

```
vacuum t1;
explain (costs false, analyze, buffers)
select count(*) from t1 where c2 between 14999001 and 15000000;
                        QUERY PLAN
-----------------------------------------------------------------
 Aggregate (actual time=1.454..1.454 rows=1 loops=1)
   Buffers: shared hit=70
   ->  Bitmap Heap Scan on t1
         Recheck Cond: ((c2 >= 14999001) AND (c2 <= 15000000))
         Rows Removed by Index Recheck: 2520
         Heap Blocks: lossy=61
         Buffers: shared hit=70
         ->  Bitmap Index Scan on t1_c2_brin
                  Index Cond: ((c2 >= 14999001) AND (c2 <= 15000000))
                  Buffers: shared hit=9
 Planning time: 0.071 ms
 Execution time: 1.490 ms
```

Will BRIN use low-level lock?

Use low-level lock. Consider the example below.

Test environment

Insert only 1,000 for testing. From the results below, we can see that all records are managed by one key.

```
drop table t3;
create table t3 (c1 integer, dummy char(100));

insert into t3 select generate_series(1,1000), 'dummy';
create index t3_c1_brin on t3 using brin (c1);
```

```
analyze t3;

select itemoffset,blknum,value
from   brin_page_items(get_raw_page('t3_c1_brin',2), 't3_c1_brin');
 itemoffset | blknum |    value
------------+--------+--------------
          1 |      0 | {1 .. 1000}
```

Session #1: Delete 1 row

```
postgres=# \set AUTOCOMMIT off
postgres=# delete from t3 where c1=1;
DELETE 1
```

Session #2: Delete another record

The record is deleted.

```
postgres=# delete from t3 where c1=2;
DELETE 1
```

📄 **Note** As of 9.5, autocommit can't be controlled as a parameter. To control autocommit, you need to use psql's set clause.

Can large table be effectively accessed using the BITAND operation?

Yes. If the table is well sorted, very dramatic tuning is possible. This is my main focus. Taking advantage of this feature will dramatically improve the performance of DW query queries. Consider the example below.

Test environment

If you type below, NDV for all columns except the `amount` column is very small and is generated in an even distribution.

```
drop table fact_t;
create table fact_t (
  age integer,              -- 20,30,40,50,60,70  (NDV=6)
  gender char(1),           -- M, F (NDV=2)
  blood_type char(2),       -- A,B,O,AB  (NDV=4)
  region integer,           -- 1,2,3,4,5,6,7,8  (NDV=8)
```

```
    amount   integer                  -- Insert random number
);

do $$
begin
  for i in 1..130000 loop
    for j in 2..7 loop -- age
      for k in 1..2 loop -- gender
        for l in 1..4 loop -- blood_type
          for m in 1..8 loop -- region
              insert into fact_t
            select j*10,
                    case when mod(k,2)=0 then 'M'
                         when mod(k,2)=1 then 'F'
                    end,
                    case when mod(l,4)=0 then 'A'
                         when mod(l,4)=1 then 'B'
                         when mod(l,4)=2 then 'O'
                         when mod(l,4)=3 then 'AB'
                    end,
                    m,
                    cast(random()*1000000 as integer);
          end loop;
        end loop;
      end loop;
    end loop;
  end loop;
end$$;
```

Create BRIN index

Due to the nature of BRIN, the index size is only 10 blocks

```
create index fact_t_age_brin on fact_t using brin (age);
create index fact_t_gender_brin on fact_t using brin (gender);
create index fact_t_blood_brin on fact_t using brin (blood_type);
create index fact_t_region_brin on fact_t using brin (region);
analyze fact_t;

select relname, relpages, round(relpages*8/1024,0) "size(MiB)"
from   pg_class where relname like 'fact_t%';
      relname         | relpages | size(MiB)
----------------------+----------+----------
 fact_t               |   317962 |     2484
 fact_t_age_brin      |       10 |        0
 fact_t_blood_brin    |       10 |        0
 fact_t_gender_brin   |       10 |        0
 fact_t_region_brin   |       10 |        0
```

Results before sorting

The following query extracts 130,000 out of about 50 million rows. It is very slow because the sorting status is bad. It takes about 29 seconds because of the large amount of IO. The BITAND operation was performed on only two columns. Let's test again after sorting.

```
explain (costs false, analyze, buffers)
select age, gender, blood_type, region, count(*), sum(amount)
from    fact_t
where   age=30
and     gender='F'
and     blood_type='AB'
and     region=2
group by age, gender, blood_type, region;
                        QUERY PLAN
-----------------------------------------------------------------
 GroupAggregate (actual time=28864.160..28864.161 rows=1 loops=1)
   Group Key: age, gender, blood_type, region
   Buffers: shared hit=148466 read=169518
   -> Bitmap Heap Scan on fact_t
         Recheck Cond: ((region = 2) AND (age = 30))
         Rows Removed by Index Recheck: 48880000
         Filter: ((gender = 'F'::bpchar) AND (blood_type = 'AB'...)))
         Rows Removed by Filter: 910000
         Heap Blocks: lossy=317962
         Buffers: shared hit=148466 read=169518
         -> BitmapAnd (actual time=62.383..62.383 rows=0 loops=1)
               Buffers: shared hit=22
               -> Bitmap Index Scan on fact_t_region_brin
                     Index Cond: (region = 2)
                     Buffers: shared hit=11
               -> Bitmap Index Scan on fact_t_age_brin
                     Index Cond: (age = 30)
                     Buffers: shared hit=11
 Planning time: 0.123 ms
 Execution time: 28864.202 ms
```

Table sorting

```
create table fact_t2
as select * from fact_t order by age, gender, blood_type, region;

create index fact_t2_age_brin    on fact_t2 using brin (age);
create index fact_t2_gender_brin on fact_t2 using brin (gender);
create index fact_t2_blood_brin  on fact_t2 using brin (blood_type);
create index fact_t2_region_brin on fact_t2 using brin (region);
```

Test after sorting

Test results after sorting are very dramatic. As we sorted the data, the BITAND operation was very efficient and the number of IO dropped sharply. Since the execution speed is less than 1 second, it is 28 times faster than before. And the number of columns participating in BITAND operation increased to three. It would be better to involve the age column in the BITAND operation rather than the gender column. Let's test it again with a few modifications to the query.

```
explain (costs false, analyze, buffers)
select  age, gender, blood_type, region, count(*), sum(amount)
from    fact_t2
where   age=30
and     gender='F'
and     blood_type='O'
and     region=3
group by age, gender, blood_type, region;
                          QUERY PLAN
-----------------------------------------------------------------------
 GroupAggregate (actual time=945.178..945.179 rows=1 loops=1)
   Group Key: age, gender, blood_type, region
   Buffers: shared hit=2465 read=5120
   -> Bitmap Heap Scan on fact_t2
         Recheck Cond: ((region=3) AND (blood_type='O') AND (gender='F')
         Rows Removed by Index Recheck: 405664
         Filter: (age = 30)
         Rows Removed by Filter: 650000
         Heap Blocks: lossy=7552
         Buffers: shared hit=2465 read=5120
         -> BitmapAnd (actual time=27.185..27.185 rows=0 loops=1)
               Buffers: shared hit=33
               -> Bitmap Index Scan on fact_t2_region_brin
                     Index Cond: (region = 3)
                     Buffers: shared hit=11
               -> Bitmap Index Scan on fact_t2_blood_brin
                     Index Cond: (blood_type = 'O'::bpchar)
                     Buffers: shared hit=11
               -> Bitmap Index Scan on fact_t2_gender_brin
                     Index Cond: (gender = 'F'::bpchar)
                     Buffers: shared hit=11
 Planning time: 0.136 ms
 Execution time: 945.231 ms
```

Using Age column instead of Gender in BITAND operation

If you disable the index by trimming the `gender` column, the `age` column participates in the BITAND operation. This way, performance is better than before.

```
explain (costs false, analyze, buffers)
select age, gender, blood_type, region, count(*), sum(amount)
from   fact_t2
where  age=30
and    trim(gender)='F'
and    blood_type='O'
and    region=3
group by age, gender, blood_type, region;
                        QUERY PLAN
-----------------------------------------------------------------
 GroupAggregate (actual time=279.397..279.397 rows=1 loops=1)
   Group Key: age, gender, blood_type, region
   Buffers: shared hit=2465, temp read=477 written=477
   -> Sort (actual time=217.052..239.543 rows=130000 loops=1)
         Sort Key: gender
         Sort Method: external sort  Disk: 3816kB
         Buffers: shared hit=2465, temp read=477 written=477
      -> Bitmap Heap Scan on fact_t2
            Recheck Cond: ((region = 3) AND (blood_type = 'O')
                                          AND (age = 30))
            Rows Removed by Index Recheck: 121824
            Filter: (btrim((gender)::text) = 'F'::text)
            Rows Removed by Filter: 130000
            Heap Blocks: lossy=2432
            Buffers: shared hit=2465
            -> BitmapAnd (actual time=23.977..23.977 rows=0 loops=1)
                  Buffers: shared hit=33
                  -> Bitmap Index Scan on fact_t2_region_brin
                        Index Cond: (region = 3)
                        Buffers: shared hit=11
                  -> Bitmap Index Scan on fact_t2_blood_brin
                        Index Cond: (blood_type = 'O'::bpchar)
                        Buffers: shared hit=11
                  -> Bitmap Index Scan on fact_t2_age_brin
                        Index Cond: (age = 30)
                        Buffers: shared hit=11
 Planning time: 0.118 ms
 Execution time: 280.743 ms
```

Can I get a partition-like effect with BRIN?

Yes. This is also a dramatic improvement in performance using BRIN. Consider the example below.

Test environment

Insert 1 million rows per day, and 100,000 rows per day by CODE.

```
drop table sales_t;
create table sales_t
(
  seqno    SERIAL,
  logdate  date,
  code     integer,
  amount   integer,
  dummy    char(10)
);

do $$
begin
  for i in 0..30 loop -- logdate
    for j in 1..10 loop   -- code
      for k in 1..100000 loop -- loop
        insert into sales_t(logdate,code,amount,dummy) values
(to_date('20170101','YYYYMMDD')+i, j, random()*10000000::integer,'dummy');
      end loop;
    end loop;
  end loop;
end$$;
```

Create BRIN index

```
create index sales_t_brin_logdate on sales_t using brin (logdate);
create index sales_t_brin_code    on sales_t using brin (code);

analyze sales_t;

select relname, relpages, round(relpages*8/1024,0) "size(MiB)"
from   pg_class where relname like 'sales_t%';
      relname         | relpages | size(MiB)
----------------------+----------+----------
 sales_t              |  227942  |   1780
 sales_t_brin_code    |       8  |      0
 sales_t_brin_logdate |       8  |      0
 sales_t_seqno_seq    |       1  |      0
```

BETWEEN condition

The BETWEEN condition is not performed with the BITAND operation. This process took 3.1 seconds. Let's test it by changing it to the IN clause.

```
explain (costs false, analyze, buffers)
select logdate, code, count(*), sum(amount)
from    sales_t
where   logdate BETWEEN to_date('20170101','YYYYMMDD')
                   AND to_date('20170107','YYYYMMDD')
and     code=2
group by logdate, code;
                        QUERY PLAN
-----------------------------------------------------------------
 HashAggregate (actual time=3113.039..3113.041 rows=7 loops=1)
   Group Key: logdate, code
   Buffers: shared hit=30613
   -> Bitmap Heap Scan on sales_t
        Recheck Cond: (code = 2)
        Rows Removed by Index Recheck: 1060512
        Filter: ((logdate >= to_date('20170101', 'YYYYMMDD'::text.)
        Rows Removed by Filter: 2400000
        Heap Blocks: lossy=30592
        Buffers: shared hit=30613
        -> Bitmap Index Scan on sales_t_brin_code
             Index Cond: (code = 2)
             Buffers: shared hit=21
 Planning time: 2.425 ms
 Execution time: 3113.113 ms
```

IN condition

After changing to IN clause, it is performed by BITAND operation. As a result, the execution speed is 0.5 seconds.

```
explain (costs false, analyze, buffers)
select logdate, code, count(*), sum(amount)
from    sales_t
where   logdate IN
('20170101','20170102','20170103','20170104','20170105','20170106','20170107')
and     code=2
group by logdate, code;
                        QUERY PLAN
-----------------------------------------------------------------
 HashAggregate (actual time=499.396..499.398 rows=7 loops=1)
   Group Key: logdate, code
   Buffers: shared hit=6984
   -> Bitmap Heap Scan on sales_t
        Recheck Cond:
        Rows Removed by Index Recheck: 240032
        Heap Blocks: lossy=6912
        Buffers: shared hit=6984
        -> BitmapAnd (actual time=9.970..9.970 rows=0 loops=1)
```

```
                 Buffers: shared hit=72
           ->  Bitmap Index Scan on sales_t_brin_code
                     Index Cond: (code = 2)
                     Buffers: shared hit=9
           ->  Bitmap Index Scan on sales_t_brin_logdate
                     Index Cond: (logdate = ANY ('{2017-01-01,..)
                     Buffers: shared hit=63
Planning time: 3.230 ms
Execution time: 499.464 ms
```

Equal Condition

If you enter a specific date and code as an equal condition, it will be executed within 0.1 second.

```
explain (costs false, analyze, buffers)
select logdate, code, count(*), sum(amount)
from    sales_t
where   logdate='20170101'
and     code=2
group by logdate, code;
                            QUERY PLAN
----------------------------------------------------------------
GroupAggregate (actual time=76.044..76.044 rows=1 loops=1)
  Group Key: logdate, code
  Buffers: shared hit=1042
  ->  Bitmap Heap Scan on sales_t
         Recheck Cond: ((logdate = '2017-01-01'::date) AND (code = 2))
         Rows Removed by Index Recheck: 39264
         Heap Blocks: lossy=1024
         Buffers: shared hit=1042
         ->  BitmapAnd (actual time=3.402..3.402 rows=0 loops=1)
                Buffers: shared hit=18
                ->  Bitmap Index Scan on sales_t_brin_logdate
                       Index Cond: (logdate = '2017-01-01'::date)
                       Buffers: shared hit=9
                ->  Bitmap Index Scan on sales_t_brin_code
                       Index Cond: (code = 2)
                       Buffers: shared hit=9
Planning time: 0.073 ms
Execution time: 76.080 ms
```

Summary

In this chapter, we have learned about Partial Indexes and BRIN.

Partial indexes are very useful when processing skewed data.

BRIN is a new indexing technique provided in 9.5. We were able to clearly identify the nature and strengths and weaknesses of BRIN through a variety of questions related to BRIN.

chapter **6**.

Understanding Partition

Understanding Partition

In this chapter, we will explain the basics of partition and some tips for tuning.

Partition Basic

Create partition

PostgreSQL creates partition using inheritance. Let's look at the picture below.

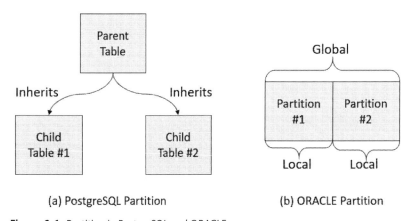

(a) PostgreSQL Partition   (b) ORACLE Partition

Figure 6-1. *Partition in PostgreSQL and ORACLE*

ORACLE has multiple partitions in a table. In other words, a table is a combination of several partitions. At this time, the partition level is called LOCAL and the table level is called GLOBAL. In PostgreSQL, after creating the parent table, it creates the child table by inheriting the properties of the parent table. Therefore, the parent table and the child table are separate tables.

PostgreSQL implements partitions through inheritance, which makes it very important that each partition can be managed at an independent table level. With this in mind, please read the following explanation.

Partition Pruning

Accessing only partitions corresponding to the input conditions is called 'partition pruning'. To do this, you must set the `constraint_exclusion` parameter to `'on'` or `'partition'`. The difference between `'on'` and `'partition'` is as follows.

- `partition`: Check only the CHECK condition of the partition table

- on: Check the CHECK condition of all tables

Partition Type and Pruning Test

Let's look at how to create a Range partition, a List partition, a hash partition, and a sub partition, as well as partition pruning for each partition.

Range Partition

By using CHECK condition when creating partitions, you can create Range and List partitions. You can use the modular operator to create a hash partition.

Let's first look at the Range partition.

Test environment

Create a parent table.

```
create table range_p1
(
    c1       integer,
    logdate  date,
    dummy    char(100)
```

```
);
```

Create partition table. At this time, the range is specified by the CHECK condition, and the parent table to be inherited is specified.

```
create table range_p1_y201701
(CHECK( logdate >= DATE '2017-01-01' AND logdate < DATE '2017-02-01' )) INHERITS
(range_p1);

create table range_p1_y201702
(CHECK( logdate >= DATE '2017-02-01' AND logdate < DATE '2017-03-01' )) INHERITS
(range_p1);

create table range_p1_y201703
(CHECK( logdate >= DATE '2017-03-01' AND logdate < DATE '2017-04-01' )) INHERITS
(range_p1);

create table range_p1_y201704
(CHECK( logdate >= DATE '2017-04-01' AND logdate < DATE '2017-05-01' )) INHERITS
(range_p1);
```

Create trigger and function for insert. This is a disadvantage of PostgreSQL partitions. Use of a trigger (or RULE) at input will reduce insert performance. Therefore, if the input target partition is known, it is preferable to directly input it into the corresponding partition table.

```
CREATE OR REPLACE FUNCTION range_p1_insert_func()
RETURNS TRIGGER AS $$
BEGIN
IF    (NEW.logdate >= DATE '2017-01-01' AND NEW.logdate < DATE '2017-02-01')
THEN INSERT INTO range_p1_y201701 VALUES (NEW.*);
ELSIF (NEW.logdate >= DATE '2017-02-01' AND NEW.logdate < DATE '2017-03-01')
THEN INSERT INTO range_p1_y201702 VALUES (NEW.*);
ELSIF (NEW.logdate >= DATE '2017-03-01' AND NEW.logdate < DATE '2017-04-01')
THEN INSERT INTO range_p1_y201703 VALUES (NEW.*);
ELSIF (NEW.logdate >= DATE '2017-04-01' AND NEW.logdate < DATE '2017-05-01')
THEN INSERT INTO range_p1_y201704 VALUES (NEW.*);
ELSE  RAISE EXCEPTION 'Out of range!';
END IF;
RETURN NULL;
END;
$$
LANGUAGE plpgsql;

-- Create an INSERT trigger
CREATE TRIGGER range_p1_insert_trig
    BEFORE INSERT ON range_p1
    FOR EACH ROW EXECUTE PROCEDURE range_p1_insert_func();
```

The partition of PostgreSQL 10

PostgreSQL 10, which is expected to be released later this year, will use ORACLE-like table partitioning techniques. See the link below.

https://www.depesz.com/2017/02/06/waiting-for-postgresql-10-implement-table-partitioning/

Insert a total of 1.2 million, 10,000 per day.

```
do $$
begin
  for i in 1..120 loop
    for j in 1..10000 loop
      insert into range_p1 values
          (j+(10000*(i-1)), to_date('20170101','YYYYMMDD')+i-1, 'dummy');
    end loop;
  end loop;
end$$;
```

Analyze by partition. As mentioned earlier, partitions are independent tables. Therefore, tasks such as `Analyze` and `Vacuum` should be performed separately for each partition.

```
analyze range_p1_y201701;
analyze range_p1_y201702;
analyze range_p1_y201703;
analyze range_p1_y201704;

select relname, relpages, reltuples
from   pg_class where relname like 'range_p1%';
     relname        | relpages | reltuples
--------------------+----------+-----------
 range_p1           |        0 |         0
 range_p1_y201701   |     5345 |    310000
 range_p1_y201702   |     4828 |    280000
 range_p1_y201703   |     5345 |    310000
 range_p1_y201704   |     5173 |    300000
```

Partition pruning test

```
show constraint_exclusion;
 constraint_exclusion
----------------------
 partition

explain (costs false)
```

```
select sum(c1), min(c1), max(c1)
from    range_p1
where   logdate = to_date('20170212','YYYYMMDDD');
                        QUERY PLAN
--------------------------------------------------------------------
Aggregate
  -> Append
        ->  Seq Scan on range_p1
              Filter: ((logdate >= to_date('20170101', 'YYYYMMDD'))
                  AND (logdate <= to_date('20170131', 'YYYYMMDD')))
        ->  Seq Scan on range_p1_y201701
              Filter: ((logdate >= to_date('20170101', 'YYYYMMDD'))
                  AND (logdate <= to_date('20170131', 'YYYYMMDD')))
        ->  Seq Scan on range_p1_y201702
              Filter: ((logdate >= to_date('20170101', 'YYYYMMDD'))
                  AND (logdate <= to_date('20170131', 'YYYYMMDD')))
        ->  Seq Scan on range_p1_y201703
              Filter: ((logdate >= to_date('20170101', 'YYYYMMDD'))
                  AND (logdate <= to_date('20170131', 'YYYYMMDD')))
        ->  Seq Scan on range_p1_y201704
              Filter: ((logdate >= to_date('20170101', 'YYYYMMDD'))
                  AND (logdate <= to_date('20170131', 'YYYYMMDD')))
```

In the above results, we entered a constant condition in the partition key column, logdate, but notice that the partition pruning does not work. Why is this? This is a problem caused by the difference between the constants and the CHECK conditions. That is, if a constant condition is input in the same form as the CHECK condition as shown below, only the P1_Y201702 partition table is accessed.

```
explain (costs false)
select sum(c1), min(c1), max(c1)
from    range_p1
where   logdate = DATE '20170212';
                    QUERY PLAN
----------------------------------------------------
Aggregate
  -> Append
        ->  Seq Scan on range_p1
              Filter: (logdate = '2017-02-12'::date)
        ->  Seq Scan on range_p1_y201702
              Filter: (logdate = '2017-02-12'::date)
```

List partition

List partition are also created using CHECK conditions. Consider the example below.

Test environment

Create a parent table.

```
create table list_p1
(
    c1        integer,
    code      integer,
    dummy     char(100)
);
```

Create partition table. At this time, list items are specified by CHECK condition.

```
create table list_p1_code1 (CHECK( code = 1)) INHERITS (list_p1);
create table list_p1_code2 (CHECK( code = 2)) INHERITS (list_p1);
create table list_p1_code3 (CHECK( code = 3)) INHERITS (list_p1);
create table list_p1_code4 (CHECK( code = 4)) INHERITS (list_p1);
```

Create trigger and function for insert.

```
CREATE OR REPLACE FUNCTION list_p1_insert_func()
RETURNS TRIGGER AS $$
BEGIN
    IF    ( NEW.code = 1 ) THEN INSERT INTO list_p1_code1 VALUES (NEW.*);
    ELSIF ( NEW.code = 2 ) THEN INSERT INTO list_p1_code2 VALUES (NEW.*);
    ELSIF ( NEW.code = 3 ) THEN INSERT INTO list_p1_code3 VALUES (NEW.*);
    ELSIF ( NEW.code = 4 ) THEN INSERT INTO list_p1_code4 VALUES (NEW.*);
    ELSE
        RAISE EXCEPTION 'Out of range!';
    END IF;
    RETURN NULL;
END;
$$
LANGUAGE plpgsql;

-- -- Create Insert Trigger
CREATE TRIGGER list_p1_insert_trig
    BEFORE INSERT ON list_p1
    FOR EACH ROW EXECUTE PROCEDURE list_p1_insert_func();
```

Insert 300,000 by CODE.

```
do $$
begin
  for i in 1..4 loop
    for j in 1..300000 loop
        insert into list_p1 values (j, i, 'dummy');
    end loop;
```

```
  end loop;
end$$;
```

Analyze by partition.

```
analyze list_p1_code1;
analyze list_p1_code2;
analyze list_p1_code3;
analyze list_p1_code4;

select relname, relpages, reltuples
from   pg_class where relname like 'list_p1%';
    relname      | relpages | reltuples
----------------+----------+-----------
 list_p1         |        0 |         0
 list_p1_code1   |     5173 |    300000
 list_p1_code2   |     5173 |    300000
 list_p1_code3   |     5173 |    300000
 list_p1_code4   |     5173 |    300000
```

Partition pruning test

```
show constraint_exclusion;
 constraint_exclusion
----------------------
 partition

explain (costs false)
select sum(c1), min(c1), max(c1)
from   list_p1
where  code=2;
             QUERY PLAN
--------------------------------------
 Aggregate
   ->  Append
         ->  Seq Scan on list_p1
               Filter: (code = 2)
         ->  Seq Scan on list_p1_code2
               Filter: (code = 2)
```

From the above results, we can see that partition pruning works well for the List partition.

Hash partition

PostgreSQL does not support hash partition syntax. However, since it is a partitioning method by CHECK condition, it is possible to create a hash partition by using the modular operator. Consider the example below.

Test environment

Create a parent table.

```
create table hash_p1
(
    c1      integer,
    code    integer,
    dummy   char(100)
);
```

Create partition table. At this time, the modular operator is used in the CHECK condition.

```
create table hash_p1_code1 (CHECK( code % 4 = 1)) INHERITS (hash_p1);
create table hash_p1_code2 (CHECK( code % 4 = 2)) INHERITS (hash_p1);
create table hash_p1_code3 (CHECK( code % 4 = 3)) INHERITS (hash_p1);
create table hash_p1_code4 (CHECK( code % 4 = 0)) INHERITS (hash_p1);
```

Create trigger and function for insert.

```
CREATE OR REPLACE FUNCTION hash_p1_insert_func()
RETURNS TRIGGER AS $$
BEGIN
    IF    ( NEW.code % 4 = 1 ) THEN INSERT INTO hash_p1_code1 VALUES (NEW.*);
    ELSIF ( NEW.code % 4 = 2 ) THEN INSERT INTO hash_p1_code2 VALUES (NEW.*);
    ELSIF ( NEW.code % 4 = 3 ) THEN INSERT INTO hash_p1_code3 VALUES (NEW.*);
    ELSIF ( NEW.code % 4 = 0 ) THEN INSERT INTO hash_p1_code4 VALUES (NEW.*);
    ELSE
        RAISE EXCEPTION 'Code out of range!';
    END IF;
    RETURN NULL;
END;
$$
LANGUAGE plpgsql;

-- Create Insert Trigger
CREATE TRIGGER hash_p1_insert_trig
    BEFORE INSERT ON hash_p1
    FOR EACH ROW EXECUTE PROCEDURE hash_p1_insert_func();
```

Insert a total of 1.2 million.

```
do $$
begin
  for i in 1..1200000 loop
      insert into hash_p1 values (i, i, 'dummy');
  end loop;
end$$;
```

Analyze by partition.

```
analyze hash_p1_code1;
analyze hash_p1_code2;
analyze hash_p1_code3;
analyze hash_p1_code4;

select relname, relpages, reltuples
from   pg_class where relname like 'hash_p1%';
    relname     | relpages | reltuples
----------------+----------+-----------
 hash_p1        |        0 |         0
 hash_p1_code1  |     5173 |    300000
 hash_p1_code2  |     5173 |    300000
 hash_p1_code3  |     5173 |    300000
 hash_p1_code4  |     5173 |    300000
```

Partition pruning test

```
show constraint_exclusion;
 constraint_exclusion
----------------------
 partition

explain (costs false)
select sum(c1), min(c1), max(c1)
from   hash_p1
where  code = 100;
            QUERY PLAN
-----------------------------------------
 Aggregate
   ->  Append
         ->  Seq Scan on hash_p1
               Filter: (code = 100)
         ->  Seq Scan on hash_p1_code1
               Filter: (code = 100)
         ->  Seq Scan on hash_p1_code2
               Filter: (code = 100)
         ->  Seq Scan on hash_p1_code3
               Filter: (code = 100)
         ->  Seq Scan on hash_p1_code4
```

```
              Filter: (code = 100)
```

From the above results, you can see that partition pruning does not work even though the value is entered in the code column. This is because the CHECK condition is not input. Therefore, if you add the CHECK condition as shown below, partition pruning will work.

```
explain (costs false)
select  sum(c1), min(c1), max(c1)
from    hash_p1
where   code = 100
and     (code % 4) = (100 % 4);
                        QUERY PLAN
-----------------------------------------------------------------
 Aggregate
   -> Append
         -> Seq Scan on hash_p1
               Filter: ((code = 100) AND ((code % 4) = 0))
         -> Seq Scan on hash_p1_code4
               Filter: ((code = 100) AND ((code % 4) = 0))
```

Subpartition

When considering partitions for performance reasons, whether subpartitioning is supported is very important. This is because it is sometimes necessary to divide the primary partition by date, divide the secondary partition by CODE in the date, divide the primary partition by date, and divide the secondary partition into hash partitions. PostgreSQL uses inheritance to create partitions, so this can be done very easily. Consider the example below.

Test environment

Create a parent table.

```
create table mp1
(
    c1         integer,
    logdate    date,
    code       integer,
    dummy      char(100)
);
```

Create partition table. At this time, enter the date as the primary CHECK condition, and set the parent table to mp1.

```
create table mp1_y201701
(CHECK ( logdate >= DATE '2017-01-01' AND logdate < DATE '2017-02-01' )) INHERITS (mp1);
create table mp1_y201702
(CHECK ( logdate >= DATE '2017-02-01' AND logdate < DATE '2017-03-01' )) INHERITS (mp1);
```

Create a subpartition table. At this time, the CODE value is input for the CHECK condition, and the parent table to be inherited is set to mp1_y201701 and mp1_y201702, respectively.

```
-- Create subpartition table
create table mp1_y201701_code1 (CHECK(code = 1)) INHERITS (mp1_y201701);
create table mp1_y201701_code2 (CHECK(code = 2)) INHERITS (mp1_y201701);

-- Create subpartition table
create table mp1_y201702_code1 (CHECK(code = 1)) INHERITS (mp1_y201702);
create table mp1_y201702_code2 (CHECK(code = 2)) INHERITS (mp1_y201702);
```

Create trigger and function for input.

```
CREATE OR REPLACE FUNCTION mp1_insert_func()
RETURNS TRIGGER AS $$
BEGIN
    IF      ( NEW.logdate >= DATE '2017-01-01' AND
              NEW.logdate <   DATE '2017-02-01')
              AND ( NEW.code=1 )
              THEN INSERT INTO mp1_y201701_code1 VALUES (NEW.*);
    ELSIF ( NEW.logdate >= DATE '2017-01-01' AND
              NEW.logdate <   DATE '2017-02-01')
              AND ( NEW.code=2 )
              THEN INSERT INTO mp1_y201701_code2 VALUES (NEW.*);
    ELSIF ( NEW.logdate >= DATE '2017-02-01' AND
              NEW.logdate <   DATE '2017-03-01')
              AND ( NEW.code=1 )
              THEN INSERT INTO mp1_y201702_code1 VALUES (NEW.*);
    ELSIF ( NEW.logdate >= DATE '2017-02-01' AND
              NEW.logdate <   DATE '2017-03-01')
              AND ( NEW.code=2 )
              THEN INSERT INTO mp1_y201702_code2 VALUES (NEW.*);
    ELSE
        RAISE EXCEPTION 'Out of range!';
    END IF;
    RETURN NULL;
END;
$$
LANGUAGE plpgsql;

-- Create Insert Trigger
CREATE TRIGGER mp1_insert_trig
    BEFORE INSERT ON mp1
    FOR EACH ROW EXECUTE PROCEDURE mp1_insert_func();
```

Insert 10,000 per day, per code.

```
do $$
begin
  for i in 1..59 loop
    for j in 1..2 loop
      for k in 1..10000 loop
          insert into mp1
          values (k, to_date('20170101','YYYYMMDD')+i-1, j, 'dummy');
      end loop;
    end loop;
  end loop;
end$$;
```

Analyze by partition.

```
analyze mp1_y201701_code1;
analyze mp1_y201701_code2;
analyze mp1_y201702_code1;
analyze mp1_y201702_code2;

select relname, relpages, reltuples
from   pg_class where relname like 'mp1%';
      relname         | relpages | reltuples
----------------------+----------+-----------
 mp1                  |        0 |         0
 mp1_y201701          |        0 |         0
 mp1_y201701_code1    |     5637 |    310000
 mp1_y201701_code2    |     5637 |    310000
 mp1_y201702          |        0 |         0
 mp1_y201702_code1    |     5091 |    280000
 mp1_y201702_code2    |     5091 |    280000
```

Partition pruning test

If you enter only the LOGDATE column condition, which is the primary CHECK condition, only the primary partition is pruned. The results below show that two subpartition belonging to the mp1_y201701 partition have been accessed.

```
show constraint_exclusion;
 constraint_exclusion
----------------------
 partition

explain (costs false)
select sum(c1), min(c1), max(c1)
```

```
from    mp1
where   logdate between DATE '20170101'
            and     DATE '20170131';
                        QUERY PLAN
------------------------------------------------------------------
Aggregate
  -> Append
        -> Seq Scan on mp1
              Filter: ((logdate >= '2017-01-01'::)
                  AND (logdate <= '2017-01-31'::date))
        -> Seq Scan on mp1_y201701
              Filter: ((logdate >= '2017-01-01'::date)
                  AND (logdate <= '2017-01-31'::date))
        -> Seq Scan on mp1_y201701_code1
              Filter: ((logdate >= '2017-01-01'::date)
                  AND (logdate <= '2017-01-31'::date))
        -> Seq Scan on mp1_y201701_code2
              Filter: ((logdate >= '2017-01-01'::date)
                  AND (logdate <= '2017-01-31'::date))
```

If the LOGDATE column condition, which is the primary CHECK condition, and the CODE column condition, which is the secondary check condition, are input, the secondary partition is pruned. The results below show that only one mp1_y201701_code2 subpartition belonging to the mp1_y201701 partition is accessed.

```
explain (costs false)
select sum(c1), min(c1), max(c1)
from    mp1
where   logdate between DATE '20170101'
            and     DATE '20170131'
and     code=2;
                        QUERY PLAN
------------------------------------------------------------------
Aggregate
  -> Append
        -> Seq Scan on mp1
              Filter: ((logdate >= '2017-01-01'::date)
                  AND (logdate <= '2017-01-31'::date) AND (code = 2))
        -> Seq Scan on mp1_y201701
              Filter: ((logdate >= '2017-01-01'::date)
                  AND (logdate <= '2017-01-31'::date) AND (code = 2))
        -> Seq Scan on mp1_y201701_code2
              Filter: ((logdate >= '2017-01-01'::date)
                  AND (logdate <= '2017-01-31'::date) AND (code = 2))
```

Partition index

Partition indexes in PostgreSQL have the following characteristics:

- Only LOCAL index of partition level is supported. That is, table-level GLOBAL index is not supported.

- Provide Partial Index for Partition.

Let's take a closer look at these features.

Provides only LOCAL index

PostgreSQL does not provide GLOBAL index because the parent and child tables are separate tables.

Provide a Partition Partial Index

Because the partition is a separate table, you can decide whether to create an index for each partition. In addition, PostgreSQL can create different indexes for different partitions. Therefore, it is advantageous to apply various tuning techniques such as creating a BRIN for a partition having a low access and creating a covering index for a partition having frequent accesses.

Tip for improving partition insert performance

Some tips for improving partition insert performance are summarized as follows.

- It is better to use Trigger than RULE.

- It is recommended to place frequently-input partitions at the top of the Trigger.

- If possible, it is recommended to specify the partition.

Let's take a look at the above by testing.

Test environment

Create a table.

```
create table list_p1
(
    c1        integer,
    code      integer,
    dummy     char(100)
);
create table list_p1_code1 (CHECK( code = 1)) INHERITS (list_p1);
create table list_p1_code2 (CHECK( code = 2)) INHERITS (list_p1);
create table list_p1_code3 (CHECK( code = 3)) INHERITS (list_p1);
create table list_p1_code4 (CHECK( code = 4)) INHERITS (list_p1);
```

Create a Trigger.

```
CREATE OR REPLACE FUNCTION list_p1_insert_func()
RETURNS TRIGGER AS $$
BEGIN
    IF     ( NEW.code = 1 ) THEN INSERT INTO list_p1_code1 VALUES (NEW.*);
    ELSIF ( NEW.code = 2 ) THEN INSERT INTO list_p1_code2 VALUES (NEW.*);
    ELSIF ( NEW.code = 3 ) THEN INSERT INTO list_p1_code3 VALUES (NEW.*);
ELSIF ( NEW.code = 4 ) THEN INSERT INTO list_p1_code4 VALUES (NEW.*);
    ELSE
        RAISE EXCEPTION 'Out of range!';
    END IF;
    RETURN NULL;
END;
$$
LANGUAGE plpgsql;
-- Create an INSERT trigger
CREATE TRIGGER list_p1_insert_trig
    BEFORE INSERT ON list_p1
    FOR EACH ROW EXECUTE PROCEDURE list_p1_insert_func();
```

Prepare RULE generation script for performance comparison with Trigger.

```
CREATE OR REPLACE RULE list_p1_code1_insert_rule AS
ON INSERT TO list_p1 WHERE ( code = 1 )
DO INSTEAD   INSERT INTO list_p1_code1 VALUES ( NEW.*);

CREATE OR REPLACE RULE list_p1_code2_insert_rule AS
ON INSERT TO list_p1 WHERE ( code = 2 )
DO INSTEAD   INSERT INTO list_p1_code2 VALUES ( NEW.*);

CREATE OR REPLACE RULE list_p1_code3_insert_rule AS
ON INSERT TO list_p1 WHERE ( code = 3 )
DO INSTEAD   INSERT INTO list_p1_code3 VALUES ( NEW.*);
```

```
CREATE OR REPLACE RULE list_p1_code4_insert_rule AS
ON INSERT TO list_p1 WHERE ( code = 4 )
DO INSTEAD  INSERT INTO list_p1_code4 VALUES ( NEW.*);
```

Create a procedure that commit every transaction.

```
CREATE OR REPLACE FUNCTION insert_list_p1(v1 integer, v2 integer) RETURNS VOID AS $$
BEGIN
PERFORM dblink('myconn','INSERT INTO list_p1
VALUES ('||v1||','||v2||')');
END;
$$ LANGUAGE plpgsql;

CREATE or replace FUNCTION loop_insert_list_p1() RETURNS VOID AS $$
BEGIN
  FOR i in 1..4 LOOP
    FOR j in 1..100000 LOOP
      PERFORM insert_list_p1(j,i);
    END LOOP;
  END LOOP;
END;
$$ LANGUAGE plpgsql;
```

(1) It is better to use Trigger than RULE.

In my test results, Trigger was faster than RULE by 20% for both Bulk Insert and Loop Insert.
Let's look at the results below.

Trigger & Bulk Insert

```
\timing
do $$
begin
  for i in 1..4 loop
    for j in 1..100000 loop
      insert into list_p1 values (j, i, 'dummy');
    end loop;
  end loop;
end$$;
Time: 6809.702 ms
```

RULE & Bulk Insert

```
do $$
begin
```

```
for i in 1..4 loop
   for j in 1..100000 loop
      insert into list_p1 values (j, i, 'dummy');
   end loop;
end loop;
end$$;
Time: 9015.100 ms
```

The above results show that Trigger is 6.8 seconds and RULE is 9.0 seconds.

Trigger: COMMIT for every transaction

```
select dblink_connect('myconn','dbname=postgres port=5436 user=postgres
password=postgres');
select loop_insert_list_p1();
Time: 252689.215 ms
```

RULE: COMMIT for every transaction

```
select dblink_connect('myconn','dbname=postgres port=5436 user=postgres
password=postgres');
select loop_insert_list_p1();
Time: 294379.413 ms
```

The above results show that the trigger is 252.7 seconds and the RULE is 294.5 seconds.

(2) It is recommended to place the frequently input partitions at the top of the Trigger.

If the input target partition is at the bottom of the Trigger. (Using an existing trigger)

```
do $$
begin
  for i in 1..1000000 loop
    insert into list_p1 values (i, 4, 'dummy');
  end loop;
end$$;
Time: 20385.491 ms
```

If the input target partition is at the top of the Trigger (Trigger recreate)

```
CREATE OR REPLACE FUNCTION list_p1_insert_func()
RETURNS TRIGGER AS $$
BEGIN
   IF    ( NEW.code = 4 ) THEN INSERT INTO list_p1_code4 VALUES (NEW.*);
   ELSIF ( NEW.code = 3 ) THEN INSERT INTO list_p1_code3 VALUES (NEW.*);
   ELSIF ( NEW.code = 2 ) THEN INSERT INTO list_p1_code2 VALUES (NEW.*);
```

```
   ELSIF ( NEW.code = 1 ) THEN INSERT INTO list_p1_code1 VALUES (NEW.*);
   ELSE
       RAISE EXCEPTION 'Out of range!';
   END IF;
   RETURN NULL;
END;
$$
LANGUAGE plpgsql;

-- Create an INSERT trigger
CREATE TRIGGER list_p1_insert_trig
   BEFORE INSERT ON list_p1
   FOR EACH ROW EXECUTE PROCEDURE list_p1_insert_func();
```

After placing the input partition at the top of the Trigger, you can see that the input speed is 20% faster. The longer the length of the IF-ELSIF-END IF of the trigger, the greater the performance improvement.

```
do $$
begin
  for i in 1..1000000 loop
    insert into list_p1 values (i, 4, 'dummy');
  end loop;
end$$;
Time: 16532.326 ms
```

(3) If possible, it is recommended to specify the partition.

This is a very natural tip. If you specify a partition, you can enter it very quickly because it does not perform the trigger logic.

```
do $$
begin
  for i in 1..1000000 loop
    insert into list_p1_code4 values (i, 4, 'dummy');
  end loop;
end$$;
Time: 8036.312 ms
```

Summary

Partitioning is a very good tool that can simultaneously improve the manageability and performance.

To properly utilize partitions, you need to know techniques such as partition type, sub partition, partition pruning, and proper indexing for each partition. In addition, it is necessary to use some techniques appropriately to minimize the load on the input of the trigger.

Parallel Processing

Parallel Processing

PostgreSQL provides parallel processing since version 9.6.

Parallel processing means that one work is executed by several processes at the same time. In other words, one query can use multiple CPU cores. In addition, IO performance is improved because several processes perform IO at the same time.

Because of this, the parallel processing function is essential for large data processing. So, it's great that PostgreSQL has begun to offer parallel processing. In some blogs, Parallel processing has been shown to speed up TPC-H (query performance measurement test for DW).

This chapter explains the basics of parallel processing and results of the Explain.

Parallel processing basic

Parallel processing related parameters

Parallel processing related parameters are as follows.

max_worker_processes

Sets the maximum number of worker processes that perform parallel processing. The default value is only 8. Therefore, if you want to use several worker processes at the same time, you have to increase this value.

max_parallel_workers_per_gather

Set the maximum number of worker processes that can be performed per query. The default value is 0, so no parallel processing is performed in any case. If you want to do parallel processing, you have to increase this value. This value can also be changed at the session level.

force_parallel_mode

If the value of the `max_parallel_workers_per_gather` parameter is greater than 0, the optimizer calculates the cost of the query and then decides whether or not to parallelize. If this value is set to `on`, parallel processing is always considered. The default setting is `off`.

parallel_setup_cost

Parallel processing requires preprocessing to allocate worker processes. This parameter means the cost required for this preliminary work. The default setting is 1000.

parallel_tuple_cost

Parallel processing requires the transfer of records between the parent process and the worker process. At this time, if the number of records to be transmitted is large, it may be burdened in parallel processing. The purpose of this parameter is to induce a single process to process when the number of records to be processed is large. The default setting is 0.1.

When the `max_parallel_workers_per_gather` parameter is greater than 0, setting this value to 0 always processes it in a parallel manner.

min_parallel_relation_size

Sets the minimum table size for parallel processing. The default setting is 8 MiB. That is, a table larger than 8 MiB is target to parallel processing. If you increase this value a lot, you get a problem that you are getting less worker processes. This will be discussed in the next paragraph.

How to calculate the number of worker processes

The number of worker processes is calculated based on the `min_parallel_relation_size` parameter value. When the default setting is 8 MiB, the number of worker processes according to the table size is shown in Table 7-1. That is, each worker process is allocated one by one every time the table size is tripled based on the parameter. For this reason, if the parameter is set large, the number of worker to be allocated may be reduced. For example, if you set the parameter to 1 GiB, only one worker is assigned to a table smaller than 3 GiB.

Table 7-1. *Number of worker processes by table size*

Table Size (MiB)	Number of Workers
< 8	0
< 24	1
< 72	2
< 216	3
< 648	4
< 1944	5
< 5822	6
> = 5822	7

Parallel process model

The PostgreSQL parallel process model is not a 'Producer - Consumer model'. It is simply a multi-threaded approach that uses multiple worker processes. (See Figure 7-1) Because of this, parallel processing is often not as fast as you might think.

Group By, hash join, group hash join after hash join, except for simple scan, must be producer-consumer model to maximize parallel processing performance.

For example, suppose a hash join is performed. The 'producer-consumer model' passes the record to the consumer group as the producer group scans the hash table. The consumer group then performs a hash build operation using the received records. After the producer group has finished scanning the hash table, it starts the probe while scanning the probe table. As such, the producer-consumer model has the advantage of being able to perform processing within the work at the same time.

However, PostgreSQL can't do this. That is, after performing a scan operation for each area, a hash build operation is performed in the own worker process, and then a probe step is performed.

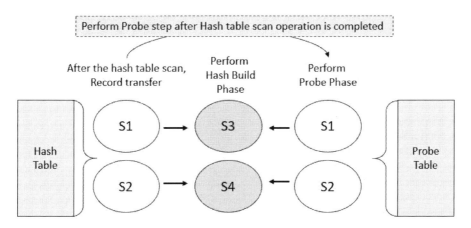

Figure 7-1. (a) *ORACLE's Parallel Process Model (Producer-Consumer Model)*

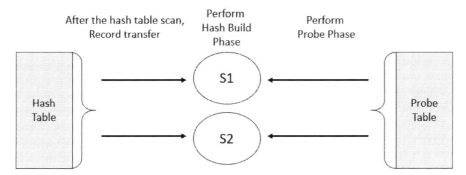

Figure 7-1. (b) *PostgreSQL's Parallel Process Model*

Parallel processing example

Currently supported Parallel processing functions are as follows.

- Parallel scan

- Parallel Group By

- Parallel join

In this section, we will check the Explain result in the above operation.

Test environment

The T1 table is approximately 1 GB and the T2 table is approximately 10 GB.

```
drop table t1;
drop table t2;

create table t1 (c1 integer, dummy char(1000));
create table t2 (c1 integer, amount integer, dummy char(1000));

insert into t1 select i, 'dummy' from generate_series(1,1000000) a(i);
insert into t2 select mod(i,10000000)+1, i*10, 'dummy' from generate_series(1,10000000)
a(i);

analyze t1;
analyze t2;

select relname, relpages, round(relpages*8/1024,0) "size(MiB)"
from   pg_class where relname in ('t1','t2');
 relname | relpages | size(MiB)
---------+----------+-----------
 t1      |   142858 |      1116
 t2      |  1428572 |     11160
```

Parallel scan

The result of parallel processing at the time of scanning is as follows.

```
set max_parallel_workers_per_gather to 8;
explain (costs false, analyze, buffers)
select count(*) from t2;
                    QUERY PLAN
-------------------------------------------------------------------
 Finalize Aggregate (actual time=33920.893..33920.893 rows=1 loops=1)
   Buffers: shared hit=567 read=1428572
   ->  Gather (actual time=33919.719..33920.887 rows=8 loops=1)
         Workers Planned: 7
         Workers Launched: 7
         Buffers: shared hit=567 read=1428572
         ->  Partial Aggregate
                 (actual time=33910.839..33910.839 rows=1 loops=8)
               Buffers: shared read=1428572
               ->  Parallel Seq Scan on t2
                       (actual time=0.441..33690.431 rows=1250000 loops=8)
                     Buffers: shared read=1428572
 Planning time: 0.040 ms
 Execution time: 33921.497 ms
```

Let's analyze some of the above Explain results.

Finalize Aggregate

This means that the parent process has finally aggregated the work of the worker processes.

Workers Planned

This means the number of worker processes calculated according to the value of `min_parallel_relation_size` parameter and the table size.

Workers Launched

This means that the number of worker processes actually performed. Depending on the number of worker processes currently running, there may be fewer worker processes actually allocated. For example, if the number of worker processes currently running is equal to the value of the `max_worker_processes` parameter, then no more worker processes are available. In this case, the value of `Workers Launched` is 0.

Partial Aggregate & Parallel Seq Scan

This means that Parallel Aggregation and Parallel scan operations are performed. At this time, since the number of loops is 8, 7 worker processes and the parent process performed the scan and aggregation tasks.

Parallel processing monitoring method

To monitor parallel processing, you must use the `ps` command. It is not possible to monitor using the `pstree` command or the `pg_stat_activity` view.

Monitoring results using ps command

You can see the worker process and the parent process (11703) using the `ps` command.

```
$ ps -ef | grep parallel
postgres 11801 11695  postgres: bgworker: parallel worker for PID 11703
postgres 11802 11695  postgres: bgworker: parallel worker for PID 11703
postgres 11803 11695  postgres: bgworker: parallel worker for PID 11703
```

```
postgres 11804 11695   postgres: bgworker: parallel worker for PID 11703
postgres 11805 11695   postgres: bgworker: parallel worker for PID 11703
postgres 11806 11695   postgres: bgworker: parallel worker for PID 11703
postgres 11807 11695   postgres: bgworker: parallel worker for PID 11703
```

pg_stat_activity view monitoring results

The pg_stat_activity view does not provide a query that the worker process performs.

```
select pid, state, query from pg_stat_activity;
  pid  | state  |        query
-------+--------+---------------------
 11703 | active | explain (costs false, analyze,buffers)  +
       |        | select count(*) from t2;
 11801 |        |
 11802 |        |
 11803 |        |
 11804 |        |
 11805 |        |
 11806 |        |
 11807 |        |
```

Parallel Group By

When performing Parallel Group By, it is a good idea to perform the operation after checking the Explain result first.

Because, even if max_parallel_workers_per_gather parameter is set as below, it is processed by single process.

```
set max_parallel_workers_per_gather to 16;
explain (costs false)
select c1, sum(amount), count(*)
from   t2
group by c1;
QUERY PLAN
----------------------------
 GroupAggregate
   Group Key: c1
   -> Sort
        Sort Key: c1
          -> Seq Scan on t2
```

At this time, let's change the force_parallel_mode parameter to on. The results below show that the parallel process is performed, but there is only one worker process. The reason for this is that if there are many records being sent as a result of the query, less worker processes are allocated to reduce communication between processes.

```
set force_parallel_mode=on;
explain (costs false)
select c1, sum(amount), count(*)
from   t2
group by c1;
              QUERY PLAN
-----------------------------------------
 Gather
   Workers Planned: 1
   Single Copy: true
   ->  GroupAggregate
         Group Key: c1
         ->  Sort
               Sort Key: c1
               ->  Seq Scan on t2
```

worker processes, you can set the value of the `parallel_tuple_cost` parameter to 0.

```
set parallel_tuple_cost=0;
explain (costs false, analyze, buffers)
select c1, sum(amount), count(*)
from   t2
group by c1;
                        QUERY PLAN
--------------------------------------------------------------------
 GroupAggregate (actual time=35664.621..42513.378 rows=10000000 loops=1)
   Group Key: c1
   Buffers: shared hit=367 read=1428572, temp read=21996 written=21996
   ->  Sort (actual time=35663.407..37860.010 rows=10000000 loops=1)
         Sort Key: c1
         Sort Method: external merge  Disk: 175960kB
         Buffers: shared hit=367 read=1428572, temp read=21996...
         ->  Gather (actual time=4.487..23567.412 rows=10000000 loops=1)
               Workers Planned: 7
               Workers Launched: 7
               Buffers: shared hit=364 read=1428572
               ->  Parallel Seq Scan on t2
                     (actual time=0.774..33280.316 rows=1250000 loops=8)
                     Buffers: shared read=1428572
```

Parallel Hash join

Finally, let's look at an example of a Parallel hash join.

```
set max_parallel_workers_per_gather to 16;
set parallel_tuple_cost=0;
explain (costs false, analyze, buffers)
select t1.c1, t2.amount
from   t1, t2
where  t1.c1 = t2.c1;
                          QUERY PLAN
-----------------------------------------------------------------------
 Hash Join (actual time=3402.936..39931.023 rows=1000000 loops=1)
   Hash Cond: (t2.c1 = t1.c1)
   Buffers: shared hit=663 read=1571430, temp read=34830 written=34800
   -> Gather (actual time=1.384..30722.302 rows=10000000 loops=1)
         Workers Planned: 7
         Workers Launched: 7
         Buffers: shared hit=385 read=1428572
         -> Parallel Seq Scan on t2
                (actual time=0.545..33064.763 rows=1250000 loops=8)
            Buffers: shared read=1428572
   -> Hash (actual time=3400.841..3400.841 rows=1000000 loops=1)
         Buckets: 131072  Batches: 16  Memory Usage: 3227kB
         Buffers: shared hit=275 read=142858, temp written=2736
         -> Gather (actual time=0.972..3079.306 rows=1000000 loops=1)
               Workers Planned: 5
               Workers Launched: 5
               Buffers: shared hit=275 read=142858
               -> Parallel Seq Scan on t1
                      (actual time=0.349..3229.414 rows=166667 loops=6)
                  Buffers: shared read=142858
```

Let's analyze some of the above Explain results.

T1 table processing part

You can see that five worker processes have performed the hash build step. Five worker processes are allocated because the size of the T1 table is about 1 GB. (See Table 7-1)

T2 table processing part

It can be seen that seven worker processes have performed the probe step.

Since the size of the T2 table is about 10 GB, seven worker processes have been allocated. But as I mentioned earlier, PostgreSQL's Parallel model is not a 'producer-consumer model'. Therefore, the total number of worker processes that execute the example query is seven.

Summary

The 9.6 version of Parallel processing is considered a start-up. On my system, parallel processing performance was not so fast compared to single processing. Of course, these results will vary depending on the system environment.

In fact, structurally, PostgreSQL is well suited for parallel processing. This is because the table and index files are managed by dividing by 1 GiB. I expect to apply various techniques such as producer-consumer model, parallel index generation, parallel index scan and parallel DML.

Index

43995347R00184

Made in the USA
Middletown, DE
01 May 2019